ALSO BY DAVID MCCUMBER

X-Rated: The Mitchell Brothers—
A True Story of Sex, Money, and Death

PLAYING OFF THE RAIL

A Pool Hustler's Journey

PLAYING OFF
THE RAIL

DAVID McCUMBER

*For Mark Measures —
Thanks for believing
in writing —
David McCumber
1/13/96*

RANDOM HOUSE ⌂ NEW YORK

For Mark Measures,
Thanks for believing in Me.
David. 1/13/96
Hollywood Athletic Club

Grateful acknowledgment is made to the following for
permission to reprint previously published material:

FIFTH FLOOR MUSIC, INC.: Four lines from "Heart of Saturday Night"
by Tom Waits. Copyright © 1974 by Fifth Floor Music, Inc.
Reprinted by permission of Fifth Floor Music, Inc.

M. T. INDUSTRIES, INC.: Excerpt from "Can't You See." Copyright © 1975
by M. T. Industries, Inc. Reprinted by permission of M. T. Industries, Inc.

MICHAEL H. GOLDSEN, INC.: Excerpt from "Farther Down the Line"
by Lyle Lovett. Copyright © 1986 by Michael H. Goldsen, Inc./LyleL (ASCAP).
All rights reserved. Reprinted by permission of Michael H. Goldsen, Inc.

SIX PICTURES MUSIC: Excerpt from "Baltimore" by Randy Newman. Copyright © 1977 by
Six Pictures Music. All rights reserved. Used by permission.

Library of Congress Cataloging-in-Publication Data

McCumber, David.
Playing off the rail: a pool hustler's journey / David McCumber.
—1st ed.
p. cm.
ISBN 0-679-42374-5
1. Annigoni, Tony. 2. Billiard players—United States—Biography.
I. Title.
GV892.2.A56M33 1995
794.7´2´092—dc20   95-6955
[B]

Manufactured in the United States of America
24689753
First Edition
Book design by JoAnne Metsch

For my boys, and for my father

Contents

1. Breaking the Rack   3

2. The Coast Starlight   26

3. Seattle   60

4. Six-by-Twelve   112

5. The Pool-Table Suite   131

6. The Human Fly   148

7. The Chelsea Rip   164

8. The City of Brotherly Love   194

9. Chinn Music   199

10. In from the Cold   208

11. The Dew Factor   230

12. Southbound   250

13. Hard Times   259

14. Nit, Nevada   284

15. Return to Platisville   310

16. Liability   317

17. The Midnight Rodeo   331

18. The Man with the Golden Gun   360

    Acknowledgments   367

PLAYING OFF THE RAIL

I

Breaking the Rack

"The trouble with shooting pool is that it's no good if
you don't win."
—Fast Eddie Felson in *The Color of Money*
by Walter Tevis

WHEN I WAS YOUNG, THE POOLROOM WHERE I LIVED WAS VERY OLD.
By the summer of 1969, when the road player walked into that
elegantly dissipated atmosphere of stale beer, stale cigar
smoke, and the stale aspirations of old men, past the big front
window where sallow, rebellious eighth-graders slouched,
eating Slim Jims and Planters peanuts, smirking nervously at
the good people who walked by on Illinois Avenue and
hoping none of them were their mothers; past the high dark
bar where Ole, the day man, stood stolid, staring rheum-eyed
at his regulars, pouring short drafts of Pabst for fifteen cents;
all the way back to the snooker table nearest the back door
where I was practicing cut-shots on the black ball, the Stag
Tavern was in its dotage. For more than fifty years the
upstanding women of Sidney, Nebraska, including my mother
and grandmother, had sniffed censoriously as they walked by,
but peered with vicarious curiosity nevertheless at a clientele
of wheat farmers and Union Pacific railroad men, along with

Farm Bureau agents and short-order cooks and insurance men, cops and farm-implement salesmen and auto-parts-house countermen and the high school basketball coach—and seventeen-year-olds like me. We had no idea that in another five years the pool hall would stand empty, waiting along with the rest of the country to be redefined by the trauma of the next decade. We had no idea that for many men the Stag Tavern and hundreds of similar pool halls would lose their allure, paling before the ruthless charms of television, video games, and singles bars. For a few like me, who could never forget the fierceness of first love, nothing would ever be quite the same.

At the time, I just felt the gaze of the road scuffler as he settled onto the end barstool and lit a cigar. He was maybe forty-five, with curly black hair and blue eyes that froze me like a ball on the rail. I didn't even know he was a player. I just knew he was watching me, and it made me self-conscious, and I missed three shots in a row. I lined up an easier one, made it, and scratched in the side.

"Kid," he said around the cigar, "can you play snooker *at all?*"

"I can play some," I said defensively.

"You got twenty bucks?"

"I've got ten."

"Well, partner, why don't you and me play any two players in the house for twenty apiece? I'll spot you the other ten."

We did, and he ran fifty points in the first game, and seventy in the second, and nobody would play after that. It was a smart move, kicking in with me—he must have known it would be easier to get action if he partnered up with one of the locals, especially one who looked pretty weak. By five o'clock that evening he was gone, and I never saw him again, but he had done more than win me forty bucks. He had fired me with for the turbulent exis-

wo YEARS, MOSTLY AS A
weeks after that after-
y first newspaper job,
ge combined to drive
road" into the realm
y a little pool, passably
skill required to make
r from home were as
all and the New York
n die hard; this one
ase of my spine, wait-
d. I had quit my job a
was published, I had a
of that road man still

y boyhood called me
ythm of balls stroked

AROUND THE BIG TABLE
like a magician, was a
igoni, and he wasn't
ticing in his own pool-
t was five minutes to
ball.
tle cut down the long
e too much—shooting
center of it, so that he

could hit the object ball more f

ball, getting in line for the r

wobbled and hung on the lip. B

game of straight pool all n

compactly to leave most of th

moving the cue ball around as

erately, rhythmically, he had

again. Make fourteen, leave on

rack the others, break, run the

again.

He was the only player in th

the way he wanted it, and after

was closed until three, and so fo

hustling over to his family on t

able to escape into his other li

defined, a brilliantly lit green

rails and six parsimonious pock

house.

He looked like the central fig

spotlit on a dark stage. The room

just barely visible in the weak g

San Francisco summer day see

dows.

He was not a physically impos

faded blue Levi's carrying no ex

were large and deep-set in a lon

ing the impression of gauntness

early thirties; he wasn't. He was

memorable feature was his thick

than the nineties' convention, p

in straight black wings across th

It was square-cut in back, just ov

khaki button-down shirt.

road fever, with an impossible yearning for the turbulent existence of the traveling gambler.

I TRAVELED PLENTY IN THE NEXT TWENTY-TWO YEARS, MOSTLY AS A journalist, never as a pool player. A few weeks after that afternoon in the Stag Tavern I had taken my first newspaper job, and over the years a career and a marriage combined to drive the whole proposition of "going on the road" into the realm of Mittyesque fantasy. I continued to play a little pool, passably well, but my proficiency and the level of skill required to make money playing pool in hostile rooms far from home were as far apart as Saturday beer-league softball and the New York Yankees. Still, the longings of seventeen die hard; this one had settled like a dormant virus at the base of my spine, waiting for an opening, and now one existed. I had quit my job a year before to write a book. The book was published, I had a little money in the bank, and the eyes of that road man still burned in my soul.

On this Monday morning in 1992, my boyhood called me insistently, beckoning me toward the rhythm of balls stroked sweet and true across green cloth.

THE MAN WHO WAS PROWLING SOUNDLESSLY AROUND THE BIG TABLE in his white Reeboks, pocketing balls like a magician, was a friend of mine, Anthony Chenier Annigoni, and he wasn't playing in the Stag Tavern; he was practicing in his own poolroom, the Q Club in San Francisco. It was five minutes to noon, and he had just missed the four ball.

It wasn't that tough, just a delicate little cut down the long rail, but he "cheated the pocket" a little too much—shooting at *one side* of the pocket instead of the center of it, so that he could hit the object ball more fully and better control the cue ball, getting in line for the next shot—and the four ball wobbled and hung on the lip. He had been playing a solitary game of straight pool all morning, breaking the balls compactly to leave most of them at the top of the table, moving the cue ball around as little as possible. Slowly, deliberately, rhythmically, he had cleared the table again and again. Make fourteen, leave one to make for the break shot, rack the others, break, run them out again. And again. And again.

He was the only player in the enormous old room. That's the way he wanted it, and after all, it was his joint. The place was closed until three, and so for a few hours, like a bigamist hustling over to his family on the other side of town, he was able to escape into his other life. It was an existence neatly defined, a brilliantly lit green rectangle bordered by the six rails and six parsimonious pockets of the tightest table in the house.

He looked like the central figure in a tragedy, soliloquizing, spotlit on a dark stage. The room was quiet and dim and cool, just barely visible in the weak gray light of a typically dreary San Francisco summer day seeping through the shaded windows.

He was not a physically imposing man, maybe five-nine, his faded blue Levi's carrying no extra weight at all. His dark eyes were large and deep-set in a long, pale, angular face, reinforcing the impression of gauntness. He looked like he was in his early thirties; he wasn't. He was thirty-nine. Perhaps his most memorable feature was his thick, glossy hair, just a little longer than the nineties' convention, parted near the crown, falling in straight black wings across the edges of his high forehead. It was square-cut in back, just over the collar of his neat cotton khaki button-down shirt.

As he played, he conveyed a power and intensity out of scale with his body, and then he no longer seemed small. Each time he prepared to make a shot his body assumed precisely the same position, as though its parts would only fit together in one way: legs slightly bent at the knee, right foot behind, precisely in line with the shot, left foot just outside that line and pointed slightly outward; left hand outstretched, first finger cocked upward and wrapped around the cue, the others splayed solidly on the cloth; body bent so low over this arm that as he moved the cue back and forth in practice stroking, it rubbed against the slight cleft in his chin, as if it had worn the little groove there itself; right arm bent at the elbow, again perfectly in line with the path of the shot to come. The only part of him that moved was his right forearm, forward and backward in the same little timing rhythm each time, stroking several times, then pausing, then delivering the actual shot.

If he had to reach for a shot, he would extend his upper body slightly more. If the cue ball was near a rail, or in front of another ball, he would elevate his cue as much as necessary, no more, and everything else stayed the same. Occasionally as he played, the cue ball would come to rest on the extreme right side of the table as he faced it, and when this happened, instead of using the mechanical bridge, he would simply reverse everything and shoot the shot left-handed.

He and the table seemed to interact as though they were two parts of the same machine, like Andre Watts and his Steinway. It was as though the table were his knowing and complaisant lover. She was flawless under his touch; he trusted every inch of her. He did not have to force the balls into the pockets; he could caress them instead.

Thirty-three other tables squatted around his in the half-light like the Greek chorus, their hulking, stolid presence passive but palpable, as if they were awaiting their chance to speak, to judge his skill and his destiny. The place was filled with history as heavy as the old tables themselves, and he was acutely aware of it. It had opened as the California Billiard Academy in 1925, part of a profusion of poolrooms within a few blocks: Graney's, the Rialto, Wright's, the Palace. Then, in the fifties, it had become Cochran's, owned by champion player Welker Cochran, who had owned Cochran's 924 Club for years, just down the street.

He had played here, at Cochran's, as a kid. If you thought you were a pool player, and you were in San Francisco, Cochran's was where you came to find out if you were right. Road players would come in to play the city's best—Jack Cooney and Jack Perkins and Filipino Gene and Denny Searcy and Pots 'n' Pans and Bucktooth and all the rest. The room was full of players and hustlers and flat-out thieves of all descriptions. One night, he had fallen asleep in a chair for a few minutes, then awakened to find his pockets slit with a razor blade and his money gone. Eventually, though, he had won a lot of money here, before the place closed in the seventies, a victim of the game's decline.

Now the game and the place were back. It had been empty and ignored for nearly two decades before being reincarnated by his force of will and a million dollars from investors into the Q Club, one of the most elegant poolrooms in the country. He loved being the proprietor, but he loved to play more, and there was a special pleasure to playing alone. He liked to compete against others, particularly for money, but he had long ago decided that the inner battle was the essence of the game.

Now, he stood up and stared at the offending four ball, still perched on the edge of the pocket like a purple insult. He drew a quick breath past his dark mustache and his small, even white teeth, making a little disapproving hissing sound. It was the fourth time he had missed a shot in the two hours he had practiced. In between his first three misses, he had made runs of twenty, seventy-three, and sixty-five balls. But this miss was even more irritating. He had run ninety-seven balls when it happened.

He pulled all the balls up to the surface of the table, then removed the ten through fifteen and racked the remaining balls in the diamond pattern used for nine-ball, with the nine in the middle and the one in the spot position at the front of the rack. He placed the cue ball an inch off the left rail, barely behind the second diamond, and bent low over the table again. This time his body was coiled tight as he aimed at an infinitesimal part of the one ball—the contact point, just left of center, where he wanted to send the cue ball on the break shot. After his practice strokes and then a pause slightly more pronounced than before, he unleashed the tension in his stance, moving his entire body behind the shot as he broke the balls with astounding force. Just like a baseball hitter, he got his hips and legs turning into the shot; his right hip even struck the table as he followed through.

The cue ball crashed into the one ball with what seemed like nuclear force, then leaped backward a foot and stopped in the middle of the table. The outside balls in the rack shot around the table like freed electrons; even the nine hit the end rail and rolled hard back down the table. The two and six balls went into the same corner pocket, one after the other, and the three rolled into the side.

Tony Annigoni allowed himself a small smile. "Even Bucktooth would like that one," he said quietly to himself, and moved around the table to line up his shot on the one ball, an easy straight shot into the bottom right corner.

"Some break, Tony."

In his concentration, he had not noticed his bartender come up the stairs, and neither had I. "Hi, Rick," he said. "Yeah, that was gin rummy right there." He got right back down over the shot, a polite signal that he didn't want to break away and talk just yet, and Rick Wallace, dark, scarred, pudgy bartender, pugilist, gambler, and occasional pool hustler, understood perfectly. He puttered around behind the gleaming, polished bar and watched with me as Tony fired his way through rack after rack of nine-ball.

If he missed, or scratched, he stopped and reracked the balls. Either way—whether he ran the table, made the nine on a combination, or made an error—he recorded the result with a brief notation on a pad before breaking again.

He played forty racks. Once, he made the nine on the break. Twice, he made the nine on a combination, striking another object ball first. Three times he scratched, the cue ball falling in on the break. Once, he scratched after the break. Fourteen times, he missed before he got to the nine. In the remaining nineteen racks, he ran the balls out in order.

After making the last nine ball, he unscrewed his cue, put it back in its black leather case, reracked all the balls, and walked back into his corner office, where he deposited the cue case. He walked back behind the bar and poured himself a tall drink over ice, half cranberry juice, half club soda. He squeezed a lime into it and sat down at the bar next to me. It was just after two.

"That'll get the money, bubba," Rick said from behind the bar.

"Yeah, not bad, but I'm still letting whitey roll a little too much on that break. I'm sticking it good about half the time but sometimes I hit it too far right, and it dunks in the side, or I hit it a little high and it rolls forward through the rack. The

Tooth's been working with me on it. He's a brutal coach. Never lets up." He sipped his drink. "How was it, late last night?"

"Good, I kept it open until four. Moro was playing Angelo in the back."

Tony looked up. "How were they playing?"

"The same. Angelo was giving him the last two, playing for two hundred a set."

"What's the last two mean?" I asked. Rick and Tony both looked at me pityingly. Tony said, "If you give somebody the last two, it means that whatever the last ball except for the nine is on the table is also a 'money' ball for them, just like the nine. It's a stronger spot than just giving up the eight, because if you make the eight on the break or on a combo or something, they still have a second money ball on the table." He turned back to Rick. "And? What happened?"

"They seesawed. It's ridiculous. Angelo should rob him like that, but he was dogging his brains out."

Tony nodded. "There's a lot of dog in that kid. Playing around for laughs, he shoots great, but he faints for the money. Did they pay the time bill?"

"No problem, two and a half." The private room in the back, through some swinging doors from the bar, rented for fifty dollars an hour.

"Did they take care of you?"

"Yeah, Moro gave me a C-note for staying." Rick added, "I took some of Angelo's action." He shook his head. "That fuckin fat pooch. He should of won easy. I thought I'd get at least five hundred." He dropped his voice a little, conspiratorially, from force of habit, even though we were alone in the place. "Moro's ready to go off like a rocket. He's got cash and he's ready. I been watchin him in here for a month. When he has money he's so hot for a game it's a joke. . . . He had a roll a hundreds the size of a grapefruit last night. Somebody'll get it, Tony. McCready will be back in here, or Delbert, or Han."

"He's serious," Tony said quietly. "He's one of the biggest scores in the game, right now. He has a lot of cash, or access to a lot of cash, and he loves to play, and he loves to lose." He shook his head. "I don't know. Maybe he's guilty about the money, or how he gets it, or whatever, but you can tell, looking at him, there just isn't any win in that boy. He's a psycho, and he's lookin to blow the cash."

"Before you opened this place he dropped two hundred thousand playing bar pool at the Third Street Station, is what I heard," Rick said.

Tony finished his drink and stood up. "I'll be back later. I'm going to empty that guy. I'm sick of him playing these short-stops."

I had been introduced to Tony Annigoni by a friend just before the Q Club opened in mid-1991. I'd been charmed by the club and taken with Mr. Annigoni and his evident skill, and he seemed quite different from the average lifelong pool-room denizen. He didn't smoke, drank a beer or a glass of wine only rarely, knew computers inside out, studied Eastern religion, listened to Charlie Parker and Miles Davis, and ate macrobiotic food most of the time. In trying to explain the way he played, he talked about "the architectural theory of dynamic symmetry" and cited Cartesian mathematic theory. I was intrigued: a Renaissance hustler.

In desultory fashion, we'd discussed going on the road; in the last couple of weeks, the talk had turned more serious. He wanted to get away from the stress of the business for a while; I wanted to live my dream. I had the money and, for once, the time; he had the talent.

"That was a hell of an audition, Tony. We need to talk about a schedule. But look—are you serious about playing this guy Moro?"

"Absolutely. I'll call you if I can when it comes off. But I already have someone to stake me in that game."

"I'd love to see it."

AT 11 P.M., OR AT 11 A.M. FOR THAT MATTER, THE STREETS AROUND the Q Club were no place to linger. It was as ugly a neighborhood as there was in urban America. Here, deep in the Tenderloin, life was a nightmare ranging from unpleasant to lethal: screamed curses, petty assaults, crack cocaine transactions, stabbings, death from overdose, exposure, disease. Maybe forty ragged street people stood and squatted and sprawled across the street from the club, at the corner of Golden Gate and Jones, in front of an abandoned porno house. Dozens more floated along the streets, some pitiful, some menacing. Golden Gate Avenue belied its name. It was a bridge to perdition, a mural of despair.

The club, therefore, employed a doorman of impressive proportion. Unlike his counterparts at the trendy South of Market clubs, he was no arbiter of taste; he didn't keep you out if you wore boring clothes. His job was simply to allow the paying customers safe entrance and egress. I was grateful for him, too, at 11 P.M. this Friday evening. As I walked into the club Paula Abdul writhed expertly on five monitors mounted high on the walls as "All Right Tonight" blared into the room from eight top-quality speakers, competing with the buzz of two hundred voices, the clatter of the bar, and the Gatling-gun clicking of pool balls. Every table in the house was in use.

I marveled at the lushness of the place. Everything was oversized, as if the place had been designed for Wilt Chamberlain. French Art Deco posters, many of them six feet high, hung in metal frames. Their bright hues found a match in the boldly swirled pile carpeting. The enormous bar bisected the room, gleaming fixtures and glassware catching the light from the tables and the video screens. Most of the players were there just to have fun, and they seemed to be succeeding. They were, in the main, young, stylish, and affluent-looking; the ten-dollars-per-hour table time weeded out the scufflers.

In fact, some of San Francisco's rich and famous could often be seen there, including novelist Amy Tan, a real pool fanatic; actor Danny Glover; singer Boz Scaggs; choreographer Tommy Tune; columnist Herb Caen; and California Speaker of the House Willie Brown. But the place wasn't just full of glitz. I'd been in the club enough to recognize the resident serious players.

Paul Silva, a kindly, soft-spoken seventy-year-old known as "Nine-Ball Paul," was playing by himself, as he so often did. He was practicing long, swooping cut-shots, one after the other, hitting them soft and smooth so the object balls just barely reached the pockets and tumbled in. For more than thirty years, Nine-Ball Paul had been the night manager at the old Palace Billiards, and hundreds of players had matched up with him and walked out light in the wallet.

A slim, bald, brown man, wearing a tie-dyed T-shirt and dirty jeans, was playing one-pocket with a kid on one of the tables in the back. It was Filipino Gene. He was only in his fifties, but he looked older than Paul Silva. Once one of the best players in San Francisco, he was now a wizened, spooky character reminiscent of Yoda, the *Star Wars* gnome. Gene was one of the first great Filipino players—right now, three of the top ten players in the world are from the Philippines—and although his acumen was indeed diminished, he still had enough "speed" (ability) and knowledge to make games he could win.

He grew up in a mansion down the road from the Manila Country Club. When he came to the United States to go to school, he did most of his learning in Cochran's, and here, thirty years later in the same room, he was conducting class himself. The kid he was playing obviously had some talent, but raw talent rarely prevails when it is matched against experience and savvy in the game of one-pocket.

A couple of tables over, a slim, stylish young Asian man was playing nine-ball with a pudgy, bearded, fortyish fellow. Both players were intense and skilled; neither ran racks consistently, but they didn't miss often, either. Crowded around the table were about twenty spectators, mostly Asians, who were clearly pulling for the younger player.

I spotted Rick Wallace behind the bar and asked him what was going on.

"That's Han. Good young player. I don't know the guy he's playing. They're playing hundred-dollar sets, races to five, and those are his friends and relatives. They're all betting on him."

They were not disappointed. Han was two sets ahead and "on the hill," having won four games and needing just one more win in the third set, Wallace told me. As I watched, his opponent missed a shot on the three ball, and Han ran the rest of the rack. As the nine went in, the other player unscrewed his cue. "That's enough," he said, "unless you want to give me some weight."

"I'll give you the breaks," Han said. Giving the breaks simply means that, win or lose, your opponent breaks every rack, as opposed to the usual rule of nine-ball, which is that the winner breaks the next rack. In nine-ball, the break is a huge advantage, since sometimes the nine rolls in on the break, which means that the breaker wins, and other times good players can run the balls out in order from the break, never giving the other player a chance to come to the table.

"Not enough," his opponent said shortly. "I'll take the seven, or the eight and the breaks." (Giving a specific numbered ball means that if that ball is legally made by your opponent, either in rotation or as the result of a legal combination, he wins. The lower the number of the ball given, the larger the handicap; when balls are made in rotation, it's much easier to get to, say, the four or the five than it is the eight. With every higher number the handicap is incrementally less. One of the reasons nine-ball is such an excellent gambling game is that there are so many ways to set an accurate handicap to even a contest when players' talent levels are very disparate, or even very slightly so.)

"No." With Han's refusal, the match was over. As he was congratulated by the crowd, I asked Wallace where Tony was.

"He's in the private room," Wallace said. "Him and Moro." He winked at me. "I'm taking a piece of it," he added. "You ought to, too."

Tony had called me earlier in the evening, exhausted but quite pleased: "When I came in last night, Moro and the kid, Angelo, were flailing away in the back room again. I watched until three, and then told Moro I had something to do, and I would be back.

"So I went home and showered, then got back into the clothes he'd seen me in—and went to bed. I slept great for five hours, and of course when I got up my clothes looked like hell, like I'd been up all night.

"When I got back to the room, Moro was just finishing up with Angelo. It was eight A.M. and he was obviously real tired. After all, he really had been up all night.

"I said to him, 'If you're finished playing kids, you can play a real player now.' And it was perfect. He fired back, 'Give me the three, the six, and the breaks and I'll play you for as much as you want, right now.'

" 'You've got that game,' I told him. 'Let's play a race to seven for a thousand.' That kid Romeo was staking me."

"Jesus!" I said. "The three, the six, and the breaks!" It was a huge spot. In addition to getting the breaks, Moro could win the rack by legally making the three, or the six, or the nine. Tony's only "money ball" remained the nine ball. "Has anybody given him that much weight?" I asked.

"No, but he hasn't been playing champions, either. Here's how I viewed the spot. First, his break is weak. He doesn't make a ball often, and he scratches a lot. A lot of the time, I'm going to run out from there. But if I can't, my more immediate goal is to get as much of his money off the table as possible, then duck." (To duck is to play a defensive shot.)

"So really, having him break is to your advantage."

"Sure. Then I broke the game up into three segments: the one through three, the four through six, and the seven through nine. Whenever I got to shoot, my goal would be first to get to the three and get it off the table. Then the six, and then, of course, the nine. But I concentrated on not giving him shots on the balls just before his money balls if I could help it. Position play is just not in his repertoire, and he's not going to run three balls very often. So how is he going to beat me in any of those three segments of the game, consistently? He isn't.

"So unless he shits out, gets really lucky—which does happen in gaffe games like this, but not often—I'm going to beat him consistently, because he just can't run three balls that regularly.

"So we start playing. Moro is a real character, you know, he's Sicilian, in his late forties, a dead ringer for Marlon Brando, he hangs out with these sort of tough-looking characters, not smooth at all, sort of like they run a garbage company or something. He's real manic when he plays, talking all the time, playing the jukebox, sort of loner blues songs."

"Songs about losing."

"Yeah. He's not what you'd expect in a high roller, that's for sure. He brought a woman with him the other night, just a friend I think, quite a bit older than he is, real tough, sort of like somebody's landlady, you know? She was drinking—he doesn't, only cranberry juice, o.j., that stuff—and she wanted to play some gin rummy for money.

"So Filipino Gene plays her some gin for fifty dollars a game. Now you can say what you want about Gene but he's a superior gin player, absolutely world-class. In pool he may be a shortstop these days but in gin he's a champion. So of course she goes off to Gene playing gin while Moro is going off to me, playing pool."

"So just how did he go off?"

"Like an alarm clock. We played for eight hours. He was never ahead, and when we quit I was eight sets up."

"Eight thousand bucks."

"You're pretty great with the numbers."

"Yeah, yeah. You and Romeo get paid?"

"All but seven hundred. But you haven't heard the best part."

"What's that?"

"He still likes the game, and we're playing again tonight, the same way."

So I was here, at ringside, for round two.

The Q Club's private room was a terrific setting for high-stakes pool. The table being used was another antique Brunswick, perfectly restored and covered with brand-new Simonis, the best cloth available. Double doors, decorated with etched glass, kept out much of the clamor from the rest of the club.

Moro had played quite a few long sessions in this room, and despite his eccentricities he was a great customer, just for the time bills alone. He would play until he dropped from exhaustion. Playing the Asian kid, Han, one night, he had actually fallen asleep over a shot. A few times, the late bartender had found him, sans pants and shirt, stretched out asleep under the table, paying fifty dollars an hour for the privilege. On one of these occasions, Tony had been horrified to discover that Moro had taken a piss in the sink of the portable bar, rather than walk clear around the club to the bathroom. "Moro," he had told him, "you're a good customer, but I'm not going to have you pissing in the sink. You want to give me twenty grand, I'll install a bathroom back here for you. But otherwise you walk around and use the other one."

Tonight, as I walked in, Moro was hitting some balls, moving around the table excitedly, chattering aimlessly, dark eyes glittering in the bright table lights. He did look like a not-quite-still-young Marlon Brando, but with a little less hair and a little more paunch.

High rollers like Moro are often equipment freaks; I was expecting to see him with some exotic piece of wood in his hand. But he was playing with a fairly inexpensive production cue, a Meucci.

Tony, by contrast, had a beautiful cue from one of the best custom makers, Southwest. It was made of bird's-eye maple and purpleheart wood, precisely to his specifications: extra-thin butt, or gripping area; eighteen ounces, very light by U.S. pool standards; normal length (fifty-eight inches) and tip circumference (thirteen millimeters). He took the butt and one of four shafts from his case and screwed them together, watching Moro as he practiced.

Tony's backer, Romeo, was in attendance. He was a mysterious guy, maybe twenty-five, six feet tall, slim, well muscled, with shoulder-length light brown hair, usually worn in a ponytail. He was strikingly handsome, soft-spoken, and well fixed for cash. Not surprisingly, given these attributes, he enjoyed the company of a dazzling assortment of women. He favored expensive name-brand sportswear; his only jewelry was a gold earring and an understated stainless steel Swiss watch. He said he was from Tennessee, and that's all anybody knew of his background. He'd just showed up at the club a couple of months previously. He was fascinated with pool, and had watched Tony play enough to appreciate his ability. He offered to back Tony if he got into a good spot, and this was the best they'd found yet.

"Hey, Moro, you owe me seven bills," Tony said by way of greeting.

"Yeah, step on up and play me for it then," Moro retorted with a smile.

This was a strange boy, all right. Here he was eight thousand dollars stuck in this game, and he wasn't in the least bit upset, or even surly, just ready to play some more. I found myself overwhelmingly curious about this professional loser. Was Tony's poolroom psychology correct? Did Moro have a compulsion to give his money away? What wacky variety of masochism was this? Or, perhaps, was his fascination not with losing, but just with playing at this level? Just his way of being one of the boys, with losing the natural result because he was so inept? He was almost bubbling with eagerness to play. There was something exquisite, I thought, in being able to wallow in the death spasm again and again, like an actor playing Macbeth night after night, knowing along with everybody else in the house that Macduff was going to run the table on him with that broadsword, the way he always did.

I wondered about the financial aspect as well as the psychological. Was he dying for real a little bit, each time? When did the thousands begin to mean something? Would he be on the street someday, short the price of a flophouse and a hamburger, thinking about the days when he lost eight thousand dollars in one night, and came back for more? Whatever the pathology of his compulsion, it was fascinating to watch the result.

Moro put up seven hundred (Tony and Romeo put up nothing, since the money was owed them) and the game began. Moro was clearly working hard on his break—he very deliberately placed the cue ball just so, put his feet in the prescribed position, carefully stroked the cue—but there was just no pop in it, and the balls didn't roll that well. Tony told me that Moro had been taking lessons on the break from a top local player. (Tony said, "How do you like it? Here we're winning thousands from Moro, and instead of trying to make a game, this guy's giving him breaking lessons for twenty an hour.")

Tony's rates were considerably higher. It took only forty minutes for him to win seven racks. Moro just couldn't get started. Every time he failed to make a ball on the break, Tony either ran out or left him safe. He made the six ball once on the break, and once he broke in the two and made the one and then the three to win, but that's it. He played very deliberately, looking the table over carefully, but he didn't execute well at all. He tried a lot of shots he couldn't make.

Now the bill was $1,400, and that became the new bet. Moro added seven more hundreds to the stack that rested under the cue cases on the next table. He began pocketing balls better, too. He jumped out to a 6–2 lead. Now he was really animated. He talked the whole time, even when Tony was shooting. "Just look at that position," he said once, when Tony got out of line.

When he was not talking to Tony, Moro was muttering to himself, standing cross-legged, nervously swaying back and forth, then moving around the table, muttering: "No shot there, shit, I should have ducked, still he's got no shot there, shit, well, looks like he might be out but if he misses I win, I win. . . . Yeah, he hit that good, shit, yes, he's out now if he makes this. . . ."

Tony ignored him; he told me he had trained himself to concentrate well enough so that his opponents distracted themselves more than they distracted him when they started "sharking"—trying to throw him off his game. Tony refused to be rushed; he walked around the table long enough to see every angle, to analyze his position carefully. Even though Moro was a relatively slow player himself, Tony's incessant walking seemed to bother him.

"I'm going to put a pedometer on you, see how far you walk in a set," he said exasperatedly.

Finally, Moro even tried to use Tony's concentration as a weapon. As Tony was ignoring everything around him and continuing to make balls, Moro said loudly, "Jesus, doesn't anything bother this guy?" Even that didn't bother Tony, and he won four games in a row to tie the set at six apiece—"hill-hill." One game left to decide the set.

Moro broke the balls—and made the one. Worse, the two-six combination was dead in the side. He drilled it and, just like that, the $1,400 was wiped off the books. Tony's mouth tightened a bit at the corners, but that was all. He was still jocular with Moro as they agreed to play another set the same way, for $1,400. Romeo added his own stack of money to Moro's stack.

Once play resumed, Tony seemed to have found another gear. He played flawlessly, both in pocketing balls and in playing defense. Moro, meanwhile, had found reverse. If there's one thing Moro did better than sharking, it was choking. He missed almost all of the few easy shots he got, and in the next four hours Tony won six straight sets for $1,400 each.

It was almost 5 A.M. Moro had been going to the bathroom, obviously to ingest more rocket fuel, with increasing frequency, but he was very tired. His chatter had become more non-sensical, and as he watched Tony shoot the balls off the table again and again, the weariness came over him in visible waves.

When he finally had enough, he had lost another $8,400—more than $16,000 in two nights. Still, he was not angry. "I'll play you some for as much as you want, twenty, thirty thousand a set, if you'll give me the three, five, seven, and the breaks," he told Tony.

"I wouldn't give my grandmother that spot," Tony retorted.

Tony and Romeo divided the winnings fifty-fifty, and Romeo gave Rick Wallace the 10 percent he had arranged earlier.

IT WAS A LARGE PAYDAY, ANY WAY YOU LOOKED AT IT, BUT TONY WAS less than ecstatic. He couldn't stop thinking about how much money he didn't win.

"If I had won that first set for $1,400, I know the next set would have been for $2,800," he said. "Even if we didn't go up from there, that would have more than doubled what I won. But imagine if he'd kept going up the ladder, double or nothing, trying to get even. Six more sets would have brought us to, what, $5,600, $11,200, $22,400, $44,800, $89,600, $179,200! I mean, that may sound absurd, but it's not impossible," he said. We were sitting at the Q Club bar, having coffee and reviewing the highlights of the match.

"This guy did pay off two hundred thou once, Rick's right, I know the guy who beat him, playing bar pool," he said. "Still, it's a good score, and if I decide I want to give him the three, five, seven, and the break, I can take another shot." He grinned. "Did you see his face when I kicked the length of the table and made the five ball and left the cue ball in perfect position to make the six? He was going buggy." He giggled like a kid, the tension of two days of high-stakes gambling draining out of him.

"Yeah, well, look on the bright side," I said. "If you'd won more than twenty K, he probably would have wanted you to install a toilet."

He laughed again.

"Tony," I said. "Is there action like this all around the country?"

He looked at me inquiringly, chewing the cappucino foam in his mustache. "Well, not exactly like this. Moro's certainly right up there. But there's action out there, sure."

"Where?"

"Shit, I don't know. Seattle, there's Harry Platis, I'll tell you about him. Chicago, my friend Curtis might be able to find me a spot there. New York, of course. Florida. L.A. Philly. Baltimore."

"How long since you've been on the road?"

"Quite a while; I mean, other than a quick run to L.A. or Reno for a tournament. I won a grand while I was playing at the L.A. Open this year, and I won a few hundred in the tournament, too. But on the road . . . not really, not for a few years." His eyes narrowed. "Do you think we should do it?"

"I don't know if we *should,* but I want to. Maybe I'm nuts, but I'm ready to take you on the road and stake you to play."

"You're kidding."

"No, I'm not." This was the best shot at the road I would ever get, and I knew it. "Can you get away from here for a while?"

He took a deep breath, and let it out in a snort. "Shit, I *should* get away from here for a while. I need to. I'm doing nothing but being in this place, you know that. It would do me good. We're having some money troubles, I'm in a huge war with the landlord, who is a stockholder.

"Paulie could keep an eye on things while I'm gone. Hell, yes, there's action out there. I'm playing pretty good now, and if we could get into some spots where I'm not known so well, particularly back East, we could do real well. You know what I've always wanted to do? Take the train around the country, playing pool, the way the old hustlers did it in the twenties and thirties, like Danny McGoorty. Probably even before that. It would be a cheap, enjoyable way to do it."

"That sounds pretty good. How much of a stake do you suppose we'd need?"

"I don't know, maybe twenty thousand to gamble with? I'd just need my expenses, and I'll have to take care of a few things here before I leave. When do you want to do this?"

"Soon," I said. "Just tend to business, get ready to go. Talk to a few people, find out where they're gambling. Take a look at the tournament schedule, too. I want to get all the way around the country." I shook my head. "Twenty thousand to gamble with. I must be nuts."

"What about Canada? We ought to try to play some snooker up there. They don't think Americans can play. We might do real good."

"Canada. Florida. New York. Los Angeles. We're going to need some time. A couple months, maybe three."

"Wow," he said. "Now that's a road trip. But you're right, it's going to take at least that long."

"Good," I said.

II

The Coast Starlight

"It was 1:08 in the morning when I got on the Seminole Limited."

—Danny McGoorty in *McGoorty* by Robert Byrne

SEPTEMBER 23—AS OF TODAY I AM A STAKEHORSE.

I was no longer an interested amateur, playing or even watching pool as a diversion. I was now a professional "sweater"—one who sits and sweats as he watches because he is *in action*, has money riding on each shot. I was staking a player, putting up the money he was playing for. If he won, I would get half of what he won. If he lost, I would lose all of what I bet.

In a reckless burst of weirdness, I had made arrangements to launch myself and my "horse," Mr. Tony Annigoni, on an ambitious international road trip. We were leaving this night, in time-honored fashion, on a train. Pool hustlers have been catching trains from town to town for most, if not all, of this century.

In *McGoorty,* Robert Byrne's wonderful oral history, billiard champion and pool hustler Danny McGoorty remembered that during the Depression, "I learned how to roll a cigarette on top of a boxcar doing sixty miles an hour. . . . I learned how to keep a fire going on the floor of a boxcar. . . . [and] I learned how to ride the rods. Under railroad cars are steel rods running from one end to the other. You didn't just hang on to them like an acrobat, you laid boards over them, cross-wise. . . . Even with a good platform, it paid to tie yourself on with your belt, and to blindfold yourself with your handker-chief—otherwise you got blinded by the sand and grit that shot in your face. Even tied on, it was dangerous to fall asleep, because you were inches from certain death."

At least Danny got to ride in a boxcar every once in a while. For California Red, a famous black hustler of the same era, the rods were the only way. The passenger trains were all-white, and a black hobo would get rousted from a boxcar every time.

It looked like we would be able to avoid hopping freights. As an integral part of my new career as a professional gambler, I had on my person $10,233.76 in cash. It was distributed like this: I had seven twenties, a ten, two ones, and $1.76 in loose change in the left-hand pocket of my jeans. This was the petty cash drawer. In the right pocket was something known in the trade as a "Chicago bankroll." This consisted of one twenty wrapped around the outside of a roll of sixty ones and secured with a rubber band. This would be useful, I hoped, as a diver-sion, if we were accosted somewhere. Bob Obici, the propri-etor of Don Q Billiards in Santa Barbara and a onetime road player, had suggested it. "If you get stuck up, just take out that roll and throw it in one direction—say 'Here, take the money'—and run in the other direction," he said. "Are they going to chase you or go get the money? They're going to go get the money, every time."

I had a slightly constricted feeling between my left knee and the calf muscle. This was caused by one hundred $100 bills, split into two stacks and encased in a cotton-elastic "leg wallet," made to look sort of like an Ace bandage. My Levi's just barely fit over the lump, but once they did you couldn't see it was there. It was not going anywhere. I knew this because I reached down and checked it surreptitiously approximately every forty seconds.

I was not used to all this. I was used to getting sixty dollars out of the ATM every once in a while. If I was really feeling reckless, eighty. But that was back before I became a professional gambler.

Tucked into one of the pockets of my briefcase was $17,000 in Visa traveler's checks—four very elegant $500 checks and fifteen books of ten more understated $100 types—along with a checkbook which, used in concert with the credit cards in my wallet, would enable us to piss away another fifteen thousand or so, if need be. I certainly hoped not. Every time I stopped to think about it I realized just how far through the looking glass I was about to go. But you have to admit, backing a pool hustler was certainly a more interesting proposition than taking a flutter with a new tax-free municipal. Security and prudence were never on my top five. You could ask my ex-wife.

All that aside, the transformation from ATM-using writer with relatively conventional fiscal habits to ramblin, gamblin, cash-flush road warrior was not easy to accomplish. Banks were not comfortable with this sort of metamorphosis, as I had discovered earlier in the day when I went to the Polk Street branch of my bank, American Savings Bank.

When I greeted teller Dolores Gonzales with a smile and said, "I'd like fifteen thousand in cash please, hundreds, and another fifteen thousand in traveler's checks, out of my checking account," the effect was similar to what I could have produced if I'd simply handed her a note that said, "I have a gun."

"What?" she said. "We can't do that."

"Excuse me, but the money's in my account, and I need to get it out."

"You have to order that kind of cash in advance."

"I didn't have to notify you in advance when I deposited the money. You were happy enough to take it right then."

"Just a minute." She withdrew, eyeing me nervously, calling for backup in the form of the branch manager.

"Sir, we don't have that kind of cash," the manager said.

"Let me get this straight," I said, raising my voice a few notches. "You don't have fifteen thousand dollars in this bank?"

"Please, sir!" the manager looked around nervously. "Why do you need so much cash?"

"Why do you need to know? Look, I'm a writer. This is a research project, and where I'm going they don't take American Express."

"Just a minute." They both retreated again. Finally, Dolores returned and said, "I can give you ten thousand in cash but I don't have that many hundreds. You'll have to take seven thousand of it in twenties."

I could see that it wasn't going to get any better, so I agreed, winning a final concession: another couple of grand in traveler's checks. Dolores put me to work signing the whole pile—it took about fifteen minutes—and then led me around the tellers' cages into a back room, where she counted out 30 hundreds and 350 twenties as I watched, put them in a canvas sack, and handed them to me.

"I've been here fifteen years, and I've never handed anybody this much cash," she said, with a hint of disapproval. "Whatever you're doing, be careful."

I stuffed the pouch into my briefcase. "If I were the careful type," I told her, "I wouldn't be doing this."

On the way out, I hit the ATM for another $200 in twenties.

I walked up the street to the Bank of America and went to the commercial teller window. "Excuse me," I said, "but I would like to trade some twenties for hundreds."

"How many?"

"Seven thousand dollars' worth."

This provoked a whispered conference with the manager, who came over and asked me, "Do you have an account with us?"

"No, my bank told me to come here. You see, they ran out of hundreds and had to give me a lot of twenties."

"Oh, I see," he said, looking at me as though I had just admitted to being a crack dealer, which of course he thought I was. "No, I don't think we'll be able to do that." Three banks later, I got an understanding manager at First Interstate who did the deed for me. Finally, I had my cash in manageable proportion.

"Be careful," she warned me.

"Yeah, yeah."

OUR FAREWELL-TO–SAN FRANCISCO DINNER AT THE HAYES STREET Grill was pleasant. In honor of the occasion Tony went off his vegetables-and-rice diet, opting for salmon, french fries, and salad. We discussed our plans over a bottle of crisp Pinot Blanc.

For the past month, Tony had gathered as much road-related gossip and rumor as he could—what an FBI agent would call "raw intelligence data." For someone so well connected, it wasn't hard to do—the pool world isn't on the Internet, yet, but word of good action gets around the country fast. Naturally, the stories are often hyperbolic, the dollar amounts inflated and some of the circumstances altered.

Some sources are more reliable than others; some, for reasons of their own, will spread false stories on purpose. This is called a "double steer"—the equivalent of a disinformation campaign in the intelligence world—and it happens often. Pool alliances can be opaque and changeable. Consider: If player A is going on the road, he might call player B and ask him what's happening in B's town. Perhaps B might say that A can get good action there with player C, who is gambling "high" and not playing that well. If C gets a favorable game with A as a result, and wins some money, he might give B a "gapper," sort of a tip, representing a percentage of what he won. Conversely, depending on how he's feeling that day, and who seems like a better long-term prospect, B might tip A off to the fact that C is indeed playing extremely well, and advise him to ask for a significant spot or refuse to play.

Everything Tony heard, therefore, had to be evaluated carefully. Some of the dispatches from the front were as vague as "there's a lot of action right now in Florida" and some were as specific as "there's a guy named Cornflakes who's playing high in Jimmy Fusco's room in Philadelphia, and you're supposed to beat him straight up."

Based on everything he'd heard, and what we already knew, we had cobbled together an ambitious foray into the poolrooms and snooker clubs of the United States and Canada.

In my briefcase, next to the traveler's checks, were four months' worth of airplane and train tickets, purchased in advance to get maximum savings, despite the fact that I realized full well we might have sudden and wrenching changes of plan along the way. I got out the itinerary and we went through it one more time: We were booked on the *Coast Starlight*, northbound to Portland, then Seattle. The night train. We'd scheduled a day's layover in Portland, to stretch legs, hit some balls, and prepare for our assault on Seattle—

specifically, on one Harry Platis, one of the preeminent pool scores in the country. Harry, Tony told me, was an attorney specializing in personal injury cases who owned a Cadillac dealership, and he loved to gamble.

After Seattle, we'd planned to head up to Vancouver, then east to Chicago. Toronto. New York. New Jersey. Philadelphia. Washington. South Carolina. Florida. Across to L.A. by air, then to Reno, then eastbound again by train, to Omaha, back to Chicago, then south to New Orleans. West through Texas to Arizona, then to Los Angeles again for the finish, during Super Bowl Week. Roughly thirteen thousand miles of travel in a little less than four months.

Our first schedule change occurred right after dinner. I called Amtrak to check on the progress of the *Starlight* as it headed up the coast from L.A. Not so good. The train was two hours late; try showing up around midnight, the operator advised.

At 11:15 we humped our luggage into the cab. Being on the edge of winter, and going across the country, we had to pack for temperatures ranging from zero to eighty, and for a full variety of social situations, or at least we thought we did. I had a huge duffel, a large soft-sided pullman, and the briefcase. Tony was even worse: three large bags plus a briefcase. And, of course, our cue cases. Tony, I noticed, treated his cue exactly as a new mother treats an infant. He almost never let it out of his hands, much less his sight.

"Oakland, the train station," I said to the driver, who smiled broadly and nodded, his long, dark Brylcreemed hair bobbing up and down. At this hour, traffic was light; we zipped over the Bay Bridge in no time. "Hey," I said. "Wasn't that the exit?"

"You know where is train station?" the driver asked, still grinning.

"Yeah, back there," I said.

"Back?" He stopped the cab and began backing up on the freeway. Light traffic or not, this didn't seem like a good plan, since the exit was at least half a mile behind us. Tony said, "Hey, pal, put it in drive, turn the meter off, and turn around at the next exit." The meter stayed on, but he did go forward again, taking the downtown Oakland exit into an area not recommended for aimless midnight touring, then finally stopped in confusion and threw up his hands. Tony was normally relatively patient and polite, at least with strangers, but this was too much. "Look, you lame-brained Liberace-looking asshole, turn the meter off before I rip it out, and get back on the freeway heading west." The driver did as he was told, sulkily. Ten minutes later he dropped us off at the station and, tipless, gunned the cab viciously out of the deserted parking lot. Not an auspicious start, I thought.

At least we didn't miss the train. It didn't show up until 1:15 A.M. An hour later, after getting the mountain of luggage loaded and our compartment located, I discovered something that would haunt me for the rest of the trip: My road partner snored.

ONE THING ABOUT TRAIN TRAVEL: IT GIVES YOU PLENTY OF TIME FOR conversation—particularly at the rate we were going. One locomotive was giving the engineers problems, and by midmorning we were more than eight hours behind schedule. As we limped upgrade through the lower Cascades toward Klamath Falls, we played penny-a-point gin and traded wisecracks, which I had discovered was Tony's favored way of communicating with his friends. I didn't need to read *Iron John* to know that it was a guy thing—the more he liked you, the more obnoxious the insults became. I decided the only thing to be done was to respond in kind. In the process, though, I found out quite a bit more about my player.

Born in San Francisco in 1953 of second-generation American parents, Tony Annigoni is 100 percent Italian (his French middle name, Chenier, came from his father, an opera fanatic who named him after the opera by Giordano). He was the youngest child in a large Bay Area extended family. Relatives of both his parents were sprinkled through the Italian enclaves of North Beach, the Mission, the Marina, and the peninsula south of the city. Being the baby meant he was a special pet to the whole family, and he remembered his early childhood as happy and filled with affection. By the time he started school, his parents had bought a house in the quiet little peninsula community of Burlingame, "City of Trees." In the late fifties and early sixties it was overwhelmingly white and middle-class, a bland, comfortable place to grow up.

Tony's father, Michael, was an electrician. He learned his trade working in the San Francisco shipyards during World War II, then started his own contracting business. Michael's father owned a cigar store at Columbus and Green in North Beach for many years, but never bought a house. Tony's maternal grandfather, Antonio Scrivani, also owned a business, a small scavenging company, started with nothing more than a horse-drawn cart. Later, he would sell it and open a little neighborhood bar on Polk Street.

The Scrivanis were different from the Annigonis; they wanted something to call their own. So, as their business prospered, they bought a big house in the Mission district, at 27 Twenty-eighth Street, in 1920, where they lived the rest of their lives.

.   .   .

"WHAT, ARE YOU ASLEEP OVER THERE? GIVE ME A CARD. . . . HEY, THAT'S good, how long you been hoarding that one? Knock for six."

"Fuck. You. Of course, nothing plays. Ten, twenty, thirty-one minus six, twenty-five."

"What a bimbo. I'm on the road with a card bimbo. Yeah, I tried to buy my grandparents' house from the estate but my cousin wouldn't let me, like it was this fuckin big deal, I don't know why. I have great memories of that house, from when I was a kid."

MICHAEL ANNIGONI WORKED HARD, BUT PROSPERITY ESCAPED HIM; the family managed to pay its bills and send the kids to Catholic school, but money was always tight. Still, despite his family's limited means, Tony knew something of wealth; Burlingame sits deferentially at the knee of baronial Hillsborough, and Tony and his friends used to sneak onto the grounds of the mansions to play. He lived just a few blocks from Bing Crosby's lavish home.

"WE USED TO ROLL OUR BASKETBALL IN FRONT OF HIS CAR, SO HE HAD TO stop. It was a white Rolls-Royce. We would croon at him, give him shit: 'I'm dreeeeeeeaming of a whiiiiiiite Rolls-Royce.' We tortured the guy. He was an asshole."

"He must have loved you, too."

AFTER A YEAR OF PUBLIC-SCHOOL KINDERGARTEN, TONY WENT TO the Capuchin Fathers School, where he was, if not among the most pious of the primary students, certainly sociable, studious, and well behaved. In fact, he got top grades for his first five years of school.

In the fifth grade, everything changed. One afternoon he

walked home from school to find just about all of his relatives' cars in front of the house. Wow, we must be having a family reunion, he thought. When he went inside, he found out why: After Tony had left for school that morning, his father had shot himself. His mother had been in the house when it happened.

"HE HAD HAD A REAL BAD BUSINESS FAILURE, AND FOR WHATEVER REASON he couldn't accept it. I mean, he was employable, and we didn't have big money problems or anything. We had a house and a house payment, but my mom was willing to get out of the house and go back to work if necessary. My sister was already married and out of the house. So it never made any sense to me."

"Was your dad a gambler at all?"

"Nah. My dad wouldn't bet four cents there was fish in the fuckin ocean. Knock for two."

HIS FATHER'S SUICIDE, COMBINED WITH HIS OWN ADOLESCENCE, changed Tony's relationship with the Capuchin Fathers in a hurry. He no longer felt like being an honor student, and he wasn't. He felt angry, disillusioned with the Church, and uncomfortable in his fatherless home.

His family did everything they could for the *bambino* who caught such a lousy break early in life. His uncles and cousins were always looking out for him. Tony always loved sports, so they took him to Giants games at Candlestick Park, and 49er football games, too. Despite his size, his eye-hand coordination and fearless pugnacity earned him respect in schoolyard basketball games, and his male relatives, doing their best to be a collective substitute father, made sure he had all the equipment he needed to play his best. His favorite player was Jerry comparison to his other life. He had also begun to display the avarice of the professional gambler.

"I HAD FOUR VICES IN HIGH SCHOOL, BASICALLY: I PITCHED COINS FOR money, I loan-sharked money, I missed a lot of school for playing pool, and I used to forge notes for people so they could get out of school. I charged them two bucks apiece. I displayed entrepreneurial spirit early in life."

"In other words, you were a filthy little hoodlum."

"Not at all. I didn't do drugs. I mean, I tried pot once or twice and I didn't like it, so I never did it. I didn't smoke tobacco so I saw no need to smoke that stuff. Of course, the padres all thought I was doing drugs, because I was nodding out in class all the time."

"Okay, you were a filthy little hoodlum who didn't do drugs."

TONY STARTED GOING TO COCHRAN'S FREQUENTLY DURING THE DAY. A school friend, Rich Setzer, was of the same mind. He lived between Tony and the Serra campus, and on many mornings Tony would be late to school, walking along, and Setzer, late too, would pull up in his car. "Cochran's?" one of them would say. The other would nod. "Hop in," Setzer would say, and thoughts of going to school were forgotten.

One day Tony's uncle called him. "Tony, I understand you're shooting some pretty good pool. Look, kid, I want you to go over to Juan's house tonight. He's got something for you. He's got a cue."

Juan Salcido was the father-in-law of one of Tony's cousins. He had owned a little poolroom in the Mission district for thirty years.

· · ·

West, the superstar Laker guard, and Tony's long hours on the playground produced a shooting touch worthy of his idol.

Tony had always been competitive, and he loved games of all kinds. He took great pride on beating the grownups in the family at whatever games they played—Monopoly, Concentration, card games.

"YEAH, I WAS AN ARROGANT LITTLE PECKERWOOD."

"You still are."

"Hey, bubba, what kind of fuckin cut was that?"

"Just the way I wanted it."

"Yeah, I bet, that's not a legal cut, cut 'em over."

"What are you talking about? You're just like the bank: I have my money in the bank, they won't give it to me. You're beating my brains out, I cut the cards, you won't accept the cut."

"That's right. If a beady-eyed motherfucker like you came into my bank, I wouldn't give you any money either. I'd make you play gin for it."

ONE AFTERNOON WHEN TONY WAS IN THE EIGHTH GRADE, HE WAS walking from school to a basketball game when he saw something that made him stop. It was a new business on Burlingame's main drag: Broadway Billiards. A poolroom, right there in River City. Tony's parents had bought him a tiny pool table when he was seven, and he wore it out, but since then he hadn't been exposed to the game. Nobody in his immediate family played, and there was no place close by. Until now. The place had a slightly disreputable ambience and the pockets on the big green tables beckoned like ten-foot jump shots. He was fourteen years old, and he was in love.

He and a few friends started playing there all the time. A

couple of them showed some promise, but none of them was like Tony. In a matter of weeks he mastered the basics of the game. He was lucky to get some good coaching, early on, from a player named Hal Houle. Houle was only an average player, but he was a tennis instructor, and he knew how to teach. Tony was an excellent pupil; he was fascinated with the game, and he worked hard, and the mechanics of the game clicked into place. Here was a game in which he could take full advantage of his razor-sharp eyes, his muscle memory and coordination, his intelligence, his love of strategy, his competitiveness, his easy way with people, even his smart-alecky side. All were assets. And for once, his size was not a roadblock to success. Before long, he was counted among the best players in town.

The social structure of the poolroom filled a void for him. It was a milieu in which he could be recognized for his talent despite his youth. The way he looked at it, it was pretty simple: The better you could play, the cooler you were, and being cool, after all, was the objective for a teenaged kid. He saw some pretty cool characters playing pool on TV, such as Peter Lawford and Robert Wagner and Dean Martin.

The gambling part of the game appealed to him, too; he appreciated the value of a buck, and he quickly figured out who he could beat, and who he had to stay away from. He lost a little, but he won far more—mostly small change, playing for quarters and dollars and occasionally five bucks. Losing meant you were a sucker, and that was the most uncool thing you could be. Winning, though, was the ultimate in coolness.

He played with his friends, but as he improved he enjoyed playing older men a lot more. You could learn something, playing better players, and they had more money to win. He worked his way through the two-dollar guys who came in, the dishwashers, gas-station attendants, truck drivers, delivery-

men, grocery-store checkers, until they wouldn't play him anymore. One day, playing four-ball, a nine-ball variation, for five bucks a game, he managed to beat a guy out of sixty-five dollars.

The owners of Broadway Billiards were two erstwhile used-car salesmen from Utah. They took a liking to the smart-mouthed, straight-shooting kid, and they began to take him around to play in tournaments here and there—San Mateo, even up to Sacramento. And they took him to San Francisco, to Palace Billiards, to Cochran's. Tony couldn't believe the scene. Walking upstairs to Cochran's, peering through the blue haze, he knew he had found his Mecca.

Cochran's had more than thirty tables, and there was action on almost every one, players betting anywhere from twenty to a hundred dollars a game, playing one-pocket, nine-ball, bank pool, straight pool. There was a big six-by-twelve snooker table, too, with tiny pockets and a day-and-night game of payball going on, where they racked six balls in a tiny triangle and the players took turns, paying on every ball made. The pink ball, the six-point ball in snooker, was racked in the middle, and it was worth twice as much as the others.

Signs were posted: NO WOMEN ALLOWED ON PREMISES. This was 1969; women who would frequent the place were likely to be hookers. The place was a temple of maleness, of gambling and cussing and smoking and spitting, of brutal humor and quick tempers.

Tony's pool education was proceeding rapidly, and he was a model student. The same could not be said, however, of his academic career. By now, the Capuchin Fathers had sent him on to Serra, the local Catholic boys' high school, where he was losing ground fast. For one thing, he was staying out all night playing pool, which didn't do much for his alertness at school or his homework. And for another, school was pretty boring i

"HERE THE GUY WAS, A ROOM OWNER ALL THIS TIME, AND BEING A PUNK kid I took it for granted that he was a square. I saw him in a different setting, you know, a family man. So I'm thinking to myself, Juan's got a cue for me, this is great. You know how it is when you're a kid. Your grandmother says to your parents, gee, what does little Tony want for Christmas? So they say Tony wants a baseball bat so she gives you the worst, most worthless bat in the world, right? You're still grateful and you love her and you appreciate it but you couldn't hit a ball ten feet with it.

"I got to Juan's house. I love Juan, he's the greatest old guy in the world, always nice to me, sending me baseball tickets, shit like that. So now we're talking and he says, let me get the cue. And so he comes with this beautiful three-shaft Willie Hoppe, beautiful, a Brunswick Willie fucking Hoppe, perfect, with a great Brunswick leather case, one of the old good ones, absolutely perfect. Holy shit, I say, this is exactly what I was looking for but I couldn't afford one.

" 'Your uncle told me you're serious about playing,' he says. 'I want you to be careful. There's a tough element out there.' I said, 'Oh yeah,' so of course it ended up getting stolen at Cochran's, just like they stole my cash that time I fell asleep."

I WAS NOT, FOR THE MOMENT, SITTING IN A DEAD TRAIN IN SOUTHern Oregon with a horrible gin hand in front of me. The thought of Willie Hoppe had taken me away. Willie Hoppe. The magical name on the butt end of a cue in my own past. By today's standards, it wasn't really a very good cue, but it was the best I'd ever seen in 1969.

I put up the forty dollars the road player won for me against a Willie Hoppe cue, and played a game of snooker for it, and won my first good cue. It was relatively light, just over eighteen ounces, and its only shaft had been sanded down over the years so that the tip was barely eleven millimeters in diameter—a real "needle," just the way I liked it for the smaller snooker balls. The cue looked right, too—like a serious player's cue, with a black leather wrap, a brass joint, and four simple, beautiful inlaid points. Right below them the name, Willie Hoppe, in a spidery, elegant hand, was burned into the wood beneath the varnish. It always reminded me of my favorite Louisville Slugger, the Mickey Mantle autograph model. It was the lance I used to joust with the wheat farmers and Union Pacific men who frequented the Stag. My favorite opponents were the two Freds.

Fred Bitterman was a brakeman, sour as his name. He was about fifty, with wire-rim specs and straight-back, Brylcreemed black hair. He would be in town on a crew change once a week. He always wore the same red and white checked shirt and Lee jeans with the cuffs turned up, and he never left anybody a good shot in his life.

We played golf, a game on the snooker table in which the object is to make your ball in each of the pockets in order before your opponent does the same thing. It is a marvelously complex game, full of three- and four-rail bank shots and lagging, or slow-rolling, your ball toward your pocket. Most important is defense, leaving your opponent no shot. It is played for a base amount, say five dollars, and a smaller amount per scratch (illegal shot, either the cue ball going into a pocket or missing the object ball), say, twenty-five cents each. It is a nasty, jabbing, parrying, chesslike battle when played correctly, and as such it perfectly suited Fred Bitterman. The only time he smiled was when he won. He was a little better than me, when we started playing, but he brought me up to his level soon enough. I liked to play him because I learned quite a few shots from him, and I began to learn how to channel the *desire* to win into the *skill* of winning. I wanted to keep that smile off his face, and his hand out of my wallet.

We played for a dollar a game and a dime a scratch, and it was rare that more than five dollars changed hands by the time we were done with an afternoon session, but that was enough, when you considered that you could eat for a week on five dollars. Railroad jobs paid well, and Freddie probably had a hell of a lot more money than I did; just out of high school, I made only seventy a week at the *Sidney Telegraph*. Still, my apartment above the Stag cost me only forty-five dollars a month.

Freddie Byers was different, and playing him was different, too. Pool, in those days, was a tribal ritual, not just a way of determining dominance among males, but a way of reliving and honoring traditions. For me, playing Freddie was an honor, a sign of respect for him as a tribal elder, and for the culture of the game. We never gambled; the game was the only thing we needed.

Freddie was in his ninety-fourth year, and he had played snooker for seventy of them, mostly during the winters when there wasn't much to do on the farm. We would play exactly two games on Tuesday and two more on Thursday, always at 11 A.M. The *Telegraph* came out on Monday, Wednesday, and Friday, and on those days I had to work in the morning. He won one, and I won one, most days.

Freddie's eyes weren't what they had once been—he wore thick bifocals—but there was no tremor in his stroke, and he didn't have to see that well because he knew every shot on the table by instinct. He would not take a shot he couldn't make, and he knew how to take care of whitey, too. Like as not, when Freddie missed, I'd be eyeing the cue ball, on the rail, and peering the length of the table to find something to shoot at.

After we played, we'd each have a hamburger, and he'd have a short beer, and I'd have a Coke because Rich Fahey, the owner, knew exactly how old I was. And we'd talk.

Freddie was the patriarch of a farming family. Farmers everywhere talk about the same things: the economy and the weather. More accurately, prices and moisture. Freddie didn't talk about prices much. Everybody knew wheat sold way too cheap, below a buck a bushel, but he still had grain stored from 1959 that he hadn't needed to sell yet. So during our lunches we talked about moisture, mostly: the dearth of it, or the excess of it, but mostly the blessing of it. "Hell of a snow, Freddie." "Yep, that winter wheat's layin down good, heh heh, real good. A couple more storms like this and we'll be just right, heh heh, just right." After ninety-three western Nebraska winters, including such highlights as the incredible Easter Day blizzard of '88, Freddie Byers was an expert on snow.

He got around forty bushels of wheat to an acre of ground, like most of the farmers in Cheyenne County, which was pretty damn good for dryland wheat, but then western Nebraska was like that: the right moisture, at the right time, most years. And plenty of time to play snooker in the winter.

"HEY, YA FUCKIN GOOFBALL, ARE YOU GOING TO SIT THERE ALL NIGHT? Gimme a card."

"Cool yourself. Take a look at the scenery. I'll give you a card when I'm good and ready."

"We've been here fifteen minutes, and I've been looking at the scenery the whole time, waiting for you to play. I can tell you where every fuckin tree is located out there. Besides, it's getting dark."

"There, take that one if you want it. Hey, I have an idea you're going to love."

"Thanks for nothing. What?"

"I don't think we ought to get off the train in Portland."

"Oh, yeah, this has been so much fun I don't think we ever ought to get off. Are you out of your mind?"

"No. We're already ten hours late. We're supposed to take tomorrow's train to Seattle, not this one, but God knows how late that train will be. Is, already. And if it isn't late we'll end up hopping off this train, getting three hours sleep or something, and getting back on. If we just ride this one straight through we'll actually get to Seattle a little earlier than planned and we can sleep for a while before we get there."

"That's not bad, if they don't have this compartment booked from Portland to Seattle tonight. But what about our bags, checked through to Portland?"

Good thinking. A helpful assistant conductor took care of switching our tickets, and rooted through the baggage car to retag our luggage. Portland, our first destination, was now expunged from the itinerary. At least we didn't lose any money there.

TONY GOT TO KNOW THE ENTIRE FOOD CHAIN AT COCHRAN'S AND the Palace, and some of the links were real beauties: Chinatown Jimmy Wong, who unnerved opponents when he set his bridge hand on the table because his little finger, broken long ago (some said in a tong dispute) was over *there*, just barely connected to the rest of his hand, like a vestigial part, or an afterthought; Filipino Gene, whom I had already met; Joe Smiley, Mexican Phil, Ears, Legs, all of them. All the way to the top of the heap, which at that time was the territory of Denny Searcy.

Denny was maybe ten years older than Tony. He was a big, good-looking Southerner, quiet and pleasant and deadly. He had a powerful, flamboyant stroke and astounding accuracy. On the snooker table with its tiny pockets, he could drive balls the length of the table, down the rails, cut them almost backwards, it didn't matter, they still went in. Mustached, with dark hair stylishly long, he was most reminiscent of Catfish Hunter, his fellow Carolinian.

Searcy played all the games well, but he was nearly unbeatable playing snooker and payball. He won when he was supposed to, and he didn't book many bad games. Tony watched him play as much as he could, and played against him some, too, particularly in the payball game, where Tony's own ball-pocketing prowess enabled him to hold his own.

Meanwhile, the padres at Serra High made it clear to Tony that the way he was going, he would not earn enough credits in his final year to graduate. His teachers and his family knew he was smart, and they all expected him to be a great student. He knew it too, and it bothered him, but it was almost like he couldn't help himself. He wasn't happy with school, or with home, but he was happy when he was playing pool. As his grades continued to suffer, the disapproving fathers, those representatives of an authority he no longer recognized, those fathers who could never be his father, were certain that he was on drugs.

"HONEST TO GOD, I WAS ON THE NATCH THE WHOLE TIME—I WASN'T even drinking. I just loved to stay out all night, playing pool and gambling. You're a little hot because I took that card, yep, you're a little hot, aren't you buddy boy?"

"Fuck you."

"Hee hee, he's takin the heat. Hey, you don't mind throwing the cards where I can see 'em, do you? Do I get multiple choice when you fuckin scramble the deck like that? Is that it? Do I get to go back and pick whichever one I want?"

"That's okay, I just did it to fuck with you. Ah, nice card there.
Gin."

FACED WITH EXPULSION, TONY TRANSFERRED TO BURLINGAME HIGH
School, where yet another significant distraction awaited him:
girls, and before long, specifically one girl: Dorothy Hepe.
She was in one of his classes, and he couldn't get over how
beautiful she was: tiny, exotic, olive-skinned, with a lush
cascade of dark hair down her back. She was part Italian, part
Castilian Spanish, and he was crazy about her. They were a
perfect match in many ways. It was first love at its headiest.

Now, for a kid of seventeen Tony had a lot on his plate. He
had, as it turned out, found both the love of his life and a lifelong obsession, and he hadn't even graduated from high
school. He felt happier than he ever had, but he was a little
frazzled, too. School, pool, and Dorothy all competed for his
time, and for his spirit.

Still, he was seeing plenty of Cochran's. By this time Tony
was an eighty-ball runner in straight pool, which put him
firmly in the "shortstop" category—a player good enough to
beat all but the very best local players, but still not a threat to
top professionals. Well, not most of the time, anyway. Occasionally, Tony showed flashes of world-class talent. He played
well enough to make money consistently—and to make his
dream of greatness a realistic pursuit.

After high school he attended the College of San Mateo,
and did well enough that the dean of instruction wrote a
letter recommending that he be accepted at Cal, despite his
horrible high school record. He was working hard on his pool
game, too, doing his "graduate work" with two coaches: Ed
Nagel, a fine player who worked with him at Town and Coun-

try Billiards in San Mateo, and then a little later Hal Mix, generally acknowledged as the best pool coach alive.

Dorothy, naturally, was beginning to wonder just where she fit in. She didn't like Tony playing pool, and she wasn't wild about him going off to college either. "If you go to Berkeley, what will I be doing?" she asked. She just wanted him to get a job and settle down in Burlingame. Tony's reaction to all the pressure was predictable—he bolted. But when pool players do it, there's another name for it. It's called going on the road.

TONY WAS NINETEEN, AND HE AND A FEW FRIENDS HAD PUT TOGETH-er two thousand dollars as a road stake. They heard there was some action in Arizona, so they drove to Phoenix.

After a little scuffling around for small money, Tony finally made a game with a low-level hustler named Three-Dollar Sam. Tony knew he could beat this guy, easy, but for one nightmarish night, playing for a hundred dollars a set, Sam got every possible roll. Tony ended the night down six hundred, and when he saw the guy the next day and tried to get another game, Three-Dollar Sam announced that he was going on vacation.

Tony and his friends decided to go south to Tucson. In the poolroom downtown, they ran into Rick Garrison, a good player Tony had known in San Mateo. "Is there any action out here?" he asked.

"I might be able to get you a game with a rich old man," Garrison said. "But you'll have to play his game, on his table."

"No problem," Tony replied. "Lead me to him."

"Okay. Meet me at the Triple T Truck Stop out on the free-way tonight at nine."

When they got there, Tony and his friends discovered that

the mark was the manager of the diesel-repair shop at the Triple T, a big, florid man in his late sixties. He led them behind the truck stop to his trailer. He had built a big cinder-block addition, and when they went inside Tony couldn't believe his eyes.

The room contained three beautiful, top-quality pool tables, two Brunswick Gold Crown 4$\frac{1}{2}$-by-9s and a custom-made 5-by-10 snooker table, absolutely pristine. Most snooker tables have fewer "diamonds," or inlays along the rails, which some players use to figure bank shots, than do the smaller pool tables, but this table had a diamond every couple of inches. Obviously, the guy had some kind of complicated geometric system of reading rails, and had had this table especially made to help him. Sure enough, it was this table he wanted to play on, and the game he wanted to play was one-pocket.

In one-pocket, one player chooses one of the two corner pockets at the head of the table, and the other player gets the other pocket. The first player to pocket eight of the fifteen balls in his pocket wins. That simple description belies the complexity of what many players feel is the hardest, most demanding game played on a pool table. In his book *The Bank Shot and Other Great Robberies,* Rudolph Wanderone, aka Minnesota Fats, opines, "The game of One Pocket . . . combines the intricacies of both billiards and pocket billiards. It is played properly only by experts."

One-pocket places a premium on "lagging," or getting balls *close* to a pocket, so they may be made easily later, and on defense. Tony preferred games like nine-ball and snooker which, while still having defensive elements, reward ball-pocketing more. Still, he had the skill to win at one-pocket, and his offensive accuracy gave him a constant edge on less talented players who simply knew how to move the cue ball well.

. . .

"A LOT OF SUCKERS PLAY ONE-POCKET BECAUSE THEY CAN'T SHOOT straight, and they always think they're smarter than players like me, and understand the nuance and strategy of the game better."

"Sort of the way you are about gin rummy."

TONY AND THE DIESEL REPAIRMAN MADE A GAME. IT BECAME CLEAR right away that the guy had played a lot of one-pocket, and he knew the table really well. It had an almost ridiculously fast cloth on it, so fast that the balls rolled twice as far as you might expect. Pretty soon, the guy was four hundred dollars ahead, but he could see that Tony was getting the hang of the table. "I'm getting kind of dizzy," he said. "I'd better quit for tonight. Let's go get a meal, over at the truck stop."

They went over, and the guy bought everybody a huge meal with Tony's money, salad, steak, pie, the works. "Come on back tomorrow night," he said. "We'll play some more."

Tony's belly was full, but his bankroll was emptying fast. Counting the six hundred he'd lost to Three-Dollar Sam, he was out about a grand for the weekend.

The next night, Tony played better, but the guy still jumped out to a two-hundred-dollar lead, and then he quit suddenly again. "I'm getting dizzy," he said. "Let's go get something to eat."

Now Tony was fuming, but he didn't want to antagonize the guy. He still had hopes of getting his money back, if not winning. He went down to the pool hall the next day to get in some practice before returning to the weird gray block building in the desert where he had left so much of his cash.

As he practiced, he noticed a couple of young longhaired guys playing nine-ball for a little money. He quickly saw that he could beat them both easily, but there was no opportunity to try to get a game.

That night, at the truck stop, three men were ostensibly unloading some crates, but not actually doing very much except watching the action. Two of them were the guys he saw playing nine-ball at the poolroom earlier. He had never seen the other man before. By now, it was obvious that Tony's skill was catching up with the older player's knowledge of one-pocket and of his own table. Tony was getting used to the fast cloth, and to the other man's style of play. After Tony won two games for $150 each, his opponent said, "Let's take a break." He went outside with the three younger men, supposedly to help them unload something. Tony was impatient. The action was going his way, and he wanted to keep playing.

The four men came back in, none of them looking at Tony at first. The room was silent for a minute. "Come on, let's play," Tony said.

The old man flashed a glance at the other men, and replied, "No, I'd like to rest for a while, but these guys play nine-ball. Maybe one of them would give you a game."

Tony said, "I'll play any of them, a hundred a set, right now. Let's go."

"Well," the old man said, "This fella here, he won't play you for a hundred. But he'll play you for five hundred."

"Okay," Tony said, and, predictably, the man he had never seen before started to put together a cue. By now, Tony knew they'd brought this guy in just to play him. The old man could see that there was a good chance Tony would eventually get to him on the one-pocket table, so he had brought in a nine-ball "ringer" to take the action. Also, getting Tony to switch from the snooker table to a smaller, slower table could be expected to throw off his game. How many times have they worked this deal with road players, Tony wondered.

Of course, Tony's new opponent was a professional-caliber nine-ball player. But for some reason, changing tables didn't throw Tony at all. The pockets on the smaller table looked as big as Minnesota Fats's pants. He won the first set 11–8. They played again, and he won again, this time 11–6.

Now he was $1,300 up for the night, and he'd recovered everything he'd lost to Three-Dollar Sam and to the old one-pocket player, who was staking the young nine-ball artist and was obviously very unhappy about the latest turn of events. "Come on, I'll play your boy again for a thousand," Tony said. "You're on," the old man snarled. Tony's backers looked nervous. One loss would put them back on the brink of being broke.

This time, Tony won 11–3.

Now the old man's face was redder than the cherry pie at the cafe next door. He went into the trailer, brought back $1,000 in twenties, and slapped the bundle of bills down on the table. "Now let's play some one-pocket, a thousand a game," he spat.

"No, thanks," Tony said. "I'm feeling kind of dizzy. Want to go to the cafe and get something to eat?"

"I'VE LEARNED A LITTLE IN THE LAST TWENTY YEARS. I HAD THAT OLD guy right where I wanted him. I could have probably heisted him for another five grand, but I couldn't resist the smart remark."

"Yeah, you never crack wise these days."

"Not when it's going to cost me money. Later on I found out the guy they brought in to play me that night was Alf Taylor, who had a great career as a road player. He and I became pretty good friends later."

THE GIN GAME WAS CALLED ON ACCOUNT OF EXHAUSTION. WE ATE A decent dinner in the club car and, thus fortified, we headed back to the compartment and talked for a while longer as our ride inched northward.

TONY DIDN'T GET INTO CAL, AND HE TRIED THE STAY-AT-HOME-IN-Burlingame plan. Dorothy put him on to a job she heard about, driving a truck for four dollars an hour, which after playing pool for a thousand a set seemed just a little dull. It seemed as if Dorothy was trying to turn him into a square—the kind of guy he used to beat at Broadway Billiards.

So Tony worked hard on his game for a couple of years, and he kept getting better. He had beaten a lot of good players in tournaments, and in gambling sessions, and it was known in the world of professional pool that the skinny Italian kid from Burlingame was no longer a shortstop. Given the chance, he could hurt you.

In 1975, he entered the Budweiser Sacramento Open at a poolroom called the Jointed Cue. It was a regular pro tour stop; most of the great players would be there. He had done pretty well in this event before, and he thought he had a good chance to get into the money.

From the start it was obvious Tony was playing some of the best pool of his life, and he beat one top player after another. He knocked off Dan Louie, an outstanding player from Seattle who was close to the peak of his career at the time, and then he beat Denny Searcy. He started horribly against Jimmy Mataya, the player they called "Pretty Boy Floyd," a top road player from Michigan. Mataya won the first six games, but Tony still managed to beat him to eleven and win the match.

He sailed on, reaching the finals of the double-elimination tournament without a loss. That meant the winner on the loser's bracket side would have to beat him twice to win the tournament. His opponent in the final turned out to be Jim

Rempe, one of the top tour players and a great road player to boot. Tony was surprised when, before the first set, Rempe offered him a "saver"—offering to split the prize money evenly no matter who won. It was Tony's first experience with that situation, and he turned it down.

"HE FIGURED TO BEAT ME. HE WAS ONE OF THE BEST IN THE GAME AND I was just local talent, but he could see I was playing good, and I was all the way out on the winner's side. I just figured, what the hell, I got this far.

"The first set I played pretty good but my cue was breaking down, I was having trouble with my tip and I miscued a couple of times in key spots and he beat me eleven–five or eleven–six.

"So we had to play again, and the last set went right down to the wire. On the case game I got hooked off his break and left him with a pretty tough runout and he messed up on the nine, he made the eight and tried to run around the nine ball and got bad on it, and missed it, and I won. But I had gotten to ten legitimately, I was up ten to eight and I actually made the nine on the break and the cue ball got kicked in the side, or I would have won it then. He got it to hill-hill and then I won."

AFTER THAT BURST OF GLORY, HE CAME HOME WITH HIS $2,000 PRIZE money and went back to work at Town and Country Billiards in San Mateo for five bucks an hour. He and Dorothy had a child, a boy named Nick, and before long they married. Their love affair continued, sweet and intense and sometimes painful; another son, Adrian, followed three years later.

In the meantime, Tony fashioned a new career for himself, in computer sales. He loved computers, and sales was a natural for him, with his outgoing personality and the psychological expertise he had acquired in the poolroom. The same capacity to learn he had displayed in school (when he went) and on the pool table served him well in his new endeavor. Soon, he was supervising his company's sales force, and he was making excellent money.

And missing pool. He continued to play tournaments sporadically; when he did play he often finished in the money, and he beat a lot of the best players: Earl Strickland, Buddy Hall, Nick Varner, Mike Sigel.

As his computer career blossomed, his marriage foundered, and he played less and less; he blamed the game, in a way, for complicating his relationship with Dorothy. He still loved her, but after four years of marriage, and ten years together, they divorced. He offered no lighthearted ripostes here; he talked about the chance they might get back together, but he feared too much had gone wrong between them for the relationship ever to go right again.

"WHERE THE FUCK ARE WE?"

"What am I, a tour guide? Shut up and go to sleep."

"Listen, you hairless pencil-pushing geek, you're the one who organized this trip. It's up to you to keep track of our whereabouts."

"I'm into serious sleep deprivation here. You snore, you play gin, you needle me, then you snore again. I get no time to sleep. We're in Portland. It's midnight. Be quiet."

"I thought you wanted to interview me."

"All right, all right, I give up. What else has happened in your miserable life?"

"I'll tell you all about it. Deal the cards."

. . .

IT WAS INEVITABLE THAT TONY ANNIGONI WOULD RETURN TO POOL; when you are among the best in the world at something, and you love it as much as he loves the game of pool, you do not walk away from it forever.

"ONE OF THE REASONS I TOOK UP THE GAME WAS I COULD SEE THAT IT was something where I could be relatively competitive just about all my life. But I didn't realize how great the psychological need to play would be as I got older. We all want to go back."

BEFORE LONG, AN OPPORTUNITY PRESENTED ITSELF FOR HIM TO combine his pool knowledge with his entrepreneurship to make a living in the game he loved. He had been successful enough in the computer business to accumulate a significant chunk of money. He bought some commercial real estate in San Francisco, and he invested in the reincarnation of the Palace Billiards, another famous old room that had fallen on hard times.

"I SAW A HUGE OPPORTUNITY IN THE PALACE. I WAS IN THE COMPUTER rental business, and basically that's what pool was, a rental business. You are renting leisure time to people, time in the game."
"Renting relaxation, and renting a dream."
"That's right."

HE WENT INTO THE PALACE AS ITS PRINCIPAL INVESTOR AND PROPRI-etor, and after some tough times it looked as if he and his part-ners were going to make a success of the place. *The Color of Money* had just been released and pool was enjoying a renaissance, just as it had twenty-plus years earlier with the release of *The Hustler.* But then they lost their lease on the space, and the room was forced to close. Tony was left with nothing for his investment and his time but a bunch of antique pool tables and nowhere to put them.

Then, with the Q Club deal, the roller coaster of Tony Annigoni's adult life took another sharp upward swing. He knew what the place should look like, and how it should run, and he bent himself to making as much of it happen as possible. He worked seven days a week, turning an abandoned building into one of the most beautiful poolrooms in the country. Finally, in the spring of 1991, the club opened. His tables, as well as his personal collection of Deco-era art, had an elegant and potentially lucrative new setting. Here was a chance to do his early life one better: The Q Club was more beautiful than Cochran's had ever been. It was what Cochran's *should* have looked like.

Now, though, a year and a half later, things didn't look so sanguine. Disappointing revenues—due, Tony maintained, to his inability to implement the business plan he had devised for the club—had led to bitter disagreements between the principals of his corporation. Meanwhile, an earthquake and California's anemic economy had turned the San Francisco real estate market decidedly sour, incidentally wiping out Tony's commercial real estate investments. All in all, the coaster car seemed to be gathering downhill momentum once again, which made it a perfect time to hit the road. Fortunately, Tony's game was in great shape. Every player reaches a peak, where experience and physical ability form a perfect partnership. Earlier, he may have had formidable skills but not much savvy and maturity at the table. Later, the player may know more, but he may be able to do a lot less. Where that point comes varies vastly, depending on health, vision, intelligence, psychological strength, and the amount of time the player is able to spend on the game. Some players peak in their twenties, some in their forties; very few remain competitive at the highest level much beyond that, although there are certainly exceptions.

When you're playing pool for a living, you'd better have a realistic idea of where you are on that performance curve. So when Tony decided to start playing seriously again, he got himself yet another coach—this one as notorious a personage as exists in the notoriety-rich pool world. His name was Richard Cook, aka Bucktooth, for two obvious reasons, and aside from being one of the best-known hustlers on the West Coast, he was an uncompromising judge of pool talent.

He liked what he saw in Tony, particularly the soundness and precision of his mechanics and his heart. "Oh, I knew he could already play good in tournaments and such," Bucktooth would say, "but I figured I could teach him to play good enough to beat all them champions out of their money."

Tony had seen Bucktooth when he was a kid, wheeling and dealing at Cochran's and elsewhere. He always played for a lot of money, he always got a spot from the best players, and he nearly always won. Tony liked his style, so when the opportunity came to work with him, years later, he jumped at it.

"HE WAS THE GREATEST POOL HUSTLER I'D EVER SEEN, AND THAT'S WHY I went to him. What was really lacking in my game was how to beat people out of their money. Too often I was just in there, just playing the game. I was accumulating yardage, as opposed to money, just like George C. Scott said.

"I never really used all the techniques I learned in sales, but I thought it was time I took those techniques right back into the game. I

needed to develop a business plan, just like I did in business. And if anybody understands the business of pool, it's Bucktooth."

TOGETHER, THEY TOOK TONY'S GAME APART AND REASSEMBLED IT, piece by piece, over hours and hours of practice: the nine-ball break, position play, rhythm, mental attitude, even some one-pocket strategy, though it would never be Tony's favorite money game. Bucktooth even gave him some tips on "matching up" or negotiating the terms of the session—the game before the game that is so crucial to the result.

During the process, Tony satisfied himself that not only could he play as well as he had before, he also had the potential to play even better. His eyes are still as sharp as they were at twenty, and the rest of him is a lot sharper, as he showed with his management of the game with Moro. By the time we left, he felt like he was playing as well as he had in a long time.

"I'M AS READY AS I'LL EVER BE, BUBBA."
"That's good, because we're finally here."

III

Seattle

"I'm just wild about Harry."
—Noble Sissle and Eubie Blake (1921),
reprised by the Tooth

SEPTEMBER 25—SEATTLE RUNS ON CAFFEINE, THANK GOD. SO DO I, and more than twenty-four hours on a train with nothing but sour transparent dripwater in a plastic cup had left me headachy, irritable, and sluggish, even after a few hours' sleep. Arriving at King Street Station red-eyed and stubble-faced, dragging the mountain of luggage off the carousel, and getting checked into a motel at 5 A.M. had been nightmarish.

At ten I staggered down to Wright's Diner, a block from the motel. You can save all that talk of Seattle's gray dripping skies. The walk was painful: It was clear and hot, and the sunlight felt like a cattle prod to the eyes.

But espresso machines are common as cockroaches in this town, and sure enough, Wright's was wired for steam. Ten minutes later survival seemed possible. Tony had been up since nine, banishing the aftereffects of the train trip in his own way. He did stretching exercises, skipped rope, and practiced his aikido for an hour and a half out by the pool.

He was serious about the discipline of the study; he approached pool as if it were a martial art, and he believed that the mental rigors of Eastern philosophy held the key to his concentration and poise at the table. Now, though, as we discussed our plans for the day over breakfast, he sounded a lot more like Bucktooth than a Zen master.

"Harry Platis has a lot of money, and he's famous for being a score," Tony said. "He can't play that well, but he loves to gamble. He's tough-minded, and he's gotten smarter about matching up, over the years, but he's still an amateur. He travels all around the country going to pool tournaments, playing champions. He wins some, don't get me wrong, but he's a hothead, and if you get his nose open—really get him in the mood to gamble—he can go off for a lot of money.

"Here's our deal. We've got to go to this joint called the Casino Club, that's where Harry hangs out. I know he wants to make a game with me, but if we can't get the right spot we should strongly consider bringing the Tooth up here."

"What?" I said. "Why?"

"Listen, you've got to see Bucktooth in action to believe him. He and Harry go back a long way. He beat Harry out of ten grand in Vegas years ago, and then in January at the L.A. Open, they made a one-handed one-pocket game, five hundred a rack.

"The Tooth hadn't played in years, but he's a great one-handed player and Harry had no chance. Bucktooth won the first rack, and Harry quit, then tried to pay off with a third-party check. Bucktooth exploded at Harry, embarrassed him, and Harry finally kicked out the cash. Now he wants Bucktooth real bad, I guarantee you. The point is, Bucktooth might get Harry to go off easier than I could."

"I'd really rather get you playing first," I said, a little nervously.

"Sure, I'll try to match up with him, but let's just remember it's an option. Bucktooth knows we're here and he'd come up in a minute to play Harry.

"In fact, here's our move. We tell Harry we're interested in opening a joint up here, me and Bucktooth, which is actually true, we're going to open a place somewhere one of these days. He knows Bucktooth's loaded so he'll believe it. I've even got a listing somebody sent me, a commercial property up here that we could tell him we're considering. Again, it's true, and it'll explain why we're here without having to simply walk in like we came to do nothing but rob him."

I wished he hadn't used those words. This planning our angle of attack was new to me, and it felt a lot like casing a bank, seeing where the cameras and the guards were. Oh, well, I thought. Willie Sutton was right. That's where the money is.

THE CASINO CLUB WAS NORTH OF THE CITY, A STRAIGHT SHOT OUT on Aurora, mile after mile of dreary commercial strip. The building was new, cheap-looking slump block construction with a garish pastel awning proclaiming CASINO CLUB—CARDS, POOL. We walked in the door and the first thing we saw was Harry Platis sitting in a red vinyl booth with two pool hustlers watching *Hellcats of the Navy* on a tiny, ancient TV.

Harry jumped up. "Hey, Tony, how are you?" He was a bear, with a big barrel body in white canvas slacks and a red cashmere sweater, black and gray chest hairs curling out of the V neck. His head was round as a bowling ball, topped by a thatch of curly black hair cropped close. He was wearing a pair of black Ben Franklin–style cheaters and an inquisitive expression on his moon face.

Tony performed the introductions to me. "Hey, this is Harry Platis, and these guys are Billy Cress and the Monk."

The Monk was built a little like Harry, only shorter and squatter. He was of an indeterminate age, with prematurely white hair and a white mustache. He looked Italian. He simply grunted and nodded at the introduction.

On the surface, Billy Cress was a lot friendlier. "How are you, Tony, long time," he said with a smile that looked distinctly predatory. He was a big boy, in his forties, maybe six-four, two-thirty, like a good small-college linebacker just gone to fat. His blond hair was slicked back, and he was wearing a rust-colored silk shirt and olive gabardine dress slacks and a flashy gold chain at his throat. He looked like a stone gambler, and nobody to fuck with, for sure.

"You guys want a drink, some coffee?" Harry said. "Hey Mike, get these guys what they need."

We both refused politely, and then Tony said, "Hey, Harry, we're just up here looking around. David here's a writer, and he had a score recently, just got a book out, and he's interested maybe in investing in a poolroom with the Tooth and me. We've got a place to look at up here."

"Where?" Platis demanded, on sure ground now. "Shit, I know the real-estate market up here, and the poolroom situation too, better than anyone. I've been tryin to open another joint, there's so much money to be made up here. I can show you some great spots."

Tony showed him the listing, and he snorted impatiently. "Shit, I can show you five or six better locations, and I can get you a deal, too, handle the whole thing, you know, Tony? Hey, you want to go out and take a look around? I'll show you some stuff that you won't find out any other way."

"Sure," Tony said. If we were to be taken seriously as potential real-estate investors, there was no way to turn down an offer like that, and besides, it kept Harry close by.

"Come on, Monk, you want to come along?" Monk grunted again and slid out of the booth behind Harry.

"We've got to get Bucktooth up here," Tony whispered to me as we headed back out into the sunshine. "I'll tell you why later."

The four of us fit nicely into the butter-soft leather interior of Harry's scarlet Cad, and off we went for a tour of the metro area north of Seattle. Harry kept up a running real-estate patter as he took us up to the massive Boeing plant at Edmonds, then farther north. "Wait 'til we get to Everett," Harry said, "I've got just the spot."

Harry turned to me, as if considering me for the first time. "Writer, eh? You ought to do a nonfiction book about pool. You're traveling with Tony, you must like the game, I see you got a cue, too." He waved a finger toward me. "You know I could give you a hell of a story, the story of a player, you could feature one player. I staked Keith McCready to play a lot, I could tell you about what it was like, staking him, you and I could have a deal." He smiled.

"Not a bad idea, Harry," was all I could say.

When we arrived in Everett the sunshine had vanished. It was a gloomy mill town afternoon; row after row of dilapidated, mildewing little clapboard labor houses belied Harry's Chamber of Commerce spiel. If a boom was coming, it had better hurry.

Harry Platis grew up there; with fierce pride he showed us the football field where he helped Everett High win championships. He was a Golden Gloves boxer, too, in this little town, and a good student, all the way through to Gonzaga where he got his law degree. He showed us the little frame house where his father's Greek restaurant was, where the family lived, and where he helped out in the kitchen, growing up poor but fired with ambition. I found myself liking the guy, admiring his intensity and his competitive drive—even though those were the qualities that we were here to exploit.

"There it is," Harry said. "It used to be a Denny's. It's a good building, you wouldn't have to do much with it, great location, great parking. They want eight hundred thousand for it but I know the guys, I could probably get it for you for maybe five, maybe even a no-cash deal." The building was vacant, garish but serviceable-looking. Tony said we'd sure have to get the Tooth up here to see it, and we started the drive back.

"How you hittin 'em, Monk?" Tony asked.

"Not great, my back's been bothering me." My God, he *does* talk, I thought.

"How about you, Harry?"

"Oh, shit, I quit playing," Harry said. "I retired. They've been robbing me so much I just quit. I broke my cue the other night, I was playing Billy, couldn't make a ball, could I, Monk, and I smashed the fuckin thing to bits."

Monk's shoulders actually jiggled, which was as close as he was going to come to showing mirth. "Sure did."

"I thought maybe we could play some, Harry, we talked about it down in L.A.," Tony said. "Bucktooth will probably be coming up tomorrow, too, so we can look at some of these spots together."

Harry looked at him sharply. "We could play some, you and me," he said, "but that fuckin Bucktooth, I don't want nothin to do with him, I don't need to play assholes like him."

When we got back to the Casino Club, Tony and I went in to hit some balls. The place had a dozen cheaper tables in front and four pretty new black Gold Crowns in back, with a nice set of seats built up on both sides. We got two trays of balls and headed back there.

I had purchased a fine cue for this trip, a handsome example of custom cue maker John Robinson's work. Nothing fancy, just bird's-eye maple with ebony points, about twenty ounces, endowed with great balance and a solid hit. It hit much better than I did. With the Robinson I was like a Sunday driver at the wheel of a Ferrari.

I hadn't been hitting balls for more than three minutes when Harry Platis sidled up next to me and said with a saccharine smile, "David, you and I could play a little."

I smiled and shook my head. "Forget it, Harry," Tony said. "He's a sweater, and he stakes me, but he doesn't play."

A few more minutes passed, and Billy Cress walked over to Tony. They chatted a little as Tony hit balls, and then Billy said, "You want to play some while you're up here?"

"Maybe," Tony said. "But I haven't been playing that much, you know, running the poolroom has taken most of my time."

"Yeah, yeah." Billy really was an imposing looking guy, despite the little spare tire he carried. He looked and acted tough; his voice sounded like twenty years of smoky poolrooms. "Want to play some one-pocket?"

"I don't play one-pocket, but I'll play you some nine-ball."

"I'll play you nine-ball, but I need the last two."

"I can't give you weight, you know that, we should play even," Tony said.

Billy didn't hesitate. "I'll play you even, maybe two hundred a game."

That was a big number, and Tony said, "I'll try you some like that, but give me until tomorrow, Billy, we came up on the fuckin train and I need to get unkinked."

"No problem, when will you be in here?"

"I don't know, in the afternoon, whenever you want."

"I'll see you in here around two."

"Fine."

After another half-hour of practice, we got out of there, and Tony could barely contain himself on the ride back down-town. "We're in major action here, bubba. There's too much action for just me, that's what I was trying to tell you." He laughed. "I can't believe it. The Monk and Billy Cress. They're getting fat off Harry, that's gotta be the only reason they're here."

"We had a few people clocking us in there, didn't we?" I said.

"A few? Man, everything else stopped in that place when we started. I like the equipment fine though. That Simonis seven-sixty is the same cloth I have in the Q Club, although it plays a little slower up here because of the humidity."

"Watching me play was enough to bring Harry out of retirement," I said.

"You looked pretty easy, pal," Tony said. "Hey, Harry will never retire from playing pool. That's all horseshit. And so's the part about not wanting to play Bucktooth. Harry wants him bad, which is just the right position for Bucktooth to be in."

"What's Monk's story?" I asked.

"The Monk," Tony said. "Warren Costanza. They call him Monk because he looks like an ape, man, check out his arms, he's so short and they're so long his knuckles nearly scrape the ground. And the name stuck because he acts like a monk, never says anything. His back may be hurting, but I tell you, that's one of the toughest guys to play this game. He's from New York, he's a famous one-pocket player, good nine-ball, too. I played a session with him when I was a kid, we played for thirty hours straight and broke even. He loves long sessions, he's a grinder, he just stays at you until he breaks you down.

"Last I heard he was living in Sacramento. He must be up here on Harry. You notice he didn't let Harry go alone with us? He knows we're after Harry too and he wants to know just what our angle is. He's a good player, real good. I may be able to beat him playing nine-ball but it's a tough game. I don't want it. There's easier.

"Now, Billy Cress, that's an interesting game. I'm supposed to beat him even, I think. Again, it's a hard game, he's a professional, but he doesn't know how good I play. This is perfect, the last time he saw me I wasn't playing that good. You saw how he jumped at the game. He was broke when I saw him last. He's won big recently or he's got a stakehorse, offering to play two-hundred-dollar nine-ball."

I was able to assist here. "I was talking to one of the cocktail waitresses and she said Billy had just come into some money, inherited a pretty good chunk."

"Really?" Tony said. "That's interesting. He's looking like he's holding a little. I just figured he'd been beating Harry. He's probably hungry for some nine-ball—everybody up here plays one-pocket because that's Harry's game." He looked sharply at me. "You didn't tell her anything, did you? Where we were staying or anything?"

"God, no," I said. "She was just talking about how much gambling there's been lately in there. She said Harry and Billy and Monk and some guy named J.D. have all been playing pretty high."

"Really! Of course, all this may be just what they want us to hear. Somebody probably told her to say it."

"Maybe," I said. "But I don't think so."

"Well, if they want to play high, we'll play high too," Tony said. "That's why we came to the dance."

WE HAD A DIFFERENT KIND OF DANCE TO ATTEND FIRST. THE HOT-test star in pool, Ewa Mataya, was giving an exhibition that

s no wonder the women players were a little peeved,
responded by setting up a promising new tour of
.

nversation was interrupted again, by a guy who shyly
he could sit next to her while a buddy snapped a
She graciously complied, tilting her head just so,
ing her dignity and distance but somehow communi-
mething in her body language that would make the
rt sing when he looked at the picture.

d Tony chatted for a while. He described our trip
ery general terms. Ewa was adamantly opposed to
in her role as spokesperson for the new, clean-image
pool, she had to be. Also, she was recently divorced
of the game's biggest gamblers, Jimmy Mataya.

bate over gambling and pool continues within the
Some say that the fear of getting hustled has kept
players out of poolrooms; they contend that the
ew image is strongly dependent on keeping the
out of the game as much as possible. Jillian's is a
xample. Gambling was strongly discouraged, and it
nd the usual sign on the wall. We had already heard
paying a $375 table-time tab for a long gambling
n the private room shortly after Jillian's opened,
tis was frostily encouraged not to return. Others say
npossible to keep gambling out of pool, and that it's
cal to even try. They make the case that gambling is
a part of the lore of the game that people expect it.
ment, of course, is offered mostly by gamblers. Still,
sputable that throughout the game's history, gam-
pool have been joined like two balls frozen on the

seems to me that the revisionists run the risk of
a lot of the color and intrigue of the game. I don't

evening at Jillian's, a big upscale billiard room and restaurant in Seattle.

We arrived just after the exhibition had started, and the place was jammed. Jillian's is a chain, with clubs in Boston, Cleveland, and Florida in addition to this pleasant, slightly pretentious poolroom, rambling through a big brick building on three levels. The surroundings were plush, although not on such a grand scale as the Q Club, and the place had a younger feel. As nice as it was, you could feel the chainness of the place, as though it was carefully following a corporate formula designed to exploit the yuppie pool craze. Most of the tables were new or reproductions of antiques, but still of excellent quality and playability.

Not that anyone was playing right now. All eyes were focused on the tall blonde making the trick shots and chatting warmly with the audience in a Lauren Bacall low register, spiced with the faintest hint of a Swedish accent.

Even from my long-distance viewpoint, standing behind the throng, it was evident that Ewa Mataya was something special. She had incredible presence. Of course, it helped to be five-ten and beautiful. She was slim and graceful in a long black dress, ash-blond curls bubbling across her shoulders. But her impact went well beyond all that.

Two local radio personalities were hosting the exhibition, a goofy-but-sincere-looking guy and a yapping, loudmouthed little woman who obviously had her facts confused and thought people were there to see *her*.

The trick shots meant little to me; they looked pretty and certainly they required skill, mostly in knowing how to set them up, but they were not a mark of a player's true ability. Ewa Mataya proved this when she set up a couple of shots and recruited the radio guy, who looked as though he had never held a cue, to make them.

She placed the balls around the table and lined him up behind the cue ball. He looked horrible over the ball, his bridge hand curled in a spastic clawlike configuration that is the mark of the true pool square. But it didn't matter. The balls were set perfectly. She chalked his cue and told him how hard to hit the cue ball. He stroked clumsily, but all the balls went in.

Meanwhile, the other host kept asking inane questions: "So, like, what's the difference between a player like you and someone like, say, *moi*, who plays a couple of times a week?"

"Just a few thousand hours of practice," Mataya said graciously, neglecting to mention talent and heart.

After the show, she answered more questions and then sat down to autograph photos in the lounge. Tony and I slipped into the line. She was smiling warmly to the people as they came up, but when she saw Tony she treated him to a total dazzler. "How wonderful to see you! Sit down here with me and tell me what you're doing up here!" Of course, I got a handshake and a lovely smile too, for a friend of a friend—I don't know if I could have taken the higher-intensity version without my knees buckling—and we sat down for a chat.

Over the past few months, Ewa Mataya had become a Name. It all started February 23 when *The New York Times Magazine* ran a story, featuring her, about the new realities of pool. There was Ewa, all over the cover, in a green sequined sheath, hugging her cue and looking fetchingly at the camera. Suddenly, she was the hottest new face in pool since Newman and Cruise. She appeared on dozens of TV shows, and played to packed houses, like this one, wherever she went. And through it all, she maintained her poise—and her devotion to the game. She was the most articulate spokesperson the game had had in a while, and because of all the exposure, she was

probably doing more to promote t[ ] player had done since Steve Mizerak [ ] commercials. And she looked a lot b[ ]

"It's been a real grind," she said [ ] graphs, "but if it improves the ima[ ] brings in more sponsorships for t[ ] interest from the public, then it's ce[ ]

Her green eyes narrowed with a[ ] about the ongoing feud between the [ ] sionally and the Professional Bil[ ] supposedly formed as an umbrella [ ] men's and women's pro tours, but [ ] nization despite calling itself "The C[ ] sional Pool."

It was a messy divorce. "Because w[ ] dictate to us, they have decided [ ] they've told promoters nobody's [ ] tioned if there's a women's division[ ] not just unfair, it's stupid." So it v[ ] advantage of the Mataya publicity [ ] would rather watch her play anybo[ ] play Buddy Hall for the umpteent[ ]

Don Mackey, the PBTA commiss[ ] the women with his abrasive, [ ] patronizing—style and his hardb[ ] men's tour. In an interview in *B[ ]* leading trade magazine, Mackey a[ ] their voice in the organization thr[ ] said bluntly, "that's the way an An[ ] you can muster the votes and seize[ ] you win." He added, "In reality, t[ ] the fact that if the men wanted so[ ]

ge[ ]
an[ ]
the[ ]
c[ ]
ask[ ]
pic[ ]
ma[ ]
cati[ ]
guy[ ]
E[ ]
only[ ]
hust[ ]
gam[ ]
from[ ]
Th[ ]
indu[ ]
woul[ ]
game[ ]
gamb[ ]
perfe[ ]
went[ ]
that a[ ]
sessio[ ]
Harry[ ]
that it[ ]
hypoc[ ]
so mu[ ]
This a[ ]
it is in[ ]
bling a[ ]
end ra[ ]
Also,[ ]
excising[ ]

think the pro pool tour shouldn't be full of cookie-cutter characters like the Professional Golfers Association, but that's exactly the model for the PBTA. Mackey and others feel that in order to get purses comparable to those on the golf tour, the PBTA must reestablish the credibility of the game, which, they reason, will be hard if many of the top players are known gamblers. I don't think you're going to keep gambling out of the game, or even out of the stands at tournaments, and I think it's not only hypocritical but damaging to try. Pool is much closer to horse racing in appeal than it is to golf. And one-on-one money matches, like prizefights, would have huge audience potential.

SEPTEMBER 26—THE NEXT MORNING FOUND US AT THE 211 CLUB.

It was one of the oldest poolrooms on the West Coast—and to my mind, one of the most beautiful. For many years, the club was located at 211 Union Street, but redevelopment recently forced it to move a couple of blocks away. Still, the room had retained its character and it looked particularly lovely after the ersatz nostalgia of Jillian's. It was a second-floor walk-up, the walls painted Depression-era pale green, the floor bare scarred pine, the tables old but beautifully cared for. Not one reproduction of an old pool picture hung on the walls; just signs prohibiting whistling and sitting on the tables.

In addition to about fifteen pool tables, there were three fine old billiard tables, with gorgeous antique light fixtures, and two stunning Brunswick Conqueror six-by-twelve snooker tables, seventy years old, the dark wood gleaming. They were in beautiful shape. (The Conqueror, appropriately, is the model you will find in Hearst Castle, and it is certainly one of the most beautiful Brunswicks ever made.) The 211 was open early, and Tony wanted to get in a little practice away from the prying eyes of the Casino Club.

If you're looking for aesthetics, not action, mornings and afternoons are the best times to be in an old poolroom, and the 211 was no exception. Pale light filtered through green skylights. A morning smell of coffee and stale beer and chalk dust pervaded the room. The house man was brushing the tables slowly, methodically, and the dust rose in soft clouds, giving the room a misty look that evoked a feeling of time travel back into the game's past. I gravitated to the big Conquerors, rented one of them, set up the snooker balls and began to practice, reveling in the soft, straight roll of the old table. Hey, Freddie Byers, I thought, it's time for our game, where are you this morning?

I was not without a game for long. A couple of local boys came in and asked politely if I wanted to play some cheap golf, five bucks and a quarter a scratch. I agreed, even though playing three-handed golf with a couple of locals in a strange poolroom is like dropping your money in the street. It is pathetically easy for two people to combine forces against a stranger in the game; the one local who is following the other in the rotation always gets shots, and the player "in the middle" doesn't. This is known as the "sandwich" or the "brother-in-law" and it is time-tested. It can be subtle or blatant, but it's a tough thing to beat. In this case, amazingly, these two guys were on the square, and just interested in the game; I managed to win one game and lose one, netting $4.75, enough to pay my table time and buy a cup of coffee: the first gambling score of the trip. I would have liked to play longer, but it was time to pick up Bucktooth at the airport.

Richard Cook. The Tooth. Tooie. Bucktooth. Millionaire ex-con high-rolling pool-hustling cash-flaunting jeweler. Onetime craps plunger, comped by every casino in Nevada,

turned into almost universally barred blackjack master.
Brutalizer of champions, owner of maybe the best winning
percentage for the money in pool. Biggest mouth since
Muhammad Ali. At any gathering of pool players, guaranteed
the Loudest and Most Likely to Piss Somebody Off. World-
class front teeth, vocal cords, and ego.

Don't worry, Tony told me, it's all a part of the smoothest
move this side of a Rolex watch.

"So how will I recognize this guy?"

"You won't have any trouble. Just look for a pair of well-
dressed front teeth with white curly hair."

Sure enough, the third person down the Jetway was a distinguished-looking gent about six feet tall, with wavy white hair
receding enough in front to give him a high forehead and
accentuate the roundness of his head. He had pale, slightly
protuberant eyes, and pleasant features dominated by a
marked overbite. He looked like what he was: a prosperous
jeweler from Alameda, California, nearing retirement age. He
did not, at first glance, look like what he also was: one of the
highest-rolling pool gamblers in the history of the game. He
was wearing black dress slacks, loafers, a silk sports jacket, and
a flashy dress shirt, open at the neck, with a greasy yellow blob
on the front. He was carrying a hanger bag and an alligator-
skin cue case.

"Tooth."

"Yeah, hi, you must be David, well, I've gotta change this
shirt, Jesus, I dogged it, I was eating the shitty little cup of
potato salad they give you on the plane and we hit a bump and
splat! right down my front, a total mess."

We walked to the car, and Bucktooth, highly embarrassed to
be wearing his lunch, peeled off in the parking garage and
changed into another Pierre Cardin shirt. "How's Tony
doing? How's he hitting 'em? What's up, does Harry know I'm

coming? So the Monk and Billy Cress are here, eh? Tony played anybody yet?" I answered the questions one by one, and the Tooth, informed right up to the minute and once again sartorially acceptable, unwound a couple of notches and sat back and watched the city go by on the long drive to the north side. "Jeez, I haven't been up here in years. Where *is* the joint?"

It was a little after one when we arrived, and the place was packed; *this is it,* I thought. This is where we start. I pushed the game-day butterflies down firmly and waited for my eyes to adjust to the darkness. Tony was hitting some balls on one of the Gold Crowns. The bleachers on both sides were almost filled with railbirds, and the tables in front were getting good play. Harry Platis and Billy Cress and the Monk were all in attendance; the bad news was that Billy and Harry were already involved in a one-pocket game—against each other. Billy was giving Harry ten to six (Billy had to make ten balls in his pocket before Harry made six in his) for a thousand dollars a game.

Harry was casual today, wearing silver iridescent Fila sweat-pants and a golf shirt. His lumpy body looked like a sackful of bowling balls in the designer sweats. He and Billy both greeted the Tooth, coolly, and returned to their game. Tony came over and said hello, then motioned to the corner table where Harry and Billy were playing. "What a bad roll," he said. "They started right before I showed up."

"No kidding," Bucktooth said. "Here are both of the guys we want, playing each other. Harry might drain Billy . . . and he might not want to play anybody else. Shit, they could play for two days. This is real bad."

Tony said, "Don't worry, they want us, this is just a way of saying, fuck you guys. They'll play, though, we just have to wait."

Waiting was obviously not one of the Tooth's favorite things to do. After about half an hour, he startled everyone by saying very loudly, "Well, this is a hell of a lot of fun, come up here to some joint in Seattle, Warshington, and sit around with all you mooches watching a couple of nits play pool. Shit, they got nits in Oakland, I could have stayed home and done this. I heard somebody up here wanted to *gamble*."

"Hey, what do you want, they're playing for a thousand bucks," a guy behind us said. The Tooth loved having a straight man.

"Thousand? *Thousand?* That ain't no kind of gambling. A thousand bucks? I didn't come up here to play for meal money. Shit, I bet I got more hundreds on me than anybody in here got bills of any denomination. When I play pool I play for stacks of money. I don't count my money, I weigh it." He took out a fat roll of hundreds and riffled through them.

Advertising that you are carrying bales of hundred-dollar bills in a strange poolroom is definitely not recommended. It is an advanced concept, but it is one that comes naturally to the Tooth. "More where these came from," he said. "I'm the early retirement plan for pool players. You beat me and you can retire."

"Fuck you, Bucktooth," Harry said, and turned his back and kept on playing.

Tony finished practicing and sat down with us. After another half an hour, Bucktooth said to Tony, "What do you think?"

"Harry's getting the best of it," Tony said, "and Billy's getting hot. This is good for us. Billy will want to play me if he ends up loser over there, and Harry will be all pumped up ready to take you on."

"Yeah, but when?" Bucktooth grumbled. "I don't want to

get in the middle of their game. Between you and me I've pushed it pretty far already."

"They know we're here, don't worry about it."

The one-pocket game continued. Harry was consistently making some impressive bank shots, and with the spot he was getting his inspired shotmaking was enough to give him the upper hand. He led by three games, but then Billy won a game, and as Harry racked the next, he banged the balls around the table in anger. "I can't believe it," Billy said in a sour aside to the sweaters watching from the rail. "He's got me stuck and he's getting hot."

But as the match dragged on, it was Billy's turn to display his displeasure. He waved his cue violently after missed shots and swore at the balls. He shook his head angrily as Harry continued to make strong shots, complaining about the handicap he had given him.

Billy's complaint about bad rolls was accurate, as far as it went, but Harry was making great shots, and that was the difference. Time after time, Billy left Harry nothing but tough bank shots, with the risk of "selling out," or leaving Billy good shots, if he missed. After four hours, Harry was up three thousand dollars, and Billy unscrewed his cue. "That's enough. You got me, Harry. Fuckin balls are spittin at me," he said savagely.

The railbirds buzzed over Harry's play; they had seen him in action often; many of them had won money from him often. Harry was the dominant player in the poolroom, by dint of his money and his gamble. "This is Platisville, and Harry is the mayor," one of the sweaters told us. Many of the spectators expected Billy to rob him, as he had before. But Harry played far above his normal game.

Harry walked over and said, "I got to go meet somebody,

but Bucktooth, I'll be in here tomorrow morning, maybe we can play if you got the heart."

"All I want is a chance," Bucktooth said. "I'm an old man, and I can't see, but I like to play high."

"I know, I know, I'll see you tomorrow." And he walked out.

Billy Cress calmed down quickly. He got a drink and sat down with us while we watched Monk play a local kid some one-pocket, spotting him ten to six. The kid, a muscular redhead named Tim, didn't play too bad, but Monk very gently and steadily blew him off the table.

Billy said to Tony, "I gotta get something to eat and take it easy for a while. I still want to play, though. How about tomorrow?"

"Fine."

A young woman wearing tight faded jeans and a tighter white blouse walked up then and dimpled at Billy, then perched on his lap. She was maybe twenty-one, about five-one, with long black hair. She looked Eurasian, with high cheekbones, green eyes slightly cantilevered, and a full red-painted mouth. Billy relinquished his chair to her, said his goodbyes, and strolled out. She made no move to follow him.

Her name was Rhonda, she giggled a lot, and she was aimed at Tony like a Scud missile. "I love excellence in anything, but pool is really *it*," she said. "Some people say I'm a pool groupie, and I guess I am. My first boyfriend was a pretty good bar-table player and I used to go watch him play. I didn't know any better and I thought he was a great player. But I found out there was a whole other world of pool players," she said, giving Tony her best Veronica Lake up-from-under look.

Rhonda said her current boyfriend was "a pretty good pool player," but confided that their relationship was finished. "He'd rather read the newspaper than—you know," she said with a giggle.

She and Monk were good friends, she said, telling us about the time right after the poolroom opened, six months before, when the heat wasn't working and she and Monk curled up under a few blankets and watched TV together. It was difficult not to laugh at the image of the simian, white-stubbled Monk and Rhonda snuggled up watching *Twin Peaks*. She prattled on about all sorts of things, but kept coming back to the main themes of pool and sex. ("I mean, these days you can't just go out and *do* everybody you'd like to.") She even discussed the tightness of her jeans. "I borrowed 'em from my fourteen-year-old sister," she said. "She's got a better figure than I do. Did you notice the little hole in the butt?" She stood up and turned around, in case we didn't.

"Don't worry," Tony said, "Everybody in the joint's been clocking your heinie all evening."

WE DROVE BACK DOWNTOWN. AFTER ALL THE CRACKERBOX UGLINESS of the north side, downtown Seattle was sparkling clean and beautiful. We feasted at McCormick and Schmick, the wonderful old seafood house that for me will always represent the best of Seattle charm and style, with its gleaming wood and glass and perfectly prepared fresh fish. A grilled steelhead fillet, baked potato, and a glass of ale made the day of watching and waiting worthwhile.

After dinner, we drove over to Jillian's. Tony wanted to show the place to Bucktooth, who displayed his aptitude for being in the right spot at the right time. He came dashing out of the men's room, hands dripping wet. "Hey," he said excitedly to Tony. "They're out of paper towels and I'm in there looking around for something to dry my hands on when this kid comes up to me, and he says, 'Somebody out there wants to play me for twenty dollars a game. How should I play him? Should I play defense or try to run out?' I told him I didn't know and he ran out the door. I think he's drunk."

"Where is he?" Tony said. Just then, from the playing area below us, came a shout: "Anybody want to play nine-ball, twenty dollars a game?"

"There he is!" the Tooth said excitedly, pointing with a wet finger at a very preppy-looking young man with a shaggy collegiate haircut, rather oddly for this chilly fall evening wearing khaki shorts and a short-sleeved button-down oxford-cloth shirt. "Go play him."

"Shit, they'll kick us all out," Tony said. "They don't allow gambling here."

"Screw that," the Tooth said impatiently. "Go get him before somebody else does."

Tony walked down into the playing area and asked the guy, "Do you know who's going to play for twenty a game? I want to watch."

"Oh, I had some guy ready to play me but he chickened out," the kid said.

"Are you a good player?" Tony asked.

"I'm a pretty good player," the young man responded.

"You're not a hustler, are you?"

"No."

"If you're not a hustler I'll play you. Guys play for that kind of money in my poolroom all the time."

So Khaki Shorts agreed, but as he started to rack the balls he said, "Let's play for ten dollars." Then, as he finished the rack, he said, "No, let's play for five a rack, okay?"

Tony looked up at Bucktooth and me, watching from the rail, smiled, and said okay. Shorts made a couple of balls, then missed an easy shot. Tony shot and missed—clearly deliberately, to my eye—and Shorts made the four and five balls before missing again. Tony, looking as awkward as I'd ever seen him, finished out the rack.

Ditto the next rack. Shorts was clearly tipsy—how much was hard to tell. He made four or five balls the next rack, but left the eight and nine for Tony.

As he racked, Shorts said, "Want to play two dollars on the five?" and then immediately said, "No, that's too confusing."

Tony shrugged and rolled his eyes.

Then Tony missed a cut on a seven ball and Shorts won a rack. That seemed to buck him up a bit, and he played pretty well to start the next rack. He had a weird style of abruptly hopping up immediately after delivering the stroke—usually a sure prescription for missing—but he seemed to shoot some shots pretty accurately. He also displayed the classic amateur technique of shooting faster and faster as if to say, now I'm in a groove and I'm going to show you how good I really am. It's a great way to guarantee your run will be short. Shorts also glanced around the room before and after his shots, playing to the crowd—another unmistakable sucker trait. He missed again, then watched as Tony finished out the rack.

His girlfriend watched nervously. As he racked the balls, she came up to him and said, just loudly enough for Tony to hear: "You're too drunk. Don't raise the bet." Tony decided then that there was no chance to do just that, so he got down to business, showing just enough to win eleven of the next twelve racks. It was closing time.

"I guess since you kicked my ass you could get the time on the table," Shorts said plaintively. Sure, Tony said.

"Well, I also owe about thirty dollars in time on that table," he said, pointing to the next table over.

"I can't help you there, pal," Tony said.

Turned out Shorts was a little short. He had to send his girlfriend to the nearest bank machine, though it was nearly 3 A.M., to get enough to pay Tony and his time bill. After Tony paid fifteen dollars in time, he had netted forty. As we walked out, he said quietly, "I've always hated that. When you're on the road you're supposed to find spots like that, but I can't stand it. It's one thing to lemon around when you're playing a pretty good player who's trying to rob you, but some dumb drunken kid . . . no thanks." Counting my golf score, we were now $44.75 winners on the trip.

We returned to the motel, only to find they had no room for the Tooth. We cadged a rollaway, which I generously volunteered to take since the other two had to play the next day. That was not the worst of it. Bucktooth is a legendary snorer. When it came to snoring he could give Tony the six.

SEPTEMBER 27—AFTER A FIVE-HOUR NIGHT ON A LUMPY MOTEL rollaway a foot too short, listening to dueling chain saws, I needed two double espressos to bring me around. Bucktooth girded for battle with scrambled eggs, sausage, hash browns, and orange juice. Tony settled for aikido, jump rope, and coffee, then proved how good he felt by dishing out a constant stream of wisecracks—on how much the Tooth and I ate, how little hair we had, and so on—all the way to our Sunday services at the Casino Club.

We had agreed last night: Tony and I would take half of the Tooth's action, assuming half the losses, if there were any, and taking half the winnings. The Tooth would take a third of any action Tony got. "But he ain't going to get away with playin cheap," Bucktooth said. "I'm going to make him play for at least two thousand a game."

When we arrived just after ten, neither Mr. Platis nor Mr. Cress were present. But word of impending action had gotten around, and the rail was very well populated for such an unlikely hour.

Bucktooth got some balls and started loosening up. "Shit, I've practiced more in the past six months than I ever did before when I played all the time," he confided to me. "I always just walked into the room and said, 'Get out your money, let's play.'"

As he rolled balls around, a tall man in his late twenties sitting in the front row struck up some conversation. He was slim but conveyed an impression of physical power, with bushy hair swept down almost over narrow, ferretlike eyes. "I've heard a lot about you," he said. The Tooth grunted noncommittally and kept shooting at balls. He made one particularly pretty cross-bank, breaking another ball out of the pack toward his pocket with the cue ball, and the guy said, "Wow, I learned something there." Then, a few moments later, he added, "Maybe you and I could play a little bit."

"Depends on what sort of a spot you'll give me," Bucktooth replied. "I haven't played anybody even in a long time. I can't see worth a shit anymore. I miss straight-in shots."

"You're making quite a few this morning," the kid said dryly.

"Oh, it's easy when you're playing by yourself," the Tooth said expansively. "I can shoot the same shot four or five times. Or if I miss I can make the next shot, where I would never see that shot in a game. It's a lot different with somebody shooting back at you."

"How could we play?" the kid persisted.

"Well, what do you give Harry?" the Tooth asked.

"Eight to six," he said. "But you're a famous pool hustler."

"Well, I'd need more than that," the Tooth said. "I need some weight from Harry. I haven't been playing for a long time."

"Looks like we won't get a game," the kid said. "Oh, well. We can say we tried."

"That's right," said the Tooth placidly, and kept on with his practice. All woofing aside, it looked like he was striking the ball extremely well. After he finished, he sat back down next to me and whispered, "Jesus, my stroke is in great shape. Did you see that long bank on the ten ball? I moved it the width of the table with English and I hit it with perfect speed, and it rolled right in."

After forty years of hustling pool, Bucktooth retained an incredible enthusiasm for the game. He got really excited when he saw something new on the table, when he or someone else hit a shot that he knew was extraordinary, or when he got that wonderful clicked-in feeling players call "dead stroke."

Suddenly, Harry was in the club. He entered through the back door and within two minutes he began to hit balls around on the same table where he had flayed Billy Cress the day before. Harry was in high-dollar warm-ups again today, and he also featured a startling new accessory: upside-down glasses.

Eyeglasses are a pain in the butt for a pool player. If you get low over the table, as you are supposed to do, then look down the table at a shot, the top of the eyeglass frame tends to be right smack in the way. Some people actually wear odd buglike frames with lenses that curve well above the eyebrows to compensate for this. Harry didn't have any of those, but he had the next best thing. He had turned the earpieces on a pair of his glasses, so that when he tucked them behind his flaps, the glasses were actually resting upside down on his nose—making him look weirder than Roy Rogers riding sidesaddle, but eliminating the eyeglass-frame problem.

I still had some first-match nervousness, but things happened so quickly that it was soon forgotten. The Tooth's braying challenge pierced the relative silence in the poolroom. "Come on, Harry, ya fuckin nit, I didn't come all the way up here just to watch you, let's play some pool. I just want one ball. One little ball. But we've got to play for some real money. You can call every applehead in Seattle. Tell 'em the Tooth's playing, I'll take nine to eight and everybody in the state of Warshington can bet. The hundred-dollar window is open."

"Ah, you ain't got no fuckin gamble, you're not a real pool player. I don't think you got the heart to play an even game," Harry said. "Come on, Bucktooth, let's see if you got any fuckin heart."

"You got to give me something. All I want is a chance, Harry, I'm old and I can't see for shit, I'm liable to miss a ball straight in the hole. Give me a ball and we'll see who's a pool player."

"You don't want a chance, you want the nuts," Harry snarled, his voice louder now, too. "Come on, Bucktooth, I'll play you some a thousand a game, dead even."

"Thousand? Thousand? Oh, no, you play me, you got to play for thousands. Plural. I didn't come up here to play for coffee money. What are you gonna do with a thousand bucks? You can't even buy fuckin doughnuts for a thousand bucks."

"Aw, horseshit," Harry said savagely, his voice matching the Tooth's in volume. "You don't have the heart to play even, that's your fuckin problem, you ain't got no fuckin heart. Why don't you just take your goddamn act outta here." The rail buzzed with nervous laughter.

The Tooth was red in the face now, and spittle flew as he screeched at Harry. "You want to play some even, motherfucker? You like the game? I'll *tell* you how I'll play you even. Get your ass up here and play for *twenty thousand a game*, even, right now." Bucktooth tossed out an enormous roll of hundreds onto the table. "Right there, motherfucker, let's play pool for some *real* money. *NOW* WHAT DO YOU HAVE TO SAY, YOU DOG-ASS SON OF A BITCH?"

The rail roared, and Harry glared at the Tooth with real hatred. He wasn't used to being high-rolled in his own poolroom. He was the man, the mayor of Platisville, and he was used to doing the trash-talking around these parts. Normally nobody dared to talk to him like that.

He stuck his jaw out and snapped, "I'll play you even, two thousand a game."

"Put up the cash and grab your cue, motherfucker, let's play some *POOL!*" the Tooth shouted, and in that instant Harry yanked up the leg of his sweats, exposing his big, white, hairy calf, and reached into a leg wallet just like the one I was wearing. He pulled out a stack of hundreds and counted out twenty of them. The Tooth took the wad he had tossed on the table and did the same. They counted each other's stacks and put the forty hundreds on top of the light over the table as the room buzzed.

"Come on, anybody else want any?" the Tooth said, grinning savagely at the railbirds. There was no response.

Harry won the coin toss and broke the balls. Perhaps he was full of adrenaline from the pregame ceremony, but he hit the break shot too hard and left Bucktooth a shot.

Bucktooth proceeded to weave the cue ball in and out of the rack of balls like a broken-field runner, shooting with perfect accuracy. He ran eight balls and out, never even looking like missing. Harry wordlessly handed him another sheaf of bills; the original stake money was left on the light.

Bucktooth broke and gained the upper hand in the second rack, as well, but Harry finally got to shoot and made a nice long bank to get back into the game. The rack seesawed until the Tooth scratched on a tough shot with just three balls left on the table and Harry made the two he needed.

But on the next rack, Bucktooth reversed the break beautifully on Harry, systematically taking each ball to his side of the table, and he won easily to go two thousand ahead.

After Bucktooth's break, the two players traded safeties for a few minutes, and then Harry tried a tough shot to break the rack and missed. As the cue ball rolled into position for him, the Tooth yelled, "Give me a shot, you dogging motherfucker." Harry's face took on the look of a large red grape as the Tooth ran the balls out.

As Harry racked the balls, he said, "I'll play for a thousand."

"What?" yelped the Tooth, truly astounded. Why would Harry reduce the bet? Normally he'd just quit if he didn't like the game. Lowering the bet was almost unheard of.

"I said we'll play for a thousand," Harry said. "Now get up there and play, you motherfucker."

"I'm not going to play for a thousand," the Tooth said.

"You cocksucker," Harry roared. "I'll break you in half." He threw off the upside-down specs, took a wild bear-paw swing at the Tooth, knocking his cue out of his hand, and charged him.

Bucktooth backed around the table and grabbed three pool balls. I jumped out of my chair and got between them, putting an arm around Bucktooth. Tony, who had been practicing on a table nearby, jumped in front of Harry.

This was not good, I thought. The first punch would inevitably start a brawl between the three of us and all of the regulars in the joint who were on Harry's side and/or payroll. It would be a short brawl. Also, we were in the home territory of one of the most prominent lawyers in Seattle, someone who was no doubt on first-name terms with every judge in town, and I knew Bucktooth had a record. For assault.

"The rotten fuck, I'll break him in two," Harry roared again. "And I'll break you in half, too, Tony, if you fuck with me."

"You don't know who I am," Bucktooth shouted. "You'd better do some fuckin research, find out what happened to the last guy who fucked with me." He had an arm cocked, the six ball in his hand, as he glared over my shoulder at Harry. (Later he would tell me, "I've been in enough poolroom fights to know that the guy with the balls has a huge advantage over the guy who swings a cue. Who do you like? You hit anything with a cue and it breaks. But these balls are heavy, man, and if you chuck them at somebody, they'll do some damage, believe me. I'm like Nolan fuckin Ryan with these pool balls, I can hit somebody in the melon with one at ten feet. And there's sixteen of them on the table.")

Meanwhile Tony stood toe to toe with Platis. I couldn't help thinking of his aikido practice, all his fucking around with martial arts, and then I thought, Jesus, don't hurt your bridge hand on his head. It never occurred to me that he was outweighed by probably a hundred pounds. But he was talking quietly to Harry, saying, "I know, you used to be a boxer, shit you could punch us all out, but look, Harry, you're a personal injury attorney and you're worth a lot of money, you know what kind of trouble you're going to get if you hit somebody." (Tony later would say, "I was about two seconds away from butting him in the bridge of his nose at that moment. If he had made a move to touch me it would have been all over.")

Bucktooth was still steaming. "Look it up, motherfucker," he spat at Harry. "You better think twice before you come after me."

"Is that a threat?" Harry asked belligerently. "Is that an implied threat?"

"Just check me out," the Tooth replied.

"Look, Harry," Tony said. "Calm down. You just threatened *me*, in front of a bunch of witnesses."

The realization that he was out of line seemed to come on Harry Platis all at once. He visibly wilted. "All right, all right, you're right, Tony, I'm sorry, but the hustling sonofabitch ought to play me for a thousand. That's all I've got left on me. It's Sunday, for Christ's sake."

"Well, why didn't you say so, instead of going buggy, you bastard?" Bucktooth snapped. Tony came over to try to help me calm Bucktooth down now that Harry wasn't in immediate danger of eruption. He took the balls out of the Tooth's hand and said quietly, "Come on, buddy, you can't afford to do anything like that. Just calm down. We're going to win the money."

"Come on, rack 'em," Harry said roughly. "Let's play for a thousand. That's all I've got on me and I'm not going to get any cash today."

The Tooth, still steaming, lost the next two racks, but then he settled down and won the following two. Harry, down four thousand again, said, "Fuck it, that's enough."

The Tooth took the last two thousand off the light and we walked over to the back of the room and sat down to watch Tony hit balls. The tall kid who had talked to the Tooth earlier came up to him and said, "I'll play you straight up for five thousand."

Now we knew this kid must play really well, which is what Bucktooth suspected before of course, and he said, "Come on, you give Harry eight to six, you've got to give me something," but the kid, named J.D., left and sat down across the room, and that was that.

After a few minutes Harry walked back to us and said, "Bucktooth, I'm sorry, I was out of line, what are you drinking?" They walked back to the bar together.

Now the poolroom's attention shifted to the back two tables, where Billy Cress and Tony were warming up.

"Hey, Tony, let's play," Billy said.

Here we had a poolroom full of gamble, with old warhorses like Billy and Monk and of course Harry, and we had walked in with more outside action than they'd seen in months—a potential payday of $30,000 to $40,000, maybe more. They were sick of playing with one another's money, or rather Harry's money, and Billy now represented the whole place's main chance at getting any of ours.

"I'm ready," Tony said.

Earlier, I had transferred a thousand dollars to my pocket from the leg wallet. Now I took two hundred of that and posted it atop the light with Billy's two hundred. Billy smiled at me; I wondered if he could tell that posting the money had sent a galvanic jolt through me stronger than any drug. It flashed me right back to playing high school football, and lining up for the first play tighter than a piano wire, waiting for that first hit that would fade everything but the action from my mind. The whole Tooth-Harry sequence had been so surreal and so quick that it felt more like a scene from an Albert Brooks movie than a gambling session. This, though, was the real thing, and money out of my pocket was in play for sure.

Billy was as hard-nosed a gambler as you could find, and he looked like it. He was wearing a wild print shirt, exposing a gold necklace with a large gold figure of a horse, studded with a diamond or two. It clacked against his cue each time he took a practice swing. I wondered how he could stand such a distraction; it seemed like a real self-sharking thing. As he bent low over the table, the cue running along the center of his chin as it does with so many good players, a curl of smoke rising from his cigarette resting on the rail beside him, he presented an image of unstoppable force. Looming behind the slim cue, his body seemed bigger than the table as he glared at the object ball with a football player's scowl, muscles bunched up all along his torso and his arms. It looked almost as though he were copulating with the table, dog-style.

Billy won the toss and broke the balls. Despite his strength he didn't seem to get that much pop on them. He made the two on the break, but tied himself up on the one. In nine-ball, on the shot after the break, the player can "push out," which means hitting the cue ball to a different position and offering the opponent the option of shooting from there, or making the first player shoot from there. Or, of course, the player can elect not to push out, but to play a regular shot. Billy tried a shot instead of pushing out, and missed.

Now it was Tony's turn. This was the first time he had played for serious money on this trip. He didn't loom over the balls like Billy, but he looked incredibly solid. As I had noticed when he played Moro, in his natural stance his legs were positioned a little oddly; he squatted a little, both legs bent at the knee, which was unorthodox. But there was method in this; his back foot was always right on the line of the shot, and his front foot was stepping into the shot, like a classic baseball hitter, striding right toward the pitcher. The upper part of his body looked dead perfect. His left arm was stretched out straight to his bridge hand, and his right was precisely aligned, the elbow cocked above his head on a line with the shot, his head down, chin on his cue, everything so still that he could have been a sculpture. His eyes were focused with cold precision on the shot. Looking at him from table level as I was, sitting against the back wall of the club maybe ten feet from where he was addressing a long cut-shot on the one ball, I saw that his cue and elbow made a perfect right triangle, with his head inside it, sighting along the cue.

He ran the table. Not in any flashy way. He hit each shot nearly center on the cue ball, except for the six, which he had to spin a little in order to get back on the seven at the other end of the table. The cue ball traveled only a few feet each time. It looked like nothing special, except that the balls all went in. He just left himself a perfect angle on each shot so he didn't have to do anything fancy to get on the next ball.

The Tooth, who had come in from the bar with his old drinking buddy Harry to watch the match, nodded calmly after his student made the nine. Billy came over and handed me two hundred dollars, then racked the balls.

It was an indelible moment of triumph. Maybe it was having the money right there in my hand, but it was more real to me somehow than Bucktooth's victory.

"Tony is intelligent, he listens well, he has great eyes and a great stroke," the Tooth told me. "If he follows the system I've taught him, he can be the greatest player in the world."

Billy was not pleased. "Motherfucking balls have been spitting at me all weekend," he growled when he returned to his chair, next to mine.

I tried to look sympathetic. "Harry made some banks on you," I said.

"Shit, that motherfucker never made banks like that in his life."

Tony broke and made a ball, but left himself hooked on the one and rolled out. Billy made a tough shot on the one and ran five more balls, but got out of line on the eight and missed. Tony's rack, and we were four hundred ahead.

He broke, and ran the rack, and now, fifteen minutes after he'd started, we'd made $600. Nine-ball for $200 a game is a lot different than, say, one-pocket for the same amount. A game of nine-ball can be over on the first shot, if the nine rolls in on the break, but even if it is played all the way down it will rarely last more than ten minutes. Many games are over inside of five. So playing for $200 a game is like playing for $2,500 an hour.

Billy won a rack, then, and he should have won the next one, too. He left himself straight in on the nine, no more than five feet away from the corner, and unaccountably dogged it, jarring the ball and leaving it in the hole.

"Mother*fucker!*" he snarled. "Rotten cocksucking balls."

He walked to the front of the club as Tony made the nine, then wheeled and walked past the table again and stuck his head out the back door and screamed— "AAAAAAAAAAAAAUGH"—then came back in and closed the door.

"Cut it, Billy," Tony said with a smile.

"That feels better," Billy said with a weak smile as he sat beside me.

It would get no better for Billy. He made a lot of balls, but against Tony his style—spinning the cue ball around the table for position, making flashy shots—was doomed to failure. He missed a lot of shots because Tony tied him up and left him safe, time after time, and after a while Billy got frustrated and missed shots he would normally have made. Tony, meanwhile, wasn't doing anything difficult—just making the balls one by one. He was not moving the cue ball any farther than he had to to get an angle on the next ball, using English sparingly, relying on getting the correct angle rather than having to juice the cue ball.

It was nine-ball *à la* Bucktooth, nine-ball for the dough rather than the show. And the real beauty of it was that the rail and the opponent really couldn't tell what he was doing unless they were very knowledgeable.

Now it was about four in the afternoon, and the joint was freezing cold. It was perfect outside, maybe sixty-five degrees, but at least fifteen degrees colder in the club, particularly on the table in the back corner by the AC vent where Tony and Billy were playing. The cold, damp air made the balls sticky; they weren't breaking apart well.

Billy got four games down, then five. He won a rack, then lost one, and then came to me and said, "Hey, did you pay me for the last rack?" Speaking calmly and evenly, I assured him I had, which of course was true, and he looked at me for a long moment then handed over the cash.

Now he was pissing and moaning at everyone, bitching at the rail for making noise, swearing at the balls, the fucking heartless balls. "Brutal weekend," he raged. "Brutal, fuckin brutal. First Harry, then this motherfuckin game."

Tony broke and made the one in the side and began moving on the other balls. "That's right, connect the fuckin dots," Billy said viciously, intimating that anybody could get out from there. But faced with a similar rack the next game, he couldn't, missing a tough seven ball. He lifted up from the table, enraged, and jabbed his cue violently into the air. "That's right, you ratfuck bastard," he growled, and walked away.

He was clearly used to being physically intimidating and had worked some of those moves into his act. His tantrums would certainly have unnerved some players, but Tony was calm and focused. That only put Billy farther out there. He, not his opponent, was being distracted by his anger, and he began to play even worse. This is known as "taking the heat," getting angry, often at yourself, which almost inevitably results in a "heat score" for your opponent.

Now, though, the phrase took on new meaning. Billy went over to the house man, who must have dialed the thermostat up, because in a few minutes the temperature went from fifty to maybe eighty.

After an hour Tony was up $1,600, and Billy said, "Tony, I'd like to play you some more in about an hour. I've got to shake this. . . . I can't play any more right now."

Tony looked at him without expression. "Okay, Billy, I'll be here." He kept hitting balls around the table. When Billy saw that Tony was planning to stay on the table and hit balls, he said, "Well, I wanted to practice on this table."

Tony said, "Well, fine, we'll go get something to eat. What time do you want to start again?"

"How about nine-fifteen?"

"Sure."

"Okay. I'm not quitting you, now. I won't quit you. I'll give you more action. I don't like the way you play."

Tony just nodded agreeably. We walked out, and Bucktooth asked, "Where do you want to eat? We don't have much time."

"Fuck him," said Tony. "I'm not going back there tonight. I'll play him tomorrow. I've never heard of such a thing. He quits, says he'd like to play in an hour, and then demands the table to roll balls around. Here I'm in dead stroke and he can't make a ball so he wants to get me out of my rhythm, get himself straightened out, and then play. That's ridiculous." He called back at 9 P.M. and left a message that he was too tired to play that night, but he'd see Billy in the morning. Billy wasn't even there.

Back at the motel, we took stock. We were $5,600 to the good. Since we took half of Bucktooth's action and he took a third of ours, Bucktooth was up about $2,600 and we were up about $3,000. A lovely beginning. Bucktooth even sprang for a room of his own. Fortunately, it was six doors down the hall. Just barely out of snoring range.

SEPTEMBER 28—WHILE TONY GOT IN HIS NINJA PRACTICE, THE Tooth and I tucked into pancakes and eggs at the hospitable Wright's Diner, and I asked him questions about his favorite subject: himself. Before long, Bucktooth the raconteur was in dead stroke.

"I was born in Oakland, 1939. My mom was Italian and my dad was Irish. He owned a little poolroom on Ninetieth Avenue. We lived there until I was going on eleven years old, and then he bought a little bar and poolroom in Fort Bragg, California, up on the Mendocino coast. It had four pool tables, a billiard table, a snooker table, a card room, and a little restaurant, and we lived right there. I think he bought the whole thing for seven thousand five hundred; I remember his payment for the business, house, everything, was a hundred a month. Of course, that was in 1950.

"Anyway, that's where I really learned how to play pool. I was big enough to help him behind the counter, you know, I'd carry a couple of cases of beer up from the stock room and back his bar. In those days you had to pull out the cold bottles, put the others in behind, put the cold ones back, and put in more ice. I suppose some high-class places had refrigeration by then, but we didn't.

"So I was in there every day, and I got to play pool all the time. I really liked it. From the first I liked nine-ball the best. I played the other games, rotation, all of them really, but nine-ball was fast, and I could gamble playing it. I remember playing nine-ball for a quarter a rack when I was eleven and twelve. My parents knew I was growing up in a poolroom so they really tried to bring me up real strict and religious, you know, Sunday school every week. My dad always said if he caught me gambling it would be my life, but of course I gambled anyway."

The Cook family moved back to Oakland when Bucktooth was fourteen, and by the time he was fifteen he was playing champions. "I kept winning in all the little towns and I'd go to Cochran's in San Francisco and I'd play these champions. They beat me at first, but I kept on playing them and I kept getting better. I didn't realize how great they were. Man, I played the best: Okie Sam, Sleepy Bob, Bignose Roberts. Hell, I beat Bignose Roberts when I was fifteen, he was only one of the greatest players who ever lived. He gave me the seven and I beat him. My father's brother was one of the best on the West Coast. They called him Oakland Blackie. He was what you would call a great regional player. It took a champion to beat him. He played Eddie Taylor, you know, the Knoxville Bear, he played Rags Fitzpatrick, he played all the greatest road players of that era. He played Minnesota Fats, of course his name was really New York Fats back then, before the movie, and he beat Fats.

"My father always told me the story about my uncle playing this guy named McDonald. They were playing one-pocket, a race to twenty-five balls, the way that works is you make 'em and then you spot 'em. My uncle had twenty-two and McDonald had eleven, and McDonald was in a tough trap. My uncle had him on the end rail. Apparently when he got in a trap like that the guy would always make these funny facial contortions and start wheezing like he had asthma or something. Anyway, this time he started making those faces and wheezing and he cut a ball backwards into his pocket and crashed into those spot balls as hard as if he was breakin a rack of nine-ball, going a hundred miles an hour, and then he ran fourteen and out to beat my uncle.

"When I was nineteen I went on a road trip and I'm in Lawton, Oklahoma, and I'm trying to catch this guy Bert to play some but Bert don't want to play me, he's staking this old guy to play me instead, I had no idea who this guy was. We're playing one-pocket and I'm beating him pretty good. We're playing forty, fifty a game and I'm six or eight games ahead, maybe three or four hundred bucks, and I get this old guy in a tough trap and he makes all these funny breathing noises, wheezing real bad like he can't breathe, and he whacked this ball and ran out on me—smacked in this unbelievable shot and asked to raise the bet.

"Right then I quit him, and told him maybe we'd play some more the next day. Meantime I ask one of the kids in the room, what's the name of the old guy I'm playing? And he says, 'That's Mac.' I ask him, 'His name isn't McDonald is it?' and he says, 'Yeah, that's right, that's his name.'

"I'd play anybody back then, I didn't care, I'd just go into a joint and play whoever was there. I played some rough places, too, black poolrooms like Trees in the Fillmore in San Francisco, places in Oakland, hell, I knew every player in there. I'd go in and say, 'All you eight balls got the eight ball,' and they'd laugh at me and say, 'Man, we just going to hang you up in the closet and leave you.' I played a lot of the great black players, Goway Jessie, Cleve, Rooster, a great player down Seventh Street in Oakland, a guy named Spare, beat him every time I played him."

Breakfast arrived, and Bucktooth tucked into the eggs with gusto, but he kept right on talking. "I kept right on learning from the great players, even while I was beating them. Some would play good up in the rack, some would play good up on the other end of the table. I just learned all the styles of play, all the old knowledge that you can't learn any other way.

"I would play Tugboat Whaley for hours, twenty, thirty hours at a time, and I robbed him playing even. It got so I would have to spot him and I still beat him, but I learned a lot about hustling from him. I beat all them old players, Hundred-Ball Blackie, Harry the Russian, Rusty Jones, Marvin Henderson, about every one you could name.

"I moved to L.A. when I was in my twenties, and started playing bar pool down there. Within a couple of years I was the best bar-table player in the world. Some say Ronnie Allen was the best but Ronnie got in the ring games I played in and I busted him just like everybody else. On a big table, too, I beat Ronnie a lot at that time; of course, he improved later. I remember he won the U.S. Open at Cochran's, Jack Perkins came in second. I didn't play in the tournament, but I played Ronnie right there after the tournament, played him one-pocket. I gave him nine to eight, twenty a game, and beat him twenty-two in a row. He didn't win a game. I busted him and his stakehorse, a guy named Fat Bill.

"We were playing in La Puente, and in Pomona, a ring game, every week. Me, Okie Sam, Glendale Johnny, Tijuana Joe, Pancho, all great players. It would be seven- or eight-handed, twenty dollars a man, and I just robbed it every week.

"We played on this real tough bar table, so tight it was almost like a snooker table only bar-sized. Ronnie Allen came to town and got in the game and went broke and I lent him the money to keep playing and he lost that, too. I played so good it just didn't make no difference who was in the game. I would just break and run out, break and run out, on this tough table where nobody can get out, man, they're having trouble running one rack and I'm just running rack after rack.

"The only guy ever to beat me on a bar table when I was playing great pool was Bakersfield Bobby, but then I came back the next week and broke him, and broke the whole town. There's only one person who ever beat me that I didn't get a chance to play again, and beat, and that was Clem, the Cincinnati Kid, he was one of the best ever. Nobody's ever beat me the second time. I have this real strong competitive thing, I can't stand losing and when I lose I go back and figure out what I need to do to win, I'm real analytical, and then I go back and beat 'em."

I ordered another coffee and managed to get a question in. "Did you ever play in the Jansco brothers' hustlers' tournaments in Johnston City, Illinois?"

"Yeah. I only went to Johnston City once, I played pretty good there, I had Nickie Vacchi in a trap, but he got out, he saw he couldn't win and pulled up. Amarillo Slim was stakin me to play there, which is funny since I was looking for Slim out there on the road in Texas and I couldn't ever find him. Him and U. J. Puckett staked me.

"That was a great show they had there in Johnston City, they did it right, everybody gambled. I wish I could have gone more years. But when I went there I said to myself, I'm so close by I think I'll go visit my uncle in West Virginia, that's where my mother and father grew up, my whole family's back there. So I went to see him, and he told me, 'Hustling pool's no way to make a living when you have a family.' I had two kids then and another on the way, and so he said, 'Come on out and I'll help you get set up in business.'

"So I went back to L.A. and loaded up the family and all our stuff in this little forty-nine Plymouth and moved everything back there. My uncle loaned me some money and I bought this little bar in Rand, West Virginia, near Charleston, a bar with three pool tables.

"I kept playing, too, I was playing at my peak. I went to New York one night, it was a freak deal, I just got a crazy notion and I took off in the middle of the night. At the time I didn't ever realize till afterward that all the players I played in New York were champions. I beat Boston Shorty, Johnny Ervalino, both of them among the best ever to play one-pocket. I beat Richie Ambrose in the Bronx in his own poolroom. Guys who see me play these days have no conception of how strong I was playing then.

"I tell people now that I went to New York and played Johnny Ervalino in his own poolroom and robbed him, playing even, and they don't believe me, but a lot of great players saw it. Cisero Murphy was there, Boston Shorty was there.

"Nobody beat me in the state of New York, or New Jersey. I went to upstate New York and it was the same. I whacked out everybody. New York Blackie. Danny DiLiberto. I played him dead even and robbed him. He still plays great today, but when I was at my peak it was no contest.

"Anyway, back then my place at Rand was doing just fine and I decided to buy another place, a bar that was for sale in the little town of Marmet. My mother and father told me not to buy it. Marmet is a tough town, the hillbillies come out of the mountains on the weekends and drink and go crazy.

"These big surly bastards would come in every day and order pitchers of orange juice, and then they'd get absolutely nuts and tear my place up. I finally figured out that they were going down to the hardware store and buying Solax paint thinner, for twelve cents a gallon, and mixing it with my orange juice. One night this six-foot-seven hillbilly came in, he'd been tush-hogging me for a couple of days, and finally when he came over the bar at me with a knife, I had enough and I told him, buddy, you brought a knife to a gunfight, and I shot him in the leg. I didn't stop there, either, I was so damn mad at 'em for tearing up my joint I just started pickin 'em off one by one as they tried to run. I didn't kill anybody, I was shooting 'em in the legs, but I got five of 'em.

"The next day I got out on bail and I went down and opened up the bar, I needed money for attorney's fees, and one of my best customers came in, bandaged nearly from head to toe, arm in a sling. I said, 'What happened to you?' and he told me, 'I saw you were going to shoot everybody in the joint and I ran right through your front door.'

"So I did my time at the penitentiary at Moundsville, West Virginia, and when I got out I came back out here to California. I never played as good after I came out, not nearly as good. It was my eyes. I used to read in the dark in the joint all the time and my eyes was really bad when I got out.

"When I got back here I started giving some exhibitions and such. I did have some flashbacks, I still could shoot good sometimes. I still beat the champions, I beat Bernie Schwartz, I beat Billy Incardona, he beat me, too, but I never beat nobody like when he came over to my poolroom in Castro Valley and I beat him fifty straight games. This was when he was the best nine-ball player in the world, I say the best. I am excluding Wimpy, Luther Lassiter, he was far and away the best but of course he couldn't get a game with nobody because everybody knew he was the best. But Incardona had beaten everybody else, and he came to my place and tried to give me the six ball and I busted him. We played five straight sets of ten ahead and he never won a game.

"All them champions, it's the same thing. I beat Jimmy Mataya, I beat Jimmy Rempe, Mike Sigel several times. Sigel never did beat me. Rempe gave me the eight ball and it was no contest, I robbed him. In my heyday I would have robbed him playing even.

"I could go on and on with all the people I beat. I'd rather not say what my best score was, you know, there could be repercussions, but you can say I won many thousands.

"Meanwhile I kept working in the business world, you know, I played pool less and less. Then I ran into Pots 'n' Pans, a great hustler who taught me a lot. His real name is Bunny Rokoff. I first met him when I was thirteen or fourteen years old. At that time he was going around hustling with a gas-station uniform on, and he came into the Midway Bowl and beat me.

"He got me into the business. I sold general merchandise for a while. I was selling anything you could imagine, and then I got into the jewelry business almost by accident. This guy came by my store and flashed a few gold chains in front of me. I bought some, and sold the majority of them right away, and bought some more, and sold them. Then eventually I hired a goldsmith and started making some rings, and got into gemology, and now I've got this jewelry business. . . . But every once in a while I really get the urge to go back and play some pool. I'll practice about a week and then I'll start playing again. Eight or nine years ago I was on vacation in Hawaii. I hadn't played at all for years, and I walked into a poolroom in thongs and a bathing suit, all sandy from swimming in the ocean, and Hawaiian Brian was there, and we started playing. We played for three days straight. I missed my plane, and I was a wreck. My feet, playing in thongs all that time, with sand on my feet, it was just like sanding the bottom of my feet with sandpaper. It's not like a cut, it's like they just start bleeding because all the skin is gone, just worn away. My feet were like hamburger. My bridge hand was black and blue from sliding the cue between my first and second fingers for three days when I hadn't been playing at all. I just wouldn't quit.

"He beat me out of a few thousand, and when I got to the mainland I started working on beating him back. I practiced a little, then when he came over here I just robbed him in Vegas and beat him again in Sacramento. I ended up breaking every pool player in Sacramento one weekend. There was a tournament, and they were all there. I beat Louie Roberts, St. Louis Louie. He asked me to play, and I had already planned what I was going to do to him. I laid down on him, lost the first set, seven ahead for five hundred dollars. I lost the first four games of the next set and then everybody jumped up to bet me. I had bets all over the rail, and then I beat him twenty in a row and busted everybody. Then I played Flyboy, and busted him. Keith McCready had won the tournament, so I played Keith and busted him, won his tournament money in about twenty minutes.

"The first time I played Harry was around then, in Las Vegas. Ronnie Allen had steered him into me earlier on a different trip to Vegas, and I was suspicious, I thought Ronnie was setting me up because he had steered me into Allen Hopkins the same trip. I remember hearing him say, 'This little fat kid can't play. Why don't you play him some?' He was only a world champion. I did play him some, and I did beat him, won a little money, but he made some fantastic shots on me or it would have been a lot more.

"So I didn't play Harry that time. I heard he was an attorney, liked to play high, but I figured he played real good, like Hopkins. Well, then I ran into him a couple of years later at this tournament at Caesar's Palace. They had one table set up and they were working on the others. Harry said, 'Let's play.' I don't think they even had spots on the tables yet. We had to mark with chalk where you were supposed to rack the balls. We played a set of one-pocket, even, seven ahead for ten thousand, and I beat him in thirty-five or forty minutes. Then I didn't play him until I came out of retirement again this year at the L.A. Open. You know what happened there.

"I also played Johnny Archer, the world's champion, there

in L.A. He was giving me the five, the seven, and the breaks. Again, I hadn't played at all in several years. The first night we played about fifteen hours. He beat me and quit me. I knew I could win at the game so we played again the next night. This time they wouldn't let me break the balls so I had Tony break for me. All these champions were there, betting against me, Billy Incardona, Ernie Gutierrez, Nicky Varner. Tony and Romeo were betting on me, and I was betting on me, that was it, everybody else was on Johnny Archer. This time we were playing a session, ten ahead. We stayed loser all night. He had up to six games on me, then down to three, back up to six, down to five, going back and forth. When I got it down to three again I made a speech: 'If it ever gets to zero again you guys can really win some money.' Well it got to zero and nobody wanted to bet anymore because they could see what was happening, and within thirty-five minutes I won the set. I won ten of the next thirteen.

"I played Mark Tadd some one-pocket, too, alternating giving me nine to six on one rack, then ten to six. I beat him twice that way and then we adjusted to straight nine to six and I beat him again.

"The capper to that trip was we went to this swell joint, someplace where they don't gamble much, the Hollywood Athletic Club, and I got into a conversation with a guy at the bar. I asked him if he'd like to play some for twenty or thirty a game, and he tried to high-roll me, and said, 'Well, I'll play you a set for five hundred.' And I barbecued him."

We started the walk back to the hotel. Tony had a date with some more of Billy Cress's money.

"Do you think the players today are better than the players you grew up watching?" I asked.

"I don't know, the equipment's so much better now, see. A lot of the modern players don't want to come out and say it, but it's true. The cue sticks are way superior. There were very few people making them back then. You just went to the bowling alley and bought a cue out of the Brunswick catalog. Plus you didn't have the high-tech balls back then, the old mud balls were a lot harder to play with. I don't think the players today would be able to execute the shots that the old-timers did with the mud balls.

"Shit, you wouldn't believe the equipment I played with. Of course, a lot of it was a hustle. I played with a broom, with a chopstick, with a mop, I played a game once where I had to wet the other end of the mop before I shot. I used to play people with my eyes closed, with a bag over my head, blindfolded, with my back to the table. I would line up a shot and then put a bag over my head and turn around and play the shot backwards. I never lost playing with my eyes closed."

We were back at the hotel. Bucktooth turned to me and said, "You know, after all these years I just like to play, to try to beat the other guy. A lot of people think it's a hustle, but I can't see well at all now, I'm terribly farsighted. People don't realize the slippage in my game. Still, every once in a while I can step up and beat someone just on natural ability and they just don't understand how it can happen that way. It's reversed on me now, though. When I was a kid I used to pick on all the old guys, the guys with the big reputations. I'd say to myself, 'He's old, he can't see as well as I can, I know I can beat him.' And now, all the young talent, all the cream rising to the top like I did, they're saying the same thing about me. But they ain't beating me too much yet."

BILLY CRESS WAS ALREADY HITTING BALLS WHEN WE WALKED BACK into the Casino Club. To the Tooth's disappointment, Harry was not around.

Billy greeted us politely, saying something about what a hard weekend he'd had, perhaps by way of apology for yesterday's tantrums. Within a few minutes, the battle was joined again.

Billy seemed much more controlled, and he was hitting the balls much better. Tony got some bad rolls off the break, and missed a couple of shots he would normally have made, and after an hour Billy was a thousand up on the day. I knew it was too good to be true. It was too smooth yesterday, too perfect. I betrayed none of this as I handed Billy's money back to him, two hundred at a time.

Fortunately, my player did not share my trepidation or my negativism. Tony kept calm and got back in stroke, and soon he pulled to within two games at four hundred down. At the same time, Billy reverted to form with a vengeance. Each time he missed a shot, there was a mini-explosion. He swung his cue farther, and more violently, and his swearing at the balls got quite exhaustive: "You cum-sipping, motherfucking, asshole-fuckin BALLS!"

Now Billy demanded to switch tables, saying, "I don't want to play anymore on this fuckin table, I'm hot at it. Let's play on that table." He pointed to the other Gold Crown.

Tony shrugged. "Sure, just let me hit a few balls on it."

"Well, if you're going to hit balls I'm going to get some breakfast."

Finally, Billy was ready on the new table—and Tony was too. He won four of the first five racks, going from four hundred down on the day to two hundred ahead.

"Let's raise the bet," Billy said, tight-lipped. "Three hundred."

"Okay," Tony said. He then won three of four at $300 a game to go ahead $800 on the day, $2,400 overall.

"That's it. I can't stand any more of this," Billy said, unscrewing his cue. We went to the front of the bar and sat around to see if Harry might come in, but he didn't appear.

Billy came up and tried a few of his desperate scuffling acts. "David, give me ten to one, a grand to a hundred, I can throw these keys into the corner pocket of that table over there." He had his car keys in his hand, and he was pointing to a table about ten feet away. "No? Here, then, how about playing cards? I'll throw cards into that pocket. What kind of odds will you give me? How many do you think I can get in there?" I laughed. I had $2,400 of his money in my pocket, and he wanted it back.

"Forget about it, Billy," I said.

Rhonda came in and sat down with us and started chatting Tony up again. After a couple of minutes, Tony went up to the bar. "Watch this," he muttered to me. He ordered Evian water and ice in a large tumbler and asked for a couple of drops of Rose's lime juice in it. He took it back to the table and sat down. "Whew," he said. "I'm glad I'm done playing for the weekend. Now I can have a drink. Rhonda, I'm sorry, do you want something?"

"Hmmm. I don't drink," Rhonda said, smiling. "What are you having there?"

"Stoly," said Tony. "Love it. Drink it all the time when I want to unwind."

Rhonda looked at the tumbler. "Stoly and what?"

"Stoly and Stoly," Tony said. "Why put anything in it? I'm not driving." He picked it up and drank about a third of it. "Aaaah," he said. "Damn, that tastes good."

In a few moments Rhonda walked over near the front counter, where Billy was standing. Billy looked up sharply at Tony, then looked away. He went over and screwed his cue together again and started hitting balls. In a few minutes he came over and waved his cue at Tony. "Come on, buddy," he said. "Round three."

I posted three hundred again, and Bucktooth and I took a front-row seat to watch the action. It looked like a replay. Tony ran two racks to start, and Billy started steaming again. On the second rack, as Tony bent down over a shot, a head-splitting static noise came from the club's speakers. It returned intermittently during the rack; apparently they had chosen this time to make repairs to the jukebox.

As Tony lined up a shot in the third rack, it happened again: "Testing, Testing." Suddenly, as he was about to shoot, the speakers nearest the table blared forth with Led Zeppelin walloping "Stairway to Heaven" at incredible volume. Just as suddenly it was gone and the static was back. But it was too late for any of that to have much effect. Tony was imperturbable, and Billy was still angry. "Cock-sucking balls!"

With Tony up six hundred this session, a player sitting right behind the Tooth and me whispered to a player we knew named Vince, "It looks like all our play money is going to California this weekend."

"Yeah," Vince said. "But you know it takes a big nut to make it down there."

A big kid sitting next to Vince growled, "Yeah, well, they aren't out of this joint yet. They haven't made it past me." I turned to look at him. He looked serious at first, and then he smiled weakly, and I smiled too. Of course, that was our primary worry now: Getting out of this place without somebody deciding to try to take us off.

Now Tony was nine hundred up in this third session. Billy missed a long cut on the three ball, pulled up and executed a full Jose Canseco swing with his cue, holding nothing back, full hip turn, extending the arms, late break on the wrists. He just missed the table lights. I was surprised the torque of the swing didn't snap the shaft. Anyone in the way would have been maimed. The rail collectively sucked in its breath. After Tony ran out, it really was over. Despite the jukebox, the thermostat, and all the firepower Billy could muster on the table, Tony had won another $1,200.

"Let's get the hell out of here right now," Tony whispered, and the Tooth concurred. "Drive a couple of exits past the hotel," Bucktooth ordered, "then double back, make sure nobody's following us." Nobody was, so we went back to the hotel and whacked up the money. Today's take from Billy was $2,000 plus yesterday's $1,600, for a total of $3,600. The Tooth booked a third of our bet, so he got $1,200 off the top. Of course, we took half of his action, so he paid us $2,000. That meant that of the corporation's gross revenues of $7,600 for the weekend, our share was $4,400, less the $625 for the Tooth's ticket: A $3,775 payday. Even my two veteran gambler road partners couldn't resist a little hollering and high-fiving.

IV

Six-by-Twelve

"I began to play snooker in 1924, and I began to take it seriously after I won the first world's championship in 1927."

—Joe Davis, *Complete Snooker for the Amateur*

SEPTEMBER 29—WHILE THE TOOTH HEADED SOUTH, HIS PLANE RIDE eased by the expanded cushion of C-notes ("Cecils," as he called them) in his pocket, we made considerably slower progress in the other direction. Amtrak's connection from Seattle to Vancouver is by "motor coach," not by rail, but the bus was strongly reminiscent of the train: it was impossibly late.

After four hours of waiting with no departure in sight, we called a cab and busted our bags over to the Greyhound station just in time for their last ride north. We had to buy a couple of fifteen-dollar tickets, but at least we were moving. No pool hustler likes to leave town on a Greyhound, but with Harry and Billy's money it seemed like we were in a Rolls.

At the border, as we hauled our nine bags off the bus and through the customs line, we were painfully reminded of what we had already become aware: We'd brought entirely too much with us. It made travel an aerobic exercise of uncomfortable proportion.

A very efficient Canadian customs inspector ran raptor's eyes over us and our belongings, finally fixing on our cue cases. After the clipped routine questions ("How long will you be in Canada? Business or pleasure?") she asked, "What are these?" Her mouth pursed just the slightest bit and she said, "Billiard cues? Are you snooker players, then?" She took in our nods and looked at me and said, "Are you going to play in a tournament, or . . . ?"

I realized at that precise moment that I was a currency smuggler. The clump of 150 hundred-dollar bills on my right calf suddenly felt radioactive. I wondered irrationally if the dope-sniffing dogs by the luggage area could also detect money in large amounts. "We're enthusiasts," I managed. "We like to play when we travel around."

"I see," she said, issuing an officially authorized smile. "Good luck to you, then."

We landed in a cheesy, overpriced tourist hotel in a marginal area of downtown Vancouver, marginal enough that it was about two blocks from an old room called Seymour Billiards. We went down right away, and discovered more six-by-twelve tables in one place than either of us had ever seen. They were Brunswick Anniversaries, very fifties-looking, streamlined but clunky and bulbous at the same time, like 1956 Packard Clippers. All but the three in the front of the room were lined up like a company of ragged, combat-weary soldiers at a mustering-out, three rows of ten tables each, all too close together, so that if one were to bend over to make a shot from the side rails, one's arse would unavoidably be hanging over the next table. A few tables were *sans* cloth, in the early stages of disassembly. The cloths on the rest were badly worn, and the rails and blinds on all the tables were scarred with cigarette burns.

Walk into any poolroom and you can immediately tell where the best table is. If you see one near the front that looks pretty clean and tight, and the players on it are slow and rhythmic and quiet, standing square and solid and impassive behind the shots, and their eyes are darting back and forth between cue ball and object ball in metronomic perfection with their practice strokes, you've found it. Nine times out of ten it will be near the cash register; the owner wants it there. Either he plays for the money himself, or he wants to watch (and probably bet on) the ones who do.

When the appleheads come in and ask for a table, the house man never gives them the best table if there's another one open. He gives them one like those tired soldiers in the back of Seymour's, and keeps the top table open for the gamblers as long as he can.

The difference between the A table and the others may seem very slight—a truer roll down the long rail, a little better cloth, slightly tighter pockets—but it is enough to make an enormous difference to the good player who knows the table well. Sometimes, the difference can be dramatic, particularly in rougher rooms where the equipment is for the most part in terrible shape. It is surprising how often a room filled with cheap, battered tables will have one excellent table, relatively well maintained, as though it represents the last vestige of pride or self-respect the place can muster.

In many rooms the best table is also the trap table, tricked up in some way the locals understand, maybe with a slight roll favoring one corner over another, crucial in one-pocket; or with a pocket that is a shade looser than the others. That makes the table invaluable to the local talent (and the rail) when road players come to town. The A table is always the nexus of the room, where the regulars, the players, and the sweaters congregate.

The A table in Seymour's was another old Brunswick six-by-twelve, structurally just like the others, but you could see the difference at a glance. Its cloth was new, and had the clean look that comes only with daily brushing; most of the tables in the joint looked as if they hadn't been brushed in a year; they were worn shiny, and there were visible lumps where the chalk dust had settled through the neglected cloth, onto the slate.

Try *that* sometime, when you're on a bad table in a strange town, playing snooker for the sheer joy of the game, and also for twenty Canadian dollars against a stranger you suspect is stalling but is still showing enough speed to match everything you've got, and you slow roll a red into the side pocket and slide whitey down toward the end rail in good position to make the black, and the red ball rolls dead center to the pocket but then turns on a lump of chalk dust—a *ridge* of chalk dust, a fucking *Sawtooth Mountain Range* of chalk dust— and jaws out and hangs like a ripe pomegranate for your smirking opponent to pluck.

SEPTEMBER 30—SEYMOUR BILLIARDS WAS THE SHELL OF A WONDER- ful poolroom, and within days it would close forever. Two or three men sat dispiritedly, backs to an already abandoned snack-bar counter, and squinted at the weak autumnal morning sunlight as it revealed the smears of dirt on Seymour's big front window.

"Hell, yes, there was big action here, how big do you want it? Cliff Thorburn played snooker for fifty dollars a point here for a month once, giving ten, twenty, thirty points. I seen him make ten thousand in a night and I seen him lose it all too."

The speaker was a shell, too, an unemployed pipe fitter who

sat the rail watching old men play two-dollar golf, a weird local variation. They played with obstacles on the table, what appeared to be neutral balls placed in a certain formation, and also skittles, like miniature bowling pins.

Who knew if the guy ever saw Thorburn anywhere but in the cozy fantasy pool realm of his tired brain? Thorburn's name in Canada is equal in stature to, say, Reggie Jackson's in the United States. He has been one of the best snooker players in the world for twenty years. He won the world championship in 1980, and in 1983 he became the first player in that event ever to score the maximum 147 points in a frame.

Now, Thorburn wasn't even the best Canadian player (Alain Robidoux held that position without much dispute), but he was still capable of beating anyone. Seymour's, though, had slipped much farther down the greased pole to oblivion.

THERE WAS NO ACTION THERE FOR US, OTHER THAN MY TWENTY-dollar game with the tall, weirdly smiling local player, blond and rangy and twenty-five, with brown eyes like polished pebbles and a sardonic toothy rictus that made him look distressingly like a marine iguana with a cigarette hanging from its mouth. He beat me by a small margin, but I felt strongly he wasn't showing me his true speed and so I pulled up.

Never mind; we would have plenty of action in the months ahead. We were there to gamble, sure, if gambling opportunities presented themselves, but we were also there to revel in the game of snooker, to venerate it, to worship at the altar of the six-by-twelve. The fifteen bloodred balls dominate the table. Each is worth but a single point, but they are the key to the game nevertheless. The reds are racked in a triangle near the head of the table. Set out in their immutable pattern, the six other colored balls each denote a different value: two points on the yellow, three on the forest green, four on the coffee-colored brown, arranged in a row near the other end. The peacock blue ball, set in the middle of the table, counts five. The pink, spotted in front of the rack of reds, is six, and the black, tucked behind the reds near the top rail, is the most valuable, and the most treacherous, at seven points. To "pot black," make the black ball, is a snooker player's delight.

Potting a red counts one point, and more importantly qualifies a player to designate a colored ball as the next target. If the colored ball is made, it is respotted and the player tries to pot another red. After all the reds are made, the players make the colored balls in sequence, starting with the yellow and continuing through the black. During this sequence the colored balls stay down after they are pocketed, and so the black is always the last object ball on the table. The maximum break of 147, *à la* Thorburn, is achieved by making every red ball ($15 \times 1 = 15$), and a black after every red ($15 \times 7 = 105$), and then the colored balls in order ($2 + 3 + 4 + 5 + 6 + 7 = 27$). Thirty-six balls without missing on a table the size of North Dakota. Cue-ball position on the black, *fifteen times in a row.*

Snooker is a lovely, dynamic game with a tremendous emphasis on defense. ("Snookering" your opponent means leaving the cue ball so he or she cannot directly hit a red ball or, if the reds are off the table, the required colored ball, and it is an art.) Still, the very best players are capable of making "breaks," or runs, of more than one hundred points at practically any time. This combination of offense and defense makes the game a hugely popular spectator sport around the world, particularly in Great Britain, where the top professional matches are watched by millions on television, and where the tour leaders make upward of $2 million per year in prize money.

Billiards has been played for 500 years, give or take, and

snooker enjoys a large slice of that history—about 120 years in its current form. It became hugely popular, from India, where it was reputedly invented by British army officers, to England to Australia to Kansas. In the United States it was particularly loved in the Midwest and West, before falling into a decline, along with the rest of pool, in the seventies. Because both Tony Annigoni and I played in our youth, we each had a special love for the game, and Tony loved it for another reason: He was unquestionably one of the best players in America.

Most U.S. nine-ball players, weaned on $4\frac{1}{2}$-by-9 tables with big pockets (and, admittedly, larger balls) had a tendency to faint when confronted with tiny pockets and an extra three feet of "green." But Tony Annigoni liked the tougher equipment.

To me, a far less skilled player, the game nevertheless represented complexity, subtlety, beauty, and a link to pool history, as well as to my own youth, to Freddie Byers and the Stag Tavern. So we were there for the soft click of memory against aspiration, rolling true toward our teenaged exuberance across the long, unforgiving green acreage of time, but of course we were also there to find a Canadian snooker player with a lot of gamble and no respect for a Yank.

BACK AT THE HOTEL I PICKED UP A BOOK WE HAD BROUGHT ALONG: *Complete Snooker for the Amateur,* consisting of two full texts: *How I Play Snooker* and *Advanced Snooker for the Average Player,* by one Joe Davis. Mr. Davis reigned as undefeated champion of the world from 1927 to 1947. He was the first to post a 147 break in tournament play, and the only man to hold the world's billiards and snooker championships simultaneously. His book, unlike most instructional texts, was an absolute delight.

It was written with an admirable precision and technical perfection; the secrets it revealed were timeless. But best of all, it was written with *politeness* toward the reader, a gentle and pleasant British formality that allowed reader and writer to marvel together at the beauty of the game.

Joe Davis wasted no time in getting you on the right path. In the front of the book was a photograph of the author, intently preparing to execute a shot. The caption read:

This is the model stance you are expected to copy down to the last detail. Salient points are:
- Balance forward and over the left knee.
- Chin-tip down to cue level.
- Straight left (bridge) arm.
- Perpendicular right forearm.
- Horizontal cue-slide.
- Cue brushing tie, just under the knot. *(Obviously, playing snooker without a tie was not even to be considered.)*
- Firm, well-arched bridge hand.
- Distance from bridge to ball twelve to fifteen inches.

As I examined it, I realized that Joe Davis's stance was more like Tony Annigoni's than any other player's I had ever seen. Tony's legs were rather more bent than Davis's, but from the waist up the two were *exactly alike.* Except I'd never seen Tony wearing a tie.

OCTOBER 1—THROUGH A FRIEND, TONY HAD BEEN STEERED TO A couple of Vancouver's elegant old private gentlemen's clubs, which revolve around snooker, fellowship, and an archaic but charming gentility.

Tony's contact, Bob McCormack, was a friend of a friend, a

member of both clubs. When Tony told him that we were visiting from the United States and were snooker enthusiasts, we received a warm and immediate invitation to lunch and a game of snooker at the Terminal City Club the next afternoon.

The Terminal City Club was the jeweled remnant of a social order long past. Built in 1916, it was rich in old oak and oil paintings and alabaster, with ornate molded ceilings twenty feet high. Octogenarian members snored peacefully in leather chairs in the reading room, and a few of the younger boys took their sport in one of the most elegant rooms ever to house billiard equipment. It had a high, lavishly festooned ceiling, exquisite chandeliers, and dark wainscoting; but instead of bookcases or memorials to war dead or overstuffed chairs, this room's dominant furniture was four magnificent English snooker tables, made around a century ago by the London firm of Burroughes & Watts. They were beautifully maintained—*burnished* seemed an appropriate word. The pockets were cut precisely, one suspected lovingly, to the international snooker tournament template, which meant they were a shade bigger than those of the toughest American tables. The balls were the best tournament class, and the like-new surface was the correct high-nap snooker cloth. "Playing the nap" is a real challenge; a ball rolled slowly against the nap will curve and lose pace, like a putt struck against the grain of a bent-grass green. The nap is another reason American players, used to playing on super-fast pool cloth, are often driven crazy by snooker in Canada and England.

If the Brunswicks at Seymour Billiards were 1956 Packards, these were 1900 Rolls-Royces. The oak and brass gleamed and the black-leather pocket linings were supple and heavy to the touch. Not that a player ever needed to touch them. Robert, the white-gloved room manager, was there to respot balls as necessary during the game; to hand players the bridge, or the long cue and bridge if needed; to wipe chalk from the cue ball from time to time—"It's supposed to be the white, not the blue, isn't it?" he said dryly—and, of course, to keep score. He would impart a little advice, if asked, and in conversation it was clear he had formidable knowledge of the history of the game.

It was the lunch hour, and all four tables were in use. Although the players talked easily among themselves, the high ceilings and the general decorum meant the room always remained hushed. It reminded me of playing golf at Pebble Beach; one had the sensation of following the ball around inside a cathedral. Joe Davis would have approved.

The two men we played obviously expected to give us Yanks a lesson. On his second turn, Tony disabused them with a text-book "break," or run, of sixty points, and we won the first game easily. Robert's eyebrows elevated several notches as he kept respotting the black, pink, and blue balls.

We were then offered menus, and the four of us ordered lunch, which was served quietly and elegantly at a small table set up just a few feet from the foot of the snooker table. I sat down to a green salad, baked potato, and a perfectly prepared sole.

What a contrast to the Casino Club. No blaring jukebox, raucous railbirds, Billy Cress swinging his cue viciously, Harry Platis taking a swipe at Bucktooth. Just Robert, replacing balls and offering the occasional murmured "Good shot, sir!" and our courteous and curious opponents, asking a few questions about play in the United States and outdoing each other in hospitality and solicitude toward us. Of course, there were no Cecils changing hands, either, and that would scotch this game for most gamblers. Minnesota Fats wrote that playing pool without serious money on the line was "like Rudolph

Valentino, being chased by 400 gorgeous tomatoes, running into his hotel room and bolting the door and reading *Playboy* magazine."

After lunch and two more games, Bob offered to take us over to the Vancouver Club next door. "They're expecting you, you know, for a few games," he said.

The Vancouver Club was slightly less formal; members were mostly working professionals, as opposed to retired CEOs. Women? No. (When I asked whether there had been pressure from women to join either club, as at the New York Athletic Club, the Bohemian Club, and so on, one of our hosts smiled and said, "No, we haven't been faced with all that yet.")

The Vancouver Club's billiards room was larger, with eight snooker tables to the Terminal City's four. All were not in perfect shape, but the Burroughes & Watts beauty we played on with members Jack Lee and Mark Green certainly was. Jack and Mark comprised the club's best two-man team. Mark, a beefy, affable shipping executive, was the best all-round player in the club, and Jack, a newspaperman turned public-relations man, was a defensive specialist.

Both played far better than I, but we still won almost every game. Tony was simply too strong for either of them, and was able to support my erratic play. In the second frame Tony put together a break of 88 that made the growing audience of club members buzz in appreciation.

Again, the hospitality was superb; a waiter in tails floated up to take drink orders as soon as introductions were made all around. At around four he returned with *finger sandwiches*—salmon and cucumber—and a plate of cheese and crackers. Mark and Jack insisted on playing for ten dollars a game, even though it was fairly clear that we had the best of it. Somehow, in this wacky decorous antique scene, it made sense. At the end, they further insisted on paying us *and* taking us to dinner in the club's dining room, which was open to the public and touted—accurately, as far as we could tell—as Vancouver's best restaurant.

They also invited us to go to Scotland with them to compete representing the United States in an international club competition. We would be in touch; Tony was interested in the possibility of competing on the English circuit, for obvious reasons. While prize money was still comparatively minuscule in U.S. pool tournaments, England's top snooker players were more on a scale with top U.S. pro athletes. The competition was vicious, and until quite recently very restrictive rules kept most foreigners from competing in qualifying tournaments. Aside from being a delight, a trip to Scotland could help Tony a great deal.

AFTER DINNER WE WENT TO LOOK FOR BILL WIEBERNUIK, ONE OF Vancouver's well-known players. We found him at the nondescript suburban snooker room where he was reputed to hang out. The only trouble was, somebody had found him first. It's a common occurrence in pool gambling: You isolate your target. You close in on him. You're late. Either he's already in action, and you get to watch him playing somebody else, or he has already played and lost, and is consequently busted, and instead of getting a game you get a mooch with a sad story.

In this instance, we got to watch a young Asian player give Wiebernuik a thrashing. It wasn't action, but it was fun to watch. Tony and I took a table nearby and played a desultory few frames of snooker and clocked the game. Wiebernuik was obviously a fine player, a bit off his game. Everything looked first-rate—his shot selection, cue-ball speed, even his stroke. But he was missing too many shots. Not that he got that much air from the young Asian, who consistently left him tough.

Tony had told me that Wiebernuik made Steve Mizerak, the blimpish former Lite beer commercial star, small. Well, maybe not small, but he was every bit as big as Mizzie, and that's saying a lot. Mizerak somehow managed to look relatively healthy. Wiebernuik didn't. He was pendulous, wrinkled, and bloated all at once, rather like a Sumatran rhinoceros.

On this night, all he did was lose. We could not tell what they were playing for, but Wiebernuik was certainly engrossed in the contest, and he sure wouldn't want a strange Yank butting in and asking for a game. So when the game ended abruptly and both players donned jackets and walked toward the door, it was clear we wouldn't get action. The way he had just played, the last thing the big man would want over the next day or two was to gamble with a road player.

That left John Bear as our only other relatively likely spot, and, of course, there was a problem with that, too: He was a superb player. Tony knew him by reputation, and said, "I don't have to win that match. There are a lot easier." But Bear did have some gamble, and maybe we could make a good game.

OCTOBER 2—AFTER A QUIET DAY, WE VISITED CLUB DYNASTY, A predominantly Asian snooker club where Bear (and his brother, also very good but not an international-class player) were known to play.

It was unassuming from the outside, a strip-center store-front in a blue-collar district across the tracks from downtown, but inside it opened up into a clean, pleasant, expansive two-story club with a well-designed tournament room. Seats surrounded a sunken area with two excellent tables in the center of the room, which was idle; no tournament tonight.

It was a semiprivate club, devoted mostly to its members,

but strangers could buy a "day pass" for ten dollars. We did so, and were given a good-looking table on the second floor. Good-looking, at least, until we rolled a ball or two on it. For some reason, the rails were about three times as lively as they should have been; the ball actually seemed to *pick up speed* off the rail. A medium-speed shot would result in a ball traveling the length of the six-by-twelve two or three times. It was probably the result of several factors in concert—very lively rubber in the rails, which seem to be set a little too high, and the dry, chilly air in that corner of the room. Even though it was irritating, I was taken with this idiosyncratic table roll. It was going to hurt a player like Tony much more than me, because he was used to being able to control the cue ball so precisely, I reasoned. Wrong.

On the way out after my thrashing, I noticed, posted on the wall, the results of the most recent club championship, with a bracket showing the outcome of each match and a posed Polaroid of the winner with trophy. It was John Bear, which was of great interest, because up to then we did not know what he looked like. "Worst thing in the world, having your picture on the wall with a trophy," Tony commented. "How are you going to get anybody to gamble with you?"

But having his cover blown didn't hurt John Bear, because he wasn't there to play. The next day we obtained an ironic bit of intelligence: While we were in Canada, trying to play John Bear at his own game, he was in the United States, playing in a nine-ball tournament. It was our cue to leave. We needed to get back to small tables and big stakes, and we had a two-day train ride ahead of us to do that.

WE RECROSSED THE BORDER TO PICK UP AMTRAK AT EVERETT ON A grayish afternoon, one of about three hundred and fifty gray-

ish afternoons per year in Everett. The train was alleged to be
damned near on time (it originated, after all, in Seattle) and
it was supposed to be leaving in about an hour. We checked
everything else but didn't dare let the cue cases out of our
sight. We drew some curious stares as we carried them up the
hill from the station in the drizzle, toward a row of down-and-
outer bars to see if we could scrounge some lunch.

We passed up the joint with a dozen Harleys splayed across
the sidewalk in front, went inside the next one, and ordered
hamburgers. I put a quarter in the bar table and Tony and I
played eight-ball with a couple of horrible house cues, not
wishing to draw any more attention than necessary.

For a true hustler, being able to play well with a house cue
is essential, and Tony Annigoni is pretty handy with one. But
if we were looking for action, which we weren't in this cheap-
jack joint, having our cues with us should have immediately
killed our chances. Weirdly, that turned out not to be the case.
I scratched on the eight in the first game and had bent to rack
them again when a young guy at the bar said, "Hey, you guys
don't look so tough. You can't be hustlers, comin in a dive like
this with yer own cues." Tony and I both looked at him. He was
maybe twenty-five, with long, lank dark hair, a New York Jets
sweatshirt and a matching accent, pulling on a Rainier draft.
Tony unerringly picked up on his twisted thought pattern and
hit him with another double reverse. "My buddy here will play
you a game or two, but we've got a train to catch in a few
minutes."

"Oh, yer steerin me onta him, eh, no thanks, whyn't
meenyou play, howbout ten bucksa game?"

Forty minutes later, plus eighty bucks, we walked bemused
back down the hill to keep our date with the train.

. . .

NOT JUST ANY TRAIN, BUT THE ARROGANTLY TITLED *EMPIRE BUILDER*, although we were taking it in the opposite direction from those who bought the Great Northern Railroad's shuck and jive in 1910 about the "empires" waiting to be built on a half-section of hard, cold northern prairie.

By sunset, if you can call it that when the sun is about as visible as a mooch's bankroll, we were rolling along the Stilliguamish River, and I was enviously watching the occasional fisherman slug streamers into the wind and rake them back, looking for Mr. Big. As night fell, I passed up Tony's gin-rummy challenge and sacked out, knowing that when dawn came we'd be jouncing through Glacier National Park.

OCTOBER 4—SURE ENOUGH, ONE OF THE FIRST THINGS I SAW THIS day was a bull elk and half a dozen cows browsing not fifty feet from the train.

A few minutes later, I saw a bear ambling along a hillside a hundred yards from the tracks. I went to the dining car for cardboard pancakes just to get a better view, and thought about how tantalizing it was to be passing through this magnificent place, hermetically sealed in stale, smoky Amtrak air with the grandeur of Glacier outside an unopenable window.

Then it struck me how much better off most of the West would be if more people saw it only like this, through a moving window, instead of stopping and succumbing to our proprietary lusts, which take varying forms and degrees. We lust to feel of the West, to caress it with our eyes and our boots, to tramp on it, ride it, fish it, hunt it. Then lust becomes obsession; we want to cut it up into ten-acre "pieces of heaven" and own it, leave our spoor on it, satellite dishes and Hamburger Huts and Quik Stops and septic systems, clearcut its flora and stuff its fauna in taxidermy shops to fuel our self-images as its conquerors, break its spirit, and take what we call riches by turning mountains into piles of toxic dust. We sell cheap bowdlerized versions of its native peoples' artifacts in gaudy towns like Jackson, Wyoming, and Aspen, Colorado, while the Native Americans themselves languish poor and debased in shabby backwaters like Gallup, New Mexico, and Crow Agency, Montana. And we struggle to honor the tradition of this, and rationalize our modern behavior by calling it "How the West Was Won."

Tony and I were ourselves a part of this ridiculously romanticized Western heritage. The railroad-traveling pool hustler is as much the stuff of legend as the itinerant gunslinger, just as full of machismo and avarice and the looseness of road life, just as heedless of the consequences of his actions as the Dalton Gang. (Or even James Hill, who built this rail line on the false hopes of those 1910 homesteaders.)

Pool hustling as a trade would have died out long ago were it not for the same American penchant for cockeyed optimism that those settlers represented. The railroad whistle has always been a clarion call for those who are looking for redefinition, for "opportunity." Just like the thunderous clack of a rack of balls breaking, it is an inescapable offer of hope, the signal that a new start is just down the tracks, pendent in your next turn at the table.

Soon after 7 P.M. a group of workers waved cheerfully from the roof of the old train station at Williston, N.D., as the *Empire Builder* pulled in. They had better be about their business, I thought, because roof-fixing season was almost over here on the High Line. The pale slanted October light outlined the young roofers in their baseball caps against the ominous darkness of an easterly storm. No one here would draw any false hope from the startling electric blue patches where the clouds had split to the northwest. This was a Siouan sky, flat, low, and yellowish, with blotches of light gray rain clouds leaking down toward the wheatfields. Those were pursued by the real thing, towering black thunderheads dwarfing grain silos on the horizon ahead. We were headed straight into the apocalypse, it seemed. What turbulence lay beyond the clouds, I wondered, on the tables of Chicago?

The early evening light was beautiful but thin, austere, lacking much nourishment or warmth, like these plains. Everything in Williston looked weather-weary. A town usually shows its ass to the railroad tracks, and this one was no exception. An oilfield supply house had a fearsome little collection of rusting fifty-five-gallon drums stacked horizontally behind it. Everywhere were the signs of reduced expectation, of the failure of this or that business enterprise spawned in foolhardy optimism. This land did not suffer fools; it did not provide succor to many; and it afforded true prosperity to almost no one. Molding hay lay rolled and abandoned in the fields next to town. Even the weeds were dying, turning brown and withered in the borrow pit next to the tracks. It was almost time for winter, but then it is always almost time for winter in Williston, except when it is July and the fields are so hot that they seem like lakes of fire.

I'd cut wheat not far from here, driving to towns much like this one with my combine crewmates at dusk in beater field cars, old Cadillacs and Buicks you bought for fifty dollars at the beginning of summer and abandoned at the end, coming into town covered with wheat dust and parched and arm-weary, looking for the welcoming neon of a cafe that served Miller beer, hoping against hope for a pool hall. Work is the lingua franca of towns like Williston, muscle and bone work. It is the coin of survival, and still on many days it is not enough to hold off the bank and the auctioneer.

We, on the other hand, had eschewed honest work, preferring the slothful days and sharp nights of the professional gambler. Despite my Nebraska wheat-country roots I felt about as separated from the relentless reality of this hard land as I could be, and I was a little ashamed to be glad of it.

V

The Pool-Table Suite

"Never give a sucker an even break."

—W. C. Fields

AFTER SPENDING FORTY-SIX AND A HALF HOURS ON THE *EMPIRE Builder,* walking under the cavernous rotunda of Chicago's Union Station was startlingly pleasant. It was a dreamlike sensation striding through a towering open space after being so restricted while rolling through the vast emptiness of the High Line.

We taxied over to the Loop and checked in at the Palmer House. Tony had great connections with Hilton Hotels and the Palmer House in particular because for several years he had been negotiating sporadically with the hotel to put in a Q Club–style poolroom. So we'd been promised a good price, which turned out to be $107 per day. It was way over our budget but about half the regular price for a nice room in a deluxe hotel. We went upstairs, began to get settled, and the phone rang. It was the bell desk. "Mr. Annigoni?" I wasn't but I didn't quibble. "Our hotel manager has asked us to move you two into one of our pool-table suites."

"Pool-table suites?"

"Yes, sir."

"All right, I guess that would be OK."

Quicker than a nine ball on the break, the bellhop moved our bags and us to the eighth floor. The first room he opened looked like our old room. Tony looked at me and said, "Sure, pool-table suite. You probably misunderstood him. He probably said Pullman suite or something."

"Just watch," I said nervously, and sure enough he opened the adjoining room and there sat a reproduction of an antique four-by-eight, a very serviceable little table. Also two sofas, a huge coffee table, two bathrooms, a wet bar, a formal dining room, a coffee bar, and a credenza or two.

Rack 'em, I said, and we played three racks of straight pool. I won the first rack 10–4, but of course didn't get another shot. The table leaned badly to one side, but so what? Don't roll a gift cue ball down the rail.

> "Crazy muthafucka named Ice Cube
> from a gang called Niggaz With Attitude . . ."

Tony's friend Curtis was not straight out of Compton like Ice Cube. He was straight out of Davenport, Iowa. But he certainly had attitude. Eazy-E, Ice Cube, and the rest of the NWA were booming forth from Curtis's red and black Mustang convertible as he pulled up to meet us in front of his Lake Shore Drive apartment building.

Curtis could be invaluable to us in Chicago. Tony knew he'd be at the center of whatever action there was. Curtis was young, hip, black, and bulging with bankroll. He was a professional blackjack player, a stakehorse, and who knew what else. He backed various players, depending on the situation, but he particularly liked to stake one of the great Filipino players, Francisco Bustamante, who competed in the United States from time to time but lived in Germany.

The three of us walked up to Curtis's apartment, which was incongruously furnished with two white-silk Louis XIV sofas and two elaborate matching French hand-painted white porcelain lamps, in addition to the huge Mitsubishi color TV and quite a few pictures of Curtis with family and friends, including Joe Louis and Michael "Second to" Nunn, the world champion middleweight boxer who grew up with Curtis in Davenport.

Curtis in the flesh looked double-slick. He was about five-nine and muscular. His hair was pulled back in a bun at the nape of his neck. He was wearing a gold crucifix set with a dozen diamonds—each a carat, a carat and a half easy—and a couple of heavy gold bracelets, along with an Italian black denim shirt with metal buttons, black jeans, and purple suede hiking shoes. Tony told me later that for Curtis, it was an understated look.

Curtis was reserved, polite, and quiet, but his sense of humor came quick and dry. He delivered lines in a monotone, without a smile or a sideways look, that were Letterman-quality funny. He got animated only when I asked him about his latest blackjack trip to Nevada. "Fifteen."

"Fifteen?"

"Dropped fifteen thousand in two days. Deck hot all the time, plus eight, plus ten, plus fourteen. Shit. I bet it up, like you got to, every time. Nothin ever came right." This little setback notwithstanding, Curtis had been doing well with the blackjack, from all accounts, since Bucktooth got him on a good card-counting system. Getting favorable decks, betting big, and losing will happen, now and then. But long-term, a good card-counter will win, and that's why casinos hate them. "That's okay," Curtis said. "I made forty, time before, twenty-five before that. It happens, that's all. It happens."

Tony had told me that Curtis was a nerveless, rock-hard gambler. He'd jam the money out whenever he liked the action, and he was not someone most people would consider "doing business" on—that is, deliberately losing to your opponent by arrangement in order to get the stakehorse's money. This is also called "dumping," and of course if you agree to do this but secretly have a superseding agreement with your stakehorse to win anyway and rob the other guy, it's called a "double dump." And such advanced concepts as the "double double" have been known to happen. But not to Curtis.

Poolrooms closed up early in this town, at 1 A.M., and so it was important to get moving. As we approached the Mustang, Curtis asked Tony to drive.

"Why?" Tony asked.

"License suspended."

"Why?"

"Speed."

"How many tickets, Curtis?"

"Shit. Six."

WE RUMBLED ON OUT TO THE NORTH SIDE WITH TONY AT THE wheel, about as unlikely looking a carful of gamblers as you could imagine, five-liter engine thrumming, Ice T banging out of Curtis's megaspeakers: *I gotta get paid I got money to earn.*

Right you are, T, I thought. We're out on the earn, looking for a payday. We had a little vacation in Vancouver, playing for the love of a game, not, as it turned out, for money. That was over. This excursion was for commerce, period. Bucktooth was fond of reminding Tony that there was only one way to keep score in this game—who had the money at the end of the session.

We headed for a place called the Billiard Cafe, in the hope of making a game with a top player named Billy Incardona. Tony thought that maybe he could get a little weight from Billy playing nine-ball, maybe the eight and the breaks, and if he could, he thought, he had a good chance to win.

While we ate dinner down the street from the poolroom, Curtis made a few calls on his handheld Motorola, looking for action elsewhere around town.

"What about Bugs Rucker?" I asked. Rucker was a famous South Side Chicago player known as maybe the best bank-pool player in the world. Bank pool simply means every shot must be a bank shot, and it is a demanding, subtle game with very few proficient practitioners. "Bugs ain't gonna play Tony no nine-ball," Curtis said succinctly, "and you don't want to play him any banks." True enough.

The Billiard Cafe was a pleasant poolroom with good equipment, maybe fifteen tournament-quality $4\frac{1}{2}$-by-9s and one pretty 6-by-12 snooker table with English rubber and felt.

On the way in, we got propositioned by an old black pool hustler named John Henry. Tony recognized him and woofed back at him a little, but it turned out John Henry didn't have the cash to play. Incardona wasn't around, so Tony got a table to hit a few balls while Curtis and I played a race of nine-ball to 10. He buried me, 10–3. My move was to get him on the snooker table, but he wouldn't go for it.

Tony meanwhile, got a game with a young Latino named Jesse who, it was obvious, could shoot pretty damn straight. Slim and intense, in Wranglers and a plaid Western shirt, this kid looked like a hick and played like a hustler. Tony stalled with the guy a little, at $50 per rack, and they traded back and forth. Tony was able to run out frequently on the lightning-fast equipment, but Jesse ran some racks too, and his break was very strong.

Tony's consistent play put him ahead six games—he ran three racks in a row twice—but suddenly Jesse caught fire and ran five straight. At that point Tony asked him to raise the bet to $100 and Jesse refused. There was no gamble in this lad, I decided, if he wouldn't raise the bet after running five racks. Tony won a few more racks and finally Jesse quit with Tony $150 ahead.

Meanwhile, Billy Incardona had arrived. Short and dark, a sort of rough-edged Clark Gable lookalike—he was once described as a welterweight Omar Sharif—Incardona was a true legend. Nicknamed Cardone, Nine-Ball Billy, Billy the Kid, he was one of the two or three best nine-ball players in the game in the late sixties and seventies. He was still a superb player, although he played more one-pocket now than nine-ball. He was also well known these days as a TV pool commentator—and as the book at pool tournaments. He handicapped the matches and anyone—rail, players, whoever—could try their hand with him. He had a reputation as an extremely careful gambler.

He sat down, feet up, legs crossed negligently on top of his cue case, and watched the end of the Monday-night football game. Philly was beating up the Cowboys, and Incardona, a Pittsburgh native, was pleased.

Billy lived up to his reputation for caution by flatly refusing to give Tony any weight—not even the eight. "You could be beating champions, I don't know, I haven't seen you play in a long time," Billy said, pleasantly but firmly. "You can't expect to come in here and get weight. You're a damn good player."

Curtis saw an opening. "Hey, Billy, I bet I can beat you, lagging, a hundred a time, a hundred a roll." Incardona looked up, interested. Curtis was a halfway decent pool player but Cardone was a champion. Curtis shouldn't be able to beat him at anything on the table, even lagging—stroking the cue ball so it went the length of the table, then back, with the winner the one who got it closest to the end rail.

That was the gaff—Curtis knew Cardone couldn't back down from a challenge like that, and Curtis happened to be able to lag very, very well.

After losing three hundred, Billy quit Curtis and matched up with a local player named Paul Jones in a one-pocket session for a hundred a game. Paul, who was being staked by Curtis, got an unusual spot: Billy gave him a ball and the breaks, and after each break Paul got to take one ball from the break, whichever one he thought was most disadvantageously placed, that is, near Billy's pocket, and put it on the spot.

Paul, a large, muscular black man about forty-five, was an unbelievably slow player, and watching him was agonizing. One-pocket is never a fast-paced game, but Paul was insanely slow. He would bend over the shot, then pull up and restudy the table, over and over. He probably did it an average of four times before each stroke. Billy looked a bit disgusted from time to time, and on a couple of occasions it looked like the slow play actually took him out of his game; he rushed shots and missed, leaving easy shots.

Nevertheless, he dominated the match. After the first two games were split 1–1, Billy ran seven balls after a scratch, then missed and left Paul a shot, and he ran six right back, including several outstanding shots. But he missed the next, a relatively easy cut down the rail to his hole, and left the ball in position for Billy to bank it across and win the game, which he did. That shot seemed to take the starch out of Paul's game, and Billy won the next two racks before closing time ended it. After the last game, Paul replayed the key shot to all who would watch or listen.

Tony asked Billy about action, and Billy said there wasn't much, right now, around Chicago. "You guys should go to Philly," he said. "They're betting it up at Jimmy Fusco's room, South Philly Billiards."

"Yeah, we heard that."

"There's a guy, Cornflakes, there who's playing real high."

"We heard that, too. How do you think we match up?"

"Flakes doesn't have to win playing you."

It was closing time, and out on the street Curtis, who clearly had more gamble than any six people, was trying to convince a young white guy named Bob to bet him bankroll to bankroll, whatever cash he was carrying versus whatever cash Curtis had, on one flip of the coin. "Come on, man, flip you for your bank, man, flip you for your BR, let's go, what you got there, I know you got less than me, whoever has the least that's what we bet, come on, what you got, open those bills, man."

"I'll flip you, I'll flip you, I've got plenty here, don't worry about it, what about you, what are you holding, Curtis, you have any money left after Paul dumped you?" After a few similar exchanges, they were ready to do it. The smaller of the two bankrolls, they agreed, would be the stake of the bet.

They threw their wads of cash on the sidewalk in the center of the circle of half a dozen men—me, Tony, Billy, a guy nicknamed Beef for obvious reasons, and a couple of others. Curtis yelled "Tails!" and threw the quarter as high as he could, above the top of the building. It came down by my foot. Heads.

Bob's bankroll was $750, Curtis's $1,500. Curtis paid the $750 with a smile, then asked, "Go again?"

Finally, after more wrangling, Bob agreed to roll dice for three hundred—less than half of what he had just won. They both would roll a single die, high number to win. Curtis flipped his with sangfroid over his shoulder behind him, and

Bob threw his high off the awning and down onto the side-walk. A cop cruised by slowly enough to seem curious, but did not stop.

Curtis had a four. Bob had a one. Curtis took the three hundred, and Bob turned to leave. He owned several gas stations and car washes, Curtis had told me, and apparently they were doing well; he was driving a black Mercedes 500SL.

Now Curtis wanted to drag-race his Mustang against the Mercedes, with a handicap. On this point the negotiations bogged down. Bob offered two car lengths, racing "from the green light to that white truck." Curtis wanted five. He was no fool, and besides, Tony would have to drive. Bobby wisely rejected giving up a five-car-length spot. "Come on, man, you got five liters in that thing, you're tryin to rob me." So the last bet of the night turned out to be no action.

Curtis was unbowed as he left us, despite his stakehorse and quarter-flipping losses. "I gamble with these guys all the time," he said. "I usually come out winners."

OCTOBER 6—LATE IN THE AFTERNOON, WATCHING PBS IN THE hotel room, I began to feel the incredible segregation of my new world from the one populated by almost everyone else.

Outside, working people hurried through the Loop, heading homeward or barward from their nine-to-five jobs. Tony, snoring next to me, would get up to meet the day shortly. On the TV David Gergen and Mark Shields were discussing the day's events in the presidential campaign; the program seemed like a dispatch from another country.

Very few of the staples of the workaday world—things like normal hours, home life, presidential politics—have much relevance to the pool world. The economy, stupid? No big deal. The poolroom economy is only tangentially linked to the one that dictates most people's lives. Sure, when unemployment is high poolrooms sell a lot of coffee and candy bars. In Robert Byrne's book Danny McGoorty told the old joke about all the mooches in the Depression: POOL HALL BURNS DOWN; 5,000 MEN HOMELESS.

But the gamblers are different. Sure, they have to get their cash somewhere, but rarely does that somewhere have much to do with the outside world. The economy is only relevant to the extent that it dictates how many suckers there are to gamble with, and most of the top players aren't gambling with suckers and appleheads anyway. They're gambling with one another. It's strictly a cash economy, and the cash is mostly just a way of keeping score in the game. Whether a gambler has ten thousand dollars or sixty dollars in his pocket, he will still gamble all of it more enthusiastically than he will spend five dollars for a meal or thirty for a place to sleep. Subsistence is dreary and necessary, but gambling is the aqua vitae, the source of all excitement, ego gratification, and joy. Gamblers are as a consequence vicious comparison shoppers. They will drive ten miles to save two bucks on a meal but think nothing of betting a thousand on a football game.

Pool players *are* news addicts, but for world events or politics, most care little. Reading about Saddam Hussein becomes subordinate to finding out who Mark Tadd beat out of three thousand last week in Florida, or how Toby Flaherty in Las Vegas is playing a ball or two better than he used to. By the time we got to Chicago, players had already heard that Bucktooth made a big score in Seattle. Fortunately, the news of Tony's game with Billy Cress hadn't made the wire, or at least nobody hit us with it. Of course, it could have had something to do with Incardona's unwillingness to give up anything.

We did hear that Cole Dickson, a renowned hustler, had beaten Moro out of several thousand dollars in the Q Club—

but, unfortunately, he let Moro play "on the wire," or on credit—a saying that comes from keeping track of money owed on the old-fashioned scorekeeping wires strung with wooden beads that adorned every old pool hall. "Damn it, that'll ruin Moro," Tony fretted. "I would never let him play on the wire. Cash posted, pay after every game. It's the only way. Now he'll quit coming in because he owes Cole the money."

When Tony woke up I was playing pool. Together we leveled the table, using a crude but effective method: I picked up the end and held it while Tony shoved playing cards under the leg at the low corner. Soon, we had it rolling very nicely.

Playing around on the table, I set up the only trick shot I knew: line up four balls, each frozen to the next, in a straight line perpendicular to the right-hand side pocket, with the end ball resting just out of the pocket. Of course, Tony had seen the shot zillions of times too, and he knew that in order for it to be made the way it was supposed to be—all four balls should go into different pockets, the two end balls in each side pocket, the two inside balls in the right-hand corner pockets—it had to be lined up perfectly. So when I said, "I'll bet you dinner I make this," he responded, "On the first try? Sure, I'll bet you dinner."

I hit the cue ball slightly below center-ball, striking the two inside balls right in the middle. Miracle! I had lined up the balls correctly, and they shot impressively into their respective pockets.

"Hey!" I said delightedly. "Dinner's on you, bubba."

Tony laughed. A little tightly, but he laughed nonetheless. Little did I realize the horror of the situation. A fateful Rubicon had just been crossed: I had just gambled with a pool hustler on a pool table. True, he was *my* hustler, but he was a hustler just the same, and both tradition and instinct dictated a regrettable, Pavlovian response when I won that bet. "Hey, I bet you haven't seen this one," he said. He went into the other room and came back with a twenty-dollar bill, which he placed just under the end rail, evenly spaced between the two corner pockets. "You're a golf player, you lag the ball pretty good. What odds do you want on lagging the cue ball so it stops on this twenty?"

"Say, four to one?"

"Okay, I'll give you four to one on each attempt, for, say, ten dollars a shot?"

"Your forty, my ten, right?"

"Right."

"Sure, I'll try you like that."

Eight shots later, I owed him eighty dollars, and something didn't seem quite right. Whenever I thought I'd hit the shot just right, the ball always just barely coasted off the bill. Finally, I admitted defeat and quit.

Then I noticed how hard Tony was laughing. "I can't believe you fell for it," he gasped. "The oldest trick in the book." He then showed me that most bills already have a fold in the middle, and if you place the bill so that the middle fold makes it slightly convex, all but an absolutely perfect shot will slide right off the slick, sloping bill. Also, each time he returned the cue ball to me, he had surreptitiously adjusted the bill's position, tucking it a little farther into the rail, until soon half of the bill was in a place, under the lip of the rail, that the cue ball never reaches.

"Very funny," I said coldly. "But dishonest."

"Hey, you were the one that wanted to bet on trick shots. And another thing—the way I asked you what odds you would take? Always ask the mark. Most of the time, like you did, he'll take much less than the true odds, which on this shot are probably twenty to one. I'd happily give anywhere up to ten to one." He chuckled again. "You asked for *four.*" That sent him into another fit of laughing.

"Well! I assumed you'd be honest with me, your road partner, of all people. To defraud me on a . . . a *carny trick*—"

"You asked me to bet."

"But—"

"Hey, if you want to bet, you have to take what comes."

"All right, asshole, I'll remember that. Over dinner."

The strain in the player-stakehorse relationship forgotten for the moment, we walked over to the headquarters of *Billiards Digest.* Publisher Mort Luby, a soft-spoken, enthusiastic, literate man, and Mike Panozzo, his tall, saturnine, talented young editor, greeted us warmly. They knew Tony well—no doubt well enough not to bet with him. We talked about trends in pool and poolrooms for an hour or so, about the sparkling new rooms feeding off the pool renaissance: the Hollywood Athletic Club in L.A., Howard Beach Billiard Club in Queens, City Billiards in Minneapolis, the Clicks and Jillian's chains, on and on. They asked Tony about the Q Club, and he enumerated the daunting problems: the neighborhood; the parking; disputes with partners; and the growing competition from other new rooms.

We talked, too, about the disputes within the professional pool tour, about Don Mackey and his feud with the women, and about the central fact that kept pool players scuffling: the relatively poor purses in professional tournaments. The PBTA, to its credit, had the right idea about that: It was continuing to struggle for more TV time, particularly live match coverage.

Panozzo joined us for the payoff dinner, then took us on a Chicago billiards tour. We went to a yuppie brewpub/poolroom named Muddlers, packed with young women and, therefore, young men; it was ladies' night, and the women were playing for free. Seeing the place doing such a great trade had to be a little depressing for Tony, whose more beautiful and interesting poolroom was suffering in San Francisco. Jeff Carter, the house pro, was a terrific player, but wasn't about to gamble in his own room. We also went to an older, more traditional poolroom, which was also doing pretty good business; there was an amateur nine-ball tournament going on. Then, at Tony's request, Mike took us to the near North Side cue factory of Joey Gold, who welcomed us warmly.

Joey Gold was one of the craftsmen at the vanguard of the cue-making revolution, which was a result of two cultural realities: an explosion of interest in pool and an obsession with technology. Joey Gold's Cognoscenti cues were certainly high-tech, and beautiful as well. Their primary distinguishing characteristic was the joint he used in them, made of an incredibly hard resin.

"I *hate* it when people call the joint plastic," he said. "This is what I do when that happens." Joey Gold is a big man, maybe six-one and two-twenty, very muscular. He took one of his cues, unscrewed it, grabbed the butt end, and without warning took an overhand swing and stabbed it violently, screw downward, into his wooden worktable. And again. The point of the screw left a couple of nasty gashes in the tabletop, but the cue was absolutely undamaged. "Resin. Not plastic," he said.

The beauty of the joint was not just in its ability to be used as a murder weapon without breaking. It gave Gold's cues a great hit and feel.

It was almost accidental, Joey Gold being in the cue business. He is a very good player, and for a long time was a representative for Southwest, famous for wonderful cues and very long waiting lists. Gold had a tournament coming up, and he needed a new shaft, so he called the Southwest factory. "Six months," they told him. "Hey, this is Joey, the guy who's sold hundreds of cues for you," he said. "Six months," they said, thereby earning themselves a competitor.

I dearly loved my Robinson; John Robinson, who lived in Phoenix, was another of the very best cue makers, and had been for many years. He, too, had a special joint that made his cues hit differently than most: He put the screw on the shaft and the female end on the butt. He made a terrific, strong joint, and he was one of the only leading cue makers who still cut his inlays by hand. I could see that Joey, like John, was on to something, both with his patented joint and his craftsmanship. Billy Incardona, I had noticed, played with a Cognoscenti, a beautiful black and white model, and Gold told me Billy was one of his main distributors.

The last stop of the night was the Billiard Cafe. Again, there was no action. It had been too long since Seattle, and I would even have welcomed another cheap game like the one with Jesse the night before—paying $107 a night for a hotel room makes almost any game look attractive—but there was nothing.

Billy Incardona would play nine-ball, straight across, but Tony was adamant that we should not make that game. "It's a lose-lose," he had said when we'd discussed it that afternoon. "Either he beats me, and we lose, or I beat him, and we don't get any action the rest of the trip. We don't have any protection unless people know he gave up some weight."

Eager as I was to get Tony back in action, I had to admit he had a point. So we were spectators, but at least the show was good. At center stage was one of the more eccentric characters in the game, Freddie "the Beard" Benavegna.

Freddie was a first-rate one-pocket player for many years. An auto accident had left him with a gimpy leg, though, and his game had deteriorated somewhat. He was a player from

central casting, a gravel-voiced, scuffling gambler, always looking for a mark. He knew Tony too well; he wanted no part of
him.

This night, Freddie settled for Paul Jones, and the two
embarked on maybe the most tedious game of one-pocket
ever played. Freddie was slow, Paul was the slowest, and they
knew each other well enough to argue over every shot, every
situation. An added spectator attraction: Freddie was wearing
baggy sweats, and whenever he stretched for a shot he displayed the crack of his ass to the poolroom.

In mid-match Freddie mentioned that he had recently
joined an est-like organization called Lifespring. The thought
of Freddie the degenerate gambler, reputedly given to violent
fits of temper at the table, in a self-improvement seminar,
merely seemed odd to me, but from Incardona and Annigoni
came horselaughs.

Freddie glared at them and said in his almost indecipher-
able Chicago dialect, "All right, youse buncha bums, always
lookin to rob somebody, scam da money. Dere's more to life
dan dat. Youse gotta give sometin back, unnastan?" This
produced more hoots, and Freddie sulkily returned to his
match. The first rack took easily an hour. Midway through the
second, Freddie tried a risky cross-bank to his pocket and jawed
the ball, leaving Paul a potential runout. "Godfuckingdamn
that cocksucking motherfuckerrrrrrrr!" Freddie screeched.

Incardona looked over and said, "Hey, Freddie. It's okay.
You've gotta give something back, you know?"

"FUCK YOUSE!!"

At closing time, the same group gathered outside the door.
Curtis was after Bob again: "Flip you for your cash, man.
Come on, let's gamble. Flip you for your bank." The bills
slapped on the sidewalk again, and Curtis yelled "tails" (he

was very consistent on this) and threw the quarter two lanes out into the street. He and Bob chased after it, dodging cars.

"TAILS!" Curtis cawed triumphantly. His take was $1,600.

Since we preferred to gamble on Tony's pool stroke rather than the flip of a coin, Chicago seemed to have little more to offer. We could scuffle a bit, wait around, but we had a lot of country to cover, and we wanted to take one more stab at the Canadians. What we did not yet know, of course, was who would get stabbed.

VI

The Human Fly

"There is but one step from the sublime to the ridiculous."

—Napoleon I, after his retreat from
Moscow in 1812

OCTOBER 7—THIS TIME, CROSSING THE BORDER WITH THE MONEY
didn't concern me in the slightest. I was so sick of sitting on
the train that all I felt was bored and tired as we crawled back
into Canada. I had become used to carrying the cash, anyway.
Most of the time, I carried the entire wad of Cecils in my left
pocket, but I couldn't get out of the habit of going to sleep at
night with the bankroll under my pillow.

Our train, now VIA, Canadian Railway, instead of Amtrak,
finally rolled into Toronto at 9 P.M., and we checked into a
clean, cheap hotel, the Strathcona, a couple of blocks from
the station. As usual, we ripped out the yellow page from the
phone book with the billiards listings. (If you stop at a pay
phone in an airport or train station and that page is missing,
it's a pretty good sign a road player's been through. This
happened to us in Seattle; the page was missing from the first
book we consulted.)

One place, grandiosely named the Billiards Academy, was relatively close by, on Queen Street. We walked the twelve blocks or so in the chill.

We were not the only visitors from Oakland. The A's were in town for the American League baseball play-offs, which had started about an hour earlier, three blocks away in the Skydome. The Jays' recent play-off failures were forgotten that night; Toronto was a city obsessed.

Queen Street was a charming combination of funk and elegance, vaguely reminiscent of the Haight in San Francisco: the same clutches of teenagers with four-foot spiked blue hair sitting on the sidewalk, the same melange of used-clothing stores, bookstores, cafes, and bars. In each bistro we passed, patrons and servers alike were riveted to the TV. Cheers and groans alternated as we walked down the street. When we got to the Billiard Academy the four TVs over the tables were all showing the game. Oakland was a run ahead, late in the game, and the tension was almost unbearable.

It ended that way, 4–3 A's, and the room was suffused with that pit-of-the-stomach flatness that comes when bitter disappointment follows excitement. Most of the players seemed to lose their interest in pool afterward, and the place emptied out fast.

The snooker tables at the Academy varied wildly in condition, and the one we got was no bargain. (It was yet another example of the truism that a house man will never give a stranger a decent table if he can help it. We were getting used to it.) The felt was loose around one side pocket, making it impossible to roll the ball slowly into the hole, and the rails were almost impossibly hard. Brush a side rail on the way to the pocket and you had no chance; the ball would bound away like a startled springbok.

A little dishearteningly, no gambling was evident; it had been so long since the Casino Club that serious action was a dim memory. Playing pool with each other was not a profitable proposition, but at least it helped to keep Tony sharp. Switching back and forth from nine-ball to snooker was probably not great for Tony's game, but it certainly didn't seem to bother him much. He made short work of me in the first frame. As I racked the balls for the second, Tony started in with the needle. "Jesus, hurry up, the glare from your bald head is blinding me."

"Look, you think I enjoy getting the shit kicked out of me every time I pick up a cue? I could have more fun being Mike Tyson's sparring partner. I have to sit here in the chair and watch you run seventy fucking points, which makes us no money, of course, and then put up with your insults."

"Maybe you need new glasses."

"Maybe you need to kiss my ass."

There was no denying it, though, playing him was great for my game. The concentration required to be a top pool player is beyond the understanding of the other 90 percent of players. Slowly, it began to filter into my consciousness, by osmosis, and it was stunning. On this night, Tony said, "Try something. Let's play mum pool."

"Mum pool? Is this another cheap hustle?"

"No, stupid, I'm trying to help you play better."

"What's mum pool?"

"See if you can figure it out."

I broke the rack, and the cue ball came down the table and snookered Tony behind the four ball. "Hey, Mumford, shoot your way out of that one," I gloated.

Tony didn't respond. He looked at the shot up and down, then hit a two-rail kick and made a red ball that was hanging

ing it up, it might not be worth it to you to give up all
dinage and camaraderie. Unless you want to play
Try playing quietly. Your friends may look at you curi-
even try to get you to break your silence. But if you
give in, you'll notice an improvement almost immedi-
You can't think about the game while you're talking, or
while you're *thinking about what you're going to say.* I had
n playing pool for twenty-five years, and I had never real-
d how draining the brainless chatter really is. Even if you
n't execute at a professional level—I certainly can't—just
etting that far into the game will ensure that you'll play
better.

Of course, just as talking can "shark" your opponent, *not
talking* can be a shark too. There's not much in pool as
unnerving as the opponent who shows no reaction, no
emotion, no matter what happens.

It was time to adopt the direct approach. As we paid the
pool time—a not inconsiderable expense on the trip; at
anywhere from three to ten bucks an hour, when you're playing for ten or twelve hours a day, it adds up—Tony asked the
house man, "Does anyone around here like to play snooker
for money?"

The counterman took the balls and looked up sharply at us.
"Not too often in here. We get the kids in here mostly. Where
are you from, then?"

"California."

"California! And you want to play snooker?"

"Yep."

"Well, you might try the Monte Carlo, out in Mississauga.
They do have a pretty good tournament once a week, and you
might get a game with some of the boys there."

"Miss what?"

"Mississauga, it's about ten miles from downtown." He

in the side pocket. "Jesus, wh
nothing, but lined up the blue
with low left English and got stra

"Shit, you're freewheeling now,
me, and potted the red, the black,
figured out what mum pool was.

After he finished his fifty-six-point b
late him on his good shooting, as I non.
instead concentrated on the shot he left n.
safety on the only exposed red. We played
game in silence, as well as the next three fran.
better than I had the entire trip.

I couldn't believe the intense mental effort
talk during play. All the urges to which I usually
the urge to congratulate, to joke, and particularly
when I missed a shot were almost impossible to con
compulsion, in particular, is the mark of the amateu
you hear a player saying things like "Shit, too much
English, I threw it right out of the hole," or "Sure is toug
make those shots down the rail on this equipment,"
"Damn, look at that, I was straight in on the next ball, and
was out from there," he or she is really saying, "Hey, I'm better
than I looked, missing that ball. I know why I missed, which
makes me smart, and I got position on that next ball, which
means I'm really good." None of which is true. The fact is, a
miss is a miss. I found out that evening that I was addicted to
talking while I played pool, and breaking the habit made playing the game a much richer experience; the silence allowed
me to focus on what was happening on the table, and on my
own game.

If you're used to going to the poolroom and shooting a few
racks of eight- or nine-ball with a friend, kidding and joking

smiled, a tiny, sly smile; mostly his face crinkled up at the eyes for a moment. "But they shoot pretty straight, hear?"

"I'll bet they do. Who shoots straightest?"

"Well, you'll have all you can handle with Jeff White, and John White, and Chris Wood, he won the Canadian nine-ball championship last year. There's quite a few."

"Thanks, partner," Tony said, then turned to me on the way out. "Nine-ball championship? Canadian nine-ball championship? Let's hit the Monte Carlo tomorrow."

OCTOBER 8—ONCE AGAIN, WE HAD TO RENT A CAR.

Train travel, as charming and historically resonant as it was for this trip, was becoming a pain in the ass. When the old-timey hustlers arrived at the downtown train station in whatever burg they had decided to fleece, they probably had at most a three-block walk to the poolroom. They didn't have to drive to north Seattle, or the North Side of Chicago, or to Missifuckingssauga, wherever that was. It looked like we were going to have to rent a car everywhere we went.

When we finally found the Monte Carlo, it seemed much more promising. The equipment was in excellent shape, it was crowded, and there was a bit of gambling going on. We struck up a conversation with one of the owners, named Vince, and he steered us toward a beefy man named "Bomber" Bob Edwards, who had just disposed of a challenger on one of the front tables. He shook hands cordially, and asked if Tony would like to play some snooker for fifty dollars a game. Tony agreed. It was better than nothing.

Bob was a very strong player, with a snooker player's uncanny accuracy on long shots, hence his nickname, but he was not prepared for Tony's level of play, and we ended up $150 winners before Bob's wife called him home to dinner.

The weekly tournament was set for the following evening, and I put up Tony's entry fee. For now, there was no other action at the Monte Carlo, but Vince steered us to a couple of other poolrooms.

One of them produced Jeff White, a pleasant, hard-eyed, sandy-haired man of about six feet and thirty-five years. He offered to play some snooker for two hundred a game—the next evening—or some nine-ball, "if the spot is big enough." None of that sounded too promising; we knew he was a champion, and playing a champion his own game on his own table, even, is a good way to lose. And if he'd really wanted to play, we figured he would have wanted to do it right then and there.

We moved on to yet another suburban room called Le Spot, and found the place we'd been seeking. It was not nearly so pretty a club as the Monte Carlo, but it was clearly an action room, divided about half and half between snooker and pool tables, and peopled with an unmistakable collection of gamblers. Serious backgammon was being played, and money changed hands at a couple of the tables in the first few minutes we were there.

Sitting at the bar was a player Tony knew well—Jerry Watson, a former player on the English snooker tour and currently an exhibition player and trick-shot artist. In his mid-fifties, Watson was urbane and distinguished-looking, somewhere between David Niven and Terry-Thomas. He was wearing a ski parka over black tie and tails; he had done an exhibition earlier in the evening. His dry humor was fueled by the Labatt's he was chain-drinking, slowly but steadily.

After a little small talk, peppered with one-liners, Watson suggested a game. "I'll play you some nine-ball, maybe a hundred a set, race to five, but I'll need the eight ball," he said calmly. He looked so calm as to be almost reptilian, as though his heart rate never climbed above forty beats a minute. Tony initially shook his head, but it had been a long time since we'd had any significant action—since Seattle, really—and so he assembled his Southwest and we moved to a table of Watson's choosing, near the bar.

As the game began, Watson's self-deprecatory patter, honed over hundreds of exhibitions, couldn't disguise his absolutely magnificent stroke. Tony was better at nine-ball strategy, but Watson played powerfully and well. He played position a little elaborately, spinning the ball around the table, but it worked most of the time. After one bad shot, he said, "Yeah, I come in here every day about noon," intimating that anybody would like to play him, which was hardly the case. Tony won the first set, but Watson won the next two, and we concluded the session a hundred dollars stuck. Afterward, Tony fumed. I had to admit we had done this completely ass-backward. We'd walked into a strange room and played probably the best player in Canada for goofball stakes—and given him a handicap. If we had won, we would probably never have gotten another game, so at least we hadn't. The hundred dollars was probably well spent as a "spread," or seed money to get other games. If all went well, we could come back and make a score.

Back at the hotel, there were messages for Tony, and the news was stunningly bad: Paul Brienza, Tony's erstwhile partner and rent-free tenant, had gone to Tony's lawyer and demanded that Tony surrender his stock in the corporation controlling the Q Club. The fact that a supposed friend and partner had turned on him was bad enough, but the fact that Brienza was staying in Tony's house made the news nothing short of catastrophic. Also, Tony's ex-wife, Dorothy, called; their sixteen-year-old son, Nick, had been involved in an auto accident and was having problems in school. Tony, three thousand miles away, was helpless to do much about either problem. He called Nick and talked to him. He called his lawyer. And he worried. Pool requires an almost unparalleled combination of physical acuity and mental toughness. Staying focused is critical, and for Tony that had just become a lot more difficult.

OCTOBER 9—WHEN WE WENT TO THE TOURNAMENT AT THE MONTE Carlo, we found that Tony's little win over Bob Edwards the night before had not gone unnoticed; the tournament director gave him a very tough handicap.

Tony played very well—probably too well for gambling purposes. He beat several well-respected players before losing a close match to the eventual winner of the tournament, a top player named John White (no relation to Jeff). Again, everyone was surprised at an American playing such excellent snooker, which was a disadvantage. Nobody was jumping up to play Tony for money.

As we watched the rest of the tournament, Tony nudged me. "Hey, there's a guy that's worth a lot of money. He's a millionaire. In fact, that's his nickname: Marty Millionaire." He hardly seemed likely to carry that sobriquet. Paunchy, balding, with glasses sliding down his nose, he looked vaguely professorial. He owned a furniture store, "Marty Millionaire Ltd.," in downtown Toronto. "I've met the guy before. He's a pool nut," Tony said. "Maybe he'd like to play some."

Sure enough, Marty came over and said, "Mr. Annigoni, let's play some nine-ball." In the next breath, he dashed our collective hopes when he said, "For fun, of course. I never bet a dollar on a pool game." I thought perhaps that he was like Harry—that he did like to gamble, but needed to be romanced into playing. Not so.

"I don't believe in gambling," he told me. "I just like to play the game, to make myself better and better, to help other players get better too. If you want to gamble, go to Las Vegas. Don't mix it with an art form. Cliff Thorburn wanted to play me for money. I always wanted to play a game with him because I respected his skill. I offered to pay him what we would have gambled for, just to play a friendly game, but he wouldn't do that."

Marty was self-appointed coach and teacher and cheerleader for every player in the place, and often his advice was exactly right. He taught snooker the old-fashioned way, the Joe Davis way. "You, how do you play?" he asked me.

"Not very well, but I love the game."

"Let's see why you don't play better. Here, get down over this shot." Uncomfortably, I complied.

"Tch, tch, no wonder," he said. "You Yanks just don't understand snooker."

"I grew up playing snooker," I said defensively, wondering what horrible flaw I had already exposed. It turned out to be my stance, so very far from Plate I in *Complete Snooker for the Amateur.* "Here, now. Stand up. Put your feet together. Yes, that's right, together. Now take one step over with your right foot. Now, oh, wait, you're left-handed. Okay, now lock that left knee, and take one step forward with the right foot. No, not that much. There. Feel that? Solid, right? Now bend over. NO! KEEP THE BACK KNEE LOCKED! BEND FROM THE WAIST! There. Now shoot." He set up a shot so easy I could have made it with my legs crossed. I dutifully bent stiff-legged and banged it into the pocket. "There! See! I love you! You listened! See how well it works? Now, let's play a game." He alternated exhorting, cheerleading, and chiding throughout the game, often stopping me just as I started to shoot. Mum pool was not Marty's game. Snooker was, though; he beat me quite easily.

OCTOBER 10—WE AGREED TO MEET MARTY THE NEXT NIGHT.
Tony and I wanted to get over to Le Spot, but Marty would have none of it. "No, that's a rough crowd over there, they'll take your money. You guys don't play well enough to play over there. Let me take you to my club, you can play for free there."

"Er, he plays quite a bit better than I do," I managed weakly.

"So he does, so he does," Marty said affably, "but not well enough."

We compromised: We told Marty we'd go to his club first, then on to Le Spot. On his home ground, Marty was more didactic than ever. "Hey, John, slow that stroke down a little," he called to a player as he walked in. The player looked up, grinned, and nodded, then returned to his game. When we got to the table, another player came up and asked Marty to settle a rules dispute, which he did, emphatically and correctly.

Tony wanted to raise a particular point. He had been trying to incorporate a key timing mechanism into his stroke: a pause between the last practice stroke and the actual hit. "Watch Buddy Hall sometime," Tony had told me. "He's the best I ever saw at it. That pause sets up his entire delivery, keeps him perfectly focused. These snooker players do it, too. Reading Joe Davis taught the pause. I want to work on it up here."

When he talked to Marty about it, he got an enthusiastic response. "Oh, yes, yes, it's essential," Marty said. "That pause allows you to focus all your power and energy on the stroke. It's one, two, pause, and three, right through the white like you're trying to split it in two." He demonstrated. Tony watched carefully, and then tried it himself.

It was hard to believe that this kindly, enthusiastic amateur player would have anything to teach Tony. But as we drove over to Le Spot afterward, Tony said, "You have to be able to learn from anyone, take what you need where you find it, or you'll never get better. He's a student of the game, and he just helped my nine-ball break a lot. That martial arts rhythm, one, two, pause, and hit, is what I need to get all my force behind the break.

"I already use the pause pretty well in my game. It enables me to get a great look at the contact point on the object ball, before I complete the stroke. I didn't need to hear that from him. But what he said about a karate stroke, that's key to my break."

Marty had left us with another warning and a little of his philosophy about gambling. "It's not respectful to the game. The pool gods don't like it," he told me. If the pool gods don't like gambling, I thought to myself as we walked into Le Spot, they're in the wrong line of work. But it was impossible not to respect Marty's platonic love of the game.

Just as we got there, the Oakland A's managed to lose the fourth game of the series, 7–6, after leading 6–0 early on, to give the Jays a 3–1 play-off lead. The place erupted in a thunderous roar. Sixty-year-old men jumped in the air and high-fived their grandsons' peers.

Jerry Watson was at his usual spot at the bar. Tony and I had discussed what we would do if we got another shot at him: lose again. Strengthen our spread. Drive home the point: We have money, we want to gamble, and Tony can't beat Jerry. Tony quickly dumped two more sets. Watson was savvy enough to suspect what was going on, but he was happy enough to take the two hundred dollars. We had done our advertising. Now, maybe, we would have things our way.

Jeff White decided not to play; he was just too careful, and he seemed to be operating with a limited bankroll. But a player named Mario Morra, a tiny, fussy player who had also tried his hand at snooker in Britain with only limited success, expressed some interest in playing nine-ball "for as much as you want." He was playing backgammon, and while we waited for him, a thin, nervous-looking kid stepped up and asked to play a set for a hundred. Tony agreed. The kid was sallow and trendy-looking with black Levi's, white T-shirt, and the big, clunky buckled shoes that have become a uniform on the club scene but aren't ideal for playing pool (you need to be able to stand flat-footed for balance and steadiness, and the last thing you need in a long session is to drag around heavy boots or shoes.) Oddly, he was using a Schon cue that had one-pocket wizard Grady Mathews's name engraved on the butt. "No, I didn't win it from him," the kid said sheepishly. "He sold it to me."

Watching him play, it was soon evident that he hadn't beaten Grady. He didn't play badly, but he was certainly no match for a pro, and Tony simply tried not to show too much speed in beating him out of a hundred dollars. During the second game of the set, a kid who could only be described as an urchin, about thirteen, maybe four-eight and thin as an unsecured note, dirty blond hair falling onto his forehead, cigarette hanging from his mouth, came up to Tony and squeaked loudly: "Hey, mister, you wanna play some nine-ball for a buck?"

Tony, who had been about to shoot, turned and said politely, "Sorry, I'm already playing a game here, for money."

"How much?" the kid demanded.

"A hundred bucks," Tony said, smiling.

"No way!" the kid said, shocked. He was quiet for a moment, staring at the table, then he nudged Tony again. Often in nine-ball sets coins are placed under the edge of the rail at the center spot on the head rail before the match begins. One is moved around the table, spot to spot, in one direction to track a player's games won, and the other is moved the other way to track his opponent's. Apparently, the young gladiator had not seen this system employed, because he said to Tony in a stage whisper, "Did you know there's fifty cents under the rail?"

After Tony won the first set, his opponent pulled up, which was okay, because Mario was ready. He had won big at backgammon, which we took to be a positive development, since it added to his bankroll. Mario was about five-three, with dark hair in a brush cut. In order to solve the problem of the spectacle frame in his field of vision, the problem that drove Harry Platis to rig his glasses upside down, Mario wore preternaturally large gogglelike glasses made especially for snooker players. He looked a little like Napoleon Bonaparte and a lot like the Human Fly.

We agreed on two hundred Canadian dollars a game, and suddenly the whole poolroom was at attention. A couple of kids came up and asked for side action, twenty apiece per game, and I said, sure. Jerry Watson whispered to me, "Your guy should win this easy." And so he should. Finally, we had the situation in our favor—a high-stakes game against an apparently weaker opponent, with side action. This could be big, I thought.

But Tony was in trouble almost immediately. The pool table was covered with the high-nap snooker cloth, and it took some getting used to, as did the table architecture itself. The side pockets just didn't take balls well at all; Tony had three or four key shots spit back out of them in the first few racks. And, pause or no pause, Tony just couldn't get the balls to fall on the break.

Mario was not a wonderful nine-ball player, but somehow

he nearly always managed to get out. He had the expected snooker player's accuracy, and, also as expected, he played terrible nine-ball position. But it didn't seem to matter. When he left himself a tough shot he would either make it or fluke into a safety. He would play a whole rack completely out of line, but make tough shot after tough shot, never get position but never miss, either. As Tony's frustration mounted—he should have been able to give this guy the seven ball and beat him—so did Mario's winnings.

After a few games, Jerry drifted over and asked if I wanted another twenty dollars a game. This was worrisome, but I took it, because I still thought Tony should win, and I told Watson so. "Of course he should, old sport," Jerry said. "But look at him. He's clearly upset with himself."

So he was, but he played through the frustration like a champ, regaining his mental equilibrium after a couple of games and grinding grimly on the task at hand: Mario was seven games up—$1,400 Canadian, about $1,100 American. Tony kept after it, getting it down to three games, but then a key shot—a beautiful length-of-the-table draw shot on a three ball with position on the four—somehow hit the back of the pocket and jumped back out.

What a backbreaking roll! Mario won the rack, and the next, and for the next hour the match seesawed, with Mario slowly gaining a rack here, a rack there. At 3 A.M. we were losers by two thousand Canadian dollars, and I was running out of the currency. I went to the owner of Le Spot and asked quietly if he would exchange another thousand with me, and he even gave me a decent rate.

But half of that went the same way, and it was clear that this was not our night. Every time Mario missed, the balls somehow got safe. It was like one of those walking-in-cement movies. I just kept handing money to Mario, to the kids who had no idea how good a player Tony was, but happened to be at the right place at the right time. And, most painful of all, to Jerry Watson.

I had tried to prepare myself for this part of the game. Losses are inevitable if you step up and play when you get the chance. Sometimes, you're not going to get the rolls, or you're going to match up with somebody tougher, or you're going to give up too much weight, or whatever. Losing is part of gambling. But it was still excruciating. I thought back to Billy Cress and how frustrated he was, and the tantrums he had thrown. That memory, at least, kept me handing the money over with a smile, and quietly encouraging Tony. But the thought of Billy also made me angrier inside. Cress could give Mario two balls and rob him, and here we were losing to the guy. Finally, stuck $2,400 Canadian, I told Tony, "We've fired enough bullets, Tony. We've got a lot of other games to get."

"I know, damn it," he said. "I just know I can beat him, but it's not going to happen tonight." The improbable had happened, and we had booked a major loss.

"Let's get back to someplace where they don't cover pool tables with shag carpet," Tony said.

VII

The Chelsea Rip

> "The present in New York is so powerful that the past is lost."
>
> —John Jay Chapman, 1909

OCTOBER 10—WE TOOK LODGING IN AN INEXPENSIVE (FOR MANHAT-tan) little hotel, the San Carlos, that was still a third more than the Palmer House cost us. In a sense, the high daily nut fed our purpose, made us sharper, conveyed a sense of urgency to our planned hustle in a city that had seen every hustle. If you can make it there, you can make it anywhere, except of course in Toronto, where Napoleon wears goggles and does not miss a shot.

One thing was certain: We couldn't just walk into a pool-room and give weight to the best players in New York. We'd get eaten alive. This situation called for some old-fashioned trickery and deceit—a billiards tradition, of course, and particularly necessary here, where everyone we met would be holding back some speed to make a game with us. If the pool players' golden rule was applicable anywhere, it was here: Do Unto Others, Before They Run the Table, Kick You in the Nuts, and Take Your Bankroll.

This required planning, and so we went to an all-night deli called Stars on Lexington Avenue for dinner and a strategy session. Compared to the San Francisco restaurant of the same name, Stars was, well, chopped liver. But the Train Rule was still in effect: Anything—food, drink, shelter—seemed luxurious after getting off the damn thing.

The plan we came up with over bagels, scrambled eggs, and coffee required the nerve of Jimmy Doolittle, or at least Willie Sutton. We proposed to go into an establishment called Chelsea Billiards, described recently as "the last bastion of the pool hustler in America," albeit by a cutesy *L.A. Times* travel writer who didn't know that there are probably twice as many card-carrying pool hustlers at Hard Times Billiards in Bellflower, California, well within his own circulation area. We would be patient, spend several days in there, showing some cash and some gamble, and clock the place well enough to find a weaker player to whom we would lay down a spread, then get the game we wanted and snap off the entire poolroom. As plans went, it was hardly original, but it was better than nothing.

It was midnight—a good-enough time to start. We put on coats and ties—we wanted to look like appleheads—and cabbed over to Chelsea. The room was on West Twenty-first Street, a vaguely ominous area of clubs and dark storefronts with seedy loiterers loitering seedily outside. Chelsea was one of the prototypical yuppie billiard places, but at this hour on a Thursday night the place didn't seem to be attracting too many MBAs—or anybody else. The place had maybe six tables going out of the thirty or so visible when we walked in. There were another twenty or so tables downstairs; not one soul was playing there.

We ordered coffee from the house man (a mistake, it was awful coffee), who was playing a desultory game of nine-ball with a racehorse-thin kid in a Duke Blue Devils T-shirt. Something was off with the kid; his movements were jerky, his eyes huge and black. He was either high or crazy or both, but he displayed a nice stroke.

A money game started on one of the back tables, just as we came back upstairs from checking out the basement. A young Latino in a baseball cap had matched up with an older Asian guy. They put a couple of hundred on the lamp and started playing nine-ball. The younger guy had a pretty nice stroke. He seemed like a shortstop; he wasn't getting out every time, but of course he could have been stalling. He definitely shot better than the guy he was playing, who was acting like a psycho, talking to himself, talking to the balls, already taking the heat in the first couple of racks.

We hadn't been watching for ten minutes when a sketchy-looking character, maybe fifty, with slicked-back black hair, missing several teeth, dressed in a ragged leather jacket and torn Levi's, came up and asked us to play.

"No, thanks."

"Me, neither, I just want to watch for a while." He turned away wordlessly.

The Asian guy gagged the eight, leaving it and the nine both hanging, and slammed his cue down viciously. As he racked the balls, the kid in the Duke shirt came up and stood in front of us. "Want to play me some nine-ball for fifty bucks?" He needed to work on his approach. When we both refused, he stared at us for maybe thirty seconds, pupils as big as quarters, then turned on his heel and glided out the front door.

"The kid's a crackhead, but he can play real good. You're smart not to mess with him." The speaker was another pretty hard case—a fortyish hippie type who featured a worn brown-leather snap-brim cap, long brown hair, jeans, sneakers, and a bad limp. "You guys wanna play *me* some, maybe some eight-ball or nine-ball?"

We demurred once again, and the guy nodded pleasantly, looked at Tony a little more closely than I would have liked, and limped over to the other side of the room, where he curled up on two chairs and went to sleep. Tony whispered in my ear, "My God, that's Waterdog."

"Who?"

"Waterdog. Fuck, I haven't seen him in damn near twenty years. He came through San Mateo when I was eighteen or nineteen, and then he was beatin everybody in the world. Jeez, he looks horrible, I heard he's had some tough times."

We watched the nine-ball game for an hour or so. The first guy who had approached us was sitting across the table with two or three other men, and they were paying close attention to the action, as though they might have a piece. But they were also clocking us from time to time. Just as we were ready to leave, Waterdog woke up and wandered back over. "You guys want to do something, before it's too late?"

"You must be a pretty good player, man, coming up and asking strangers to play. Or we must look real easy." Waterdog just smiled, and we walked out.

In the back of a cab, on the way back to the hotel, Tony told me about Waterdog. "His name's Edwards, I think, but they call him Waterdog because he's from Watertown, New York. He used to be one of the very best road players. The night he came into Town and Country, I had just beaten some stiff out of two hundred, and he and Billy Teeter came into the room. I knew Billy a little, but I'd never seen Waterdog. He asked me if I wanted to play and I was feeling pretty good after winning, so I said, 'Rack 'em.' I think he ran seven racks. He sure took that two hundred off me in a hurry. Then he went into Cochran's and beat everybody in there." Tony shook his head at the memory. "I heard he got fucked up on smack. It's too bad, he's a real nice guy. I don't think he recognized me. But we need to be careful, stay out of his way as much as possible. We don't want him to knock our game."

OCTOBER 12—WE CAME BACK THE NEXT NIGHT, AT ABOUT 1 A.M. This time Twenty-first Street was jammed with cabs, and Chelsea's tables were full of sharply dressed young people, couples, groups of friends, all rolling the balls around and having a great time. It was good to see the club doing a decent trade, but none of these players was relevant to our purpose. We watched for a while, until some of the clubsters thinned out, and then we got a table and began the floor show.

We played ragged nine-ball, grabassing around, ties at half-mast, trading hundred-dollar bills back and forth loudly and carelessly, the loser throwing the bills on the cloth after each rack. The effect was somewhat like casting a grasshopper into a streamful of hungry trout.

Within the first five minutes, a fat man waddled up to the table and said, "Can I get in?" He looked like Peter Lorre's ugly cousin, maybe fifty-five years old, five-six and rotund, with stringy black hair smeared in streaks across his scalp like bacon grease on a cheap plastic bowl.

"No, thanks, private game, we can't beat anybody but ourselves," I said, and he snorted and went over and sat down with a couple of other scraggly types, including the guy with the missing teeth from last night. We played for another half an hour, then sat down. "Fuck, I don't know, all these guys look like busted-out mooches," Tony said quietly. "Maybe this won't work."

"Don't worry, there's money here, I can smell it," I whispered back. "Let's just keep playing it out."

The tall, thin crackhead hit on us again, and Tony said, "I was watching you play, you're way too good for me."

Then the fat guy wheeled around and said, "Cut the shit, you must want to gamble or you wouldn't be in here. How about I play one-handed, you play both hands?"

"You must be a hell of a player, man, comin with that shit."

"Oh, yeah, the hell with you. I wouldn't really play that way, I just wanted to see what you'd say."

I liked it; they were getting impatient, aggressive.

Waterdog was in action across the room, I noticed, playing some kid, giving him a huge spot—what's called the "Orange Crush," meaning the five ball and the breaks. They were playing for all of ten bucks a game, and Waterdog was getting out consistently.

Missing Teeth came up and introduced himself: His name was Eddie. He wore the same skaggy leather jacket and knock-off Converse All-Stars and had a cigarette in the corner of his mouth, and he wasted no time hitting on us again. "Come on, you guys, you were just playing for some cash, why don't you try me some nine, twenty bucks a game."

We blew him off—"No thanks, Fast Eddie"—and kept watching Waterdog. He was running out, running out, running out, gimping around the table but looking solid once the bridge hand was down. I said to Tony, "This kid's going to pull up, he's getting murdered," and right then the victim shook his head and unscrewed his cue.

Waterdog came over and handed Eddie four tens and the cue he was using. Eddie didn't look too happy with the split, but he didn't argue overmuch. Then came more entertainment: On the front table, a match for a hundred dollars a set between two psychos—a thin, bespectacled sharp dresser in pleated suit pants and tie, versus a guy who looked like a trip-wire Vietnam vet: Sinéad O'Connor haircut, camouflage T-shirt, eyes like glowing charcoal.

Both of them were nuts. Suit Pants grimaced with every shot, muttering loudly when he missed. Sinéad was even more violent, using massive body English, lunging viciously into the shot, twisting the cue high over the table to urge a ball down the rail. He stepped up and fired very fast each time, as if he were playing polo or hockey instead of pool. They seemed pretty well matched, in skill level and invective. Sweating their match was tense, like watching McEnroe play Nastase, waiting for one of them to blow.

At about 2 A.M. a young Latino kid, tall, maybe eighteen or nineteen, came over and said, "Hey, you guys, let's play some for fun, maybe twenty a set."

Tony said, "Oh, man, I don't know, we're business guys, just out on the town, I've had a couple drinks . . . but I don't know, I sort of want to play." He looked at me questioningly.

"No way, buddy," I said. "You'd be giving the money away."

"I don't know," Tony said. "We do like to gamble but we don't play good like these guys in here."

"Come on," the kid said. "Hustler's move, businessmen my ass, let's play. I'm just learning, I work construction over in Jersey during the day. I tell you what, I'll give you the wild eight."

He was a likable kid, much less obnoxious than the other sleazeballs. Tony said to me, "Come on, bud, what do you say, what's the worst that could happen? Let's give the kid forty or fifty bucks, what the hell."

"Not with my money, but go ahead, knock yourself out."

The house man put us on a pretty tight table in the back, the one Waterdog had just been using. When Tony pulled out his cue, the kid said, "Southwest, holy shit, I'm a dead man, you telling me this guy ain't a player? *Shit.*"

Meanwhile he went over and got the same cheap Meucci that Waterdog had been using. Some hustler's den. This was a one-cue poolroom. Several of the railbirds came over to look at Tony's cue. "I got a deal on it, I know a guy works for them," Tony said. "Doesn't mean shit, it can't make me play any better." The Southwest *was* a bit of a knock. It was fifteen hundred bucks' worth of cue, minimum, and people did tend to notice. On the other hand, it fit our profile as well-heeled suckers.

Tony and the kid started playing, and it was ludicrous. They were both stalling so bad nobody made more than one ball for the first five minutes. Tony managed to lose the first two games, but the kid left the next nine ball right in the hole, as if he were daring Tony to miss again. It went back and forth like that, with Tony overcutting shots, undercutting, scratching, misplaying position. I was grateful that this was not our usual pattern. I hated to watch this. To me, it was a defilement, like holding Secretariat up in the stretch. As with any fine art, Tony's game was a mix of technical knowledge, expertise, and inspiration, and this adulteration was small and ugly, no good for the soul.

The young player didn't show much more speed than Tony did, but he went three games up. Both Eddie and Peter Lorre came over then, asking to bet five a game on the side. Finally I decided it would hurt our credibility if I didn't bet with them, so I did. The kid left Tony another hanging nine, but Tony managed to give away the next rack. His opponent started to let it out a bit, and he would have run the next rack, except he scratched on the nine.

Peter Lorre asked to up the bet to ten, and I agreed. Tony lost the next rack and I threatened to quit him. "Shit, my guy's drunk, he can't beat this kid, he can't beat anybody the way he's playing tonight." Meanwhile I kept a running line of abuse going with Tony. "Jesus, how could you miss that? Don't you know I'm betting on you? Shit, that's probably it, you dogging bastard, you'd rather lose just to watch me pay off, wouldn't you?" Then, as Tony lined up one shot, I sharked him brutally, saying in midstroke, "Can you handle this one? It's a hanger."

He acted really hot with me. "Hey, asshole, you're costing both of us money. Can't you shut up while I'm playing?"

"Man, it wouldn't make any difference if you were playing in a fuckin cemetery, you'd still dog those shots. Don't blame it on me."

The kid won the first set and I quit the side action and got on Tony to leave. "Come on, he kicked your ass, it's late, let's get out of here, you'll never beat him."

"Shit, what's twenty bucks? I like the game. I'm going to play him one more."

The kid, who introduced himself after the first set as Robert Saez, kept on Tony's ass about stalling. Once when Tony made four balls in a row, he said, "Hey, look out, you're showing too much." As if he agreed, Tony gagged the next ball and Saez rolled his eyes.

The entire rail was on me to bet on the side. Peter Lorre said nastily, "Come on, no balls, why don't you back your man?"

"Go fuck yourself."

As Tony continued to lose, Saez's confidence obviously grew, and I could sense doubt in the room. We were laying it down so perfectly according to the book that they were confused. They naturally assumed Tony was a road player on the stall, but he was playing worse, not better. Maybe he *was* just a drunken salesman.

Tony dropped the second twenty and said to me, "All right,

all right, you were right, fuck you, let's get out of here and get some sleep."

We refused two or three other offers to play and headed for the door. The railbirds were solicitous. "Tough luck, guys. Come on back tomorrow, you'll probably do better."

We walked out and somehow caught the same cabbie of the night before, a wonderful gravel-voiced character named Willie Owens, a black man of maybe fifty-five or sixty. "You all win?" he asked, eyeing our cue cases.

"No, we got tortured," Tony said, like an actor staying in character offstage between scenes. "We're not very good. I can beat this guy"—he gestured to me with a thumb—"but I play anybody else and I lose."

"They's some slicks around that poolroom," Willie Owens said. "You know, hustlers. They be layin down and losin on purpose like, get you playin, you know, and nex when the cabbage come out it all be over in two seconds, they shootin out the lights."

"Yeah," Tony said. "I've heard that's done."

"Hey, I used to shoot before I got so old. I don't see good now, but yeah, I used to shoot all up and down Broadway, playin those Puerto Ricans. Yeah, those boys could play."

"Do they still play high up in Harlem?"

"Shoot, yeah, they's still big games up there, some big halls. They's a good one up 145th and Broadway, but they be a lot of hustlers in there. You can look at they hands and tell they never do a hard day's work in they life. They hustlin pool, pimpin, shootin dice, sellin drugs, they gettin they fingernails taken care of just like a woman, they wearin five-hundred-dollar suits, playin pool for five hundred a game."

"Hey, that sounds like what I like," Tony said.

"You must be pretty good you like to play high like that."

"Shit, no, man, I lose, I just like to gamble."

Owens laughed, softly—heh heh heh—and lit a big cigar as he wheeled the cab around a corner against a red light. "They gamble witchou up there."

"Can you get in and out?"

"What you mean?"

"If you're a pair of honkies like us?" I added.

This time Willie Owens laughed out loud. "Oh yes, no problem," he said. "They like honkies like you up there, want to play pool for big money."

In the hotel, Tony said, "If we end up getting the action we want, watch, it's going to be with that kid. He's on the lemon, big time. He kind of reminds me of me, when I was his age. Except I was better."

"Okay, Mr. Modesty," I said. "When are you going to start firing?"

"Do you know what we're going to do tomorrow?"

"Take the whole joint off?"

"Nope. You've got to learn some patience," he said. "Patience." He laughed. "We're going to do this thing right. I'm going to pick out the worst mooch in the place and lose to him."

OCTOBER 13—TONY NEEDED PRACTICE. IT WAS HARD, PLAYING ON the lemon all night, purposely missing balls, trying to disguise your stroke. It can put a good player off his game for real, so that when he tries to come off the stall, he finds he can't. We didn't want that to happen, so in the afternoon we sought out a place to practice.

We figured we'd be relatively safe across town on the West Side. We went to a place called Amsterdam Billiards, a beautiful, modern club part-owned by comedian David Brenner, who is a pool fanatic. Amsterdam is a thoroughgoing player's room, designed beautifully to allow some natural light in during the day without interfering with the table lighting. The equipment was perfect and all around us were serious players. Tony pointed out Tony Robles, one of the best players in New York, practicing on one of the front tables.

We decided to play a game of straight pool. It is one of the most elegant and uncompromising games played on a pool table, and although it's rare anymore to find a good money game playing straight pool, Tony loves it for practice.

The rules are relatively simple. The player pockets balls until he misses; one ball is left on the table and the remaining fourteen are reracked, without the ball at the top of the rack, with the object being to make the remaining ball and break up the rack with the cue ball, in order to be able to continue making balls. A world-class player can run a hundred or more balls without missing. Tony and I made a competitive game called "Fifty No Count": He had to make fifty balls without missing in order to count any points. On the other hand, any ball I made counted, so if I made two balls, I added two points to my score; if Tony made forty-nine balls and missed the fiftieth, he got no points. Today, we were playing to a hundred, for twenty-five dollars.

Straight pool can be a very painful game. In nine-ball or straight pool, when one player is on a long run, the other player, left to watch from his perch on the sidelines, is said to be "in the electric chair," as in, "I tortured him, ran five straight racks. I really put him in the electric chair." It is an apt idiom. I did not play well that day; the longest run I could put together was ten balls. Tony was making shots with his usual easy grace, and I was spending a lot of time sitting down. It is a horrible feeling, watching your opponent firing in shots and being powerless to stop him. One feels rather like the legendary Texas A&M twelfth man, the football player who was moved to run onto the field from the sidelines to tackle the opposing ballcarrier.

My only consolation in the early going was that Tony wasn't actually scoring. He ran thirty, thirty-eight, forty, but couldn't quite break the fifty mark. So, in spite of being thrashed, my huge handicap had enabled me to take the lead, 36–0, when I overcut a ball down the rail and left the table wide open.

As Tony started making balls, there was a palpably different feeling. From my perch in the electric chair I could see that he was getting absolutely perfect position on each shot. After he cleared all but one ball, I racked the other fourteen, and he broke them, effortlessly and precisely, the cue ball exploding the rack as he made the open ball. This time, fifty was not a problem; he passed that point early in the fourth rack. Now, every ball he made on this run would count. And he didn't look like stopping.

I was squirming for a while, but after a time I could not help but be entranced. Witnessing talent on this level is a rare privilege. When straight pool is being played correctly, a rhythm develops, not too fast, not too slow, the cue ball rarely traveling more than two or three feet from shot to shot. Tony was carving up rack after rack with surgical precision, clearing lanes to the pockets whenever he could, breaking the clusters of balls apart, but not so hard that they scattered down the table, moving from shot to shot like a drill sergeant scrutinizing soldier after soldier, lined up awaiting his attention.

Everything was perfect; the table, the cloth, the balls, everything. I could tell that Tony could *feel* the way the balls were rolling, feel how much spin the cloth would take, how the ball would cut, how the rails took a bank shot, how far he could "cheat" the pocket to make the ball and maximize position on the next shot. For the first time on this trip, Tony was *there*, in that wondrous mental realm of awareness and acuity that pool players call "dead stroke," "dead punch," "having the cue ball on a string," "in a trance." It is Bill Bradley's "sense of where you are." It is a cliché in team sports like basketball and baseball to describe players as being "in the zone" or playing "in another league," when you know that twenty-foot jump shot is going in *before* you shoot it, or the baseball is going out of the park as soon as you begin to swing, but it does happen. It is not limited to sport; it happens in ballet, lovemaking, riding cutting horses, arguing before a jury, in almost every field of endeavor. There is that attainable but ephemeral "zone," born of confidence, competence, concentration, and the positive focusing of emotion and spirit, that produces spectacular results. It is the essence of success, the Holy Grail of sports psychologists. In some measure, it is what we all seek in our lives. Dead stroke.

As I watched the balls roll in their hypnotic, deadly patterns, I remembered the only other time in my life I had such an extended stay in the electric chair. I was eighteen, and I was in the Stag Tavern for the biggest evening of my young life. The legendary Cowboy Jimmy Moore was giving a trick-shot exhibition—and then he was going to play a game of straight pool. Against me. When I got to the Stag he was already there, a big square kindly grandfatherly man with short-cropped white hair and steel-rimmed glasses in front of eyes that managed to smile even though his mouth was otherwise occupied, sucking on a wet cigar butt.

He broke. I tried a safety and botched it, and he ran thirty balls. I stepped back to the table and ran nine balls before missing an easy shot in the side and then he ran one hundred twenty balls and out.

I found out that night, with all of my friends watching, what the electric chair felt like. I remember gripping my Willie

Hoppe so tightly my knuckles felt as though they would pop, willing him to miss and at the same time not wanting him to.

I asked him later that night, "Mr. Moore, do you play much snooker?"

He chuckled softly in his throat. "Boy, I was the United States champion." We went to the snooker table and he sat me down in my chair for another fifteen minutes while he danced the cue ball in and out of the rack of red balls until they had all disappeared. Now, twenty-two years later, it was all happening again.

Finally, ending the ninth rack, Tony missed position by a hair and got too close to the break ball, leaving himself an unmakeable shot. After his attempt bounced off the rail, it was over: One hundred twenty-six balls. Tony's career-high run. And, of course, it had to come against me. My tab with him had grown to $150. Wonderful. We were starved for action, and he was beating my brains out. Still, it was great to see him play like this. Over the next two days, he would run 114 and 93 in his next two practice innings.

Before we left Amsterdam Billiards, I noticed a board with names and *pictures* showing who had run more than a hundred balls in tournament competition at the club. Some of New York's well-known young players were there, including Tony Robles and a couple of other players Tony had heard of: Frankie Hernandez and the luxuriantly named Ginky Sansucci. I kidded Tony; his run would place him in the top five at the club.

"No pictures, no pictures," he said.

OCTOBER 15—AT 2 A.M. WE WALKED INTO CHELSEA, AS WE HAD THE past few nights. The upstairs was practically deserted, but as I walked downstairs to clock the basement I ran into Robert

Saez on the stairs. "I'm playing a Canadian downstairs," he said. "He's a good player. He beat me last week."

The Canadian turned out to be Paul Potier, like John Bear a converted snooker player who spends a lot of time stateside playing nine-ball. Tony was sweating; Potier knew him, and he had the potential to knock our game instantly after several days of careful preparation.

Potier was giving Robert Saez a huge spot: the wild six, meaning that the six ball got the money any time for Robert, on the break or any other way, and also the last two, meaning the ball in front of the nine, whatever it was, cashed a ticket for Robert.

They were playing on a corner table downstairs, and the biggest rail we had seen yet was sitting in judgment. All the characters from the past couple of days were there, and then some: Waterdog, Peter Lorre, Eddie, Suit Pants, Sinéad, the Asian guy, a big, silent black man in a little porkpie hat, and several other familiar faces. It was a ghostly scene; the only light on the floor came from the bulbs over that table, and the faint glow of a Coke machine clear across the room. Occasionally, a match would flare and a face would be illuminated for a second, then fade back into darkness.

These railbirds' lives were much the same, I thought, lit for a few isolated seconds by action, however it came. It was as strong as anything Waterdog ever put in his arm, and it was fueled by the memory of past triumph. Addiction is nothing more than a good memory, after all, in this case the memory of the score. They took their pleasure vicariously, to be sure; they'd tell you they loved the game, and they'd love to be the one playing for the money, but of course most of them couldn't compete at this level; to step up and play Paul Potier for the money, you'd better be able to *play*. Gambling was their way of being players, participants in the struggle.

I looked at the sweaters' faces, and I realized that I was look-ing at myself. I loved this action, the competing, the *risking*—as much as they did. That was a sobering thought; these boys had been doing this for a while, and the lines and scars and booze noses and red eyes and pot bellies and bad teeth and the cheapness of shiny pants and dull shoes told a story about how the life had treated them.

This kid, Saez, was certainly the darling of the room; the stakehorses evidently liked his scrambling safety game. He was carrying the wallets of the homies on his back. Watching this match, two things were immediately evident: One, Robert Saez was showing a lot more speed tonight, and two, the table was brutally tight. It may have been the toughest pool table we'd run across so far, tough in a way that rewarded great play: excellent condition, tiny pockets, very fast cloth. The pace of the game, therefore, was very deliberate.

Saez was not a great player, but he was inordinately careful. He played some stylish, ball-spinning safeties, giving me the feeling he'd rather play safe than run out. Sometimes he'd get burned—missing the hook or leaving a makeable kick. But not often. Potier displayed formidable all-around skills. He had a lot of offensive firepower and a fine understanding of safety play—both part of his snooker legacy. The first race to nine took nearly two hours, but Saez eventually won, 9–7.

Potier rallied to start the second set, making some spectac-ular shots and beating Saez at the safety game. But the game was ultimately a loser for him. He probably could have given that much weight fairly comfortably if it were not for the table. It was so tight that he couldn't run out consistently when Saez missed, and that changed the game, making it much easier for Saez to get to the six ball. Saez won the second set 9–7, too, and Potier pulled up, four hundred down. He was too experienced to continue in a low-percentage game, and he maintained his equanimity perfectly in defeat.

"Tough table," he said philosophically as Saez was congratulated by his backers. He saw Tony and gave him a slow, almost imperceptible wink, as if to say, I won't knock your game, clean these fuckers out.

"Just learning, eh?" I said to Saez. He shrugged and grinned. "He gave me a big spot."

"Save that, man," Tony said to him. "You tortured the guy. I got off light last night."

"Nah, we'll play again," the kid said. "You were hanging back last night, I know it."

During the match, Tony had been woofing back and forth with Eddie the Mooch, and they finally made a game. Eddie agreed to give Tony the breaks for fifteen bucks a game. Tony tossed five straight, while I bitched and whined. Finally I told him, "Pull up or I'm leaving without you," and so he did, but not before Eddie offered him the eight.

When Saez slipped up next to us on the way out and said, "Look, if you want to play for some real money, I can get a stakehorse tomorrow night and we'll see who was stalling," we figured we had it laid down right for sure.

OCTOBER 17—WE WATCHED GAME TWO OF THE WORLD SERIES IN our hotel room. Toronto's Ed Sprague was the unlikely hero, homering off Jeff Reardon with Dave Winfield on base to win the game 5–4. I was actually pleased for the Jays, although I didn't like being reminded of Le Spot.

Both of us were keyed up during the baseball game. Tony prowled the room in his sweats, washing each of his cue's four shafts with a damp washrag, meticulously, slowly, like a warrior sharpening his lance for battle, his thoughts turning inward. This was the most interesting, delicate—and dangerous—spot we'd been in so far. It had taken far more finesse to get to this point than we had needed to get in action in Seattle or Toronto, and even though there might not be quite so much money at stake it would be incredibly satisfying to make it pay off. Particularly after Toronto. But it was no sure thing. We didn't know what kind of weight we would end up getting, or if we'd even seen Saez's true speed yet. From all I'd seen Tony could give him the seven and beat him, but you never knew.

We walked in about 11 P.M. On this Sunday evening, the clubs were all closed and Chelsea Billiards was empty again, pared back to the hard core. Eddie hit us up at the door. This guy probably hadn't made a seventy-five-dollar score in years, and by God he wanted to do it again. Sorry. He was lucky to have been the beneficiary of our advertising, but enough was enough. On this night, we had come for the money.

"Shit, I'm sick of getting beat up for nickels and dimes," Tony said loudly. "If I'm going to go off I might as well spend some money. Otherwise we might as well go to Atlantic City and play some blackjack."

We sat down in the back of the room, with the rest of the rail, and in a few minutes Robert Saez came up to us. "If you guys want to play a little higher, I can get my guy here tonight."

"What kind of weight do I get?" Tony asked.

"I'll give you the seven for two hundred a game."

"Seven and the breaks."

"No way."

"Okay, I'll take the seven, but let's freeze up some money, post a grand, play five ahead."

"Just a minute."

ist two. Of course, Potier got beat, too, and
Toronto was fresh enough in my mind that I
inguine.
arted well enough. Saez hooked Tony on the
went to the long rail and kicked the ball in,
he rest. As he started to break the second rack,
e of my life. Waterdog.
up to me and whispered, "You all from Califor-
out there some."
ght?" I whispered back, not looking at him, keep-
on the game. *What the shit is this,* I wondered.
saw a lot of good players out there, Ronnie Allen,
son, boy, that guy Cole could play, he made some
ever seen."
k. "Yeah, Cole can shoot the eyes out when he's right,"
ered, still staring at the table.
about Tony Annigoni, you ever run into him out
Waterdog whispered.
h, I run onto that doggin motherfucker," I whispered
"Waterdog, step over here for a minute." We walked a
le of tables away.
'll make this quick," he whispered. "I can't talk to you for
g. These guys will know something's up. So you know who
m, too, huh?" He smiled at me.
"Of course I do. Look—"
"Don't worry, I'm not here to knock your game. I like these
guys but I knew Tony twenty years ago and I owe him one. I
hope you get 'em, just slide me a gapper, that's all I ask."

"You've got it. I'll treat you right." I was relieved; he wasn't
threatening to pull the plug on us, he just wanted a gapper—
a taste of the action—and I was happy to do that.

"I thought that was Tony. He's changed his bridge a little
bit, but he still sets up solid like he used to. He's older, but

Saez went
waited, and w
Saez came bac
got to wait for o

"Shit," Tony s
mooches can't rais

"Chill, man, it'll h

"You're nuts, we ou
to Tony. "They'll never

"Fuck you. I'll put up
me.

"We'll wait for whoever
man's hundred on the side,

"Fine with me," said Tony.

"Anybody else want any?"
drinking tonight, I warn you, an
sick of losing." I figured it would
And the rail was ready.

"I'll take fifty."

"Give me another C?"

"How about twenty a game, straight?

"Two hundred on the set?"

I went all around the sweaters covering
the money in little stacks all along one rail
the one we were going to use, with our cue
Then, sure enough, a short, dark, familiar-lo
in and walked up to Saez. He looked at Tony
and pulled out a bankroll. Saez walked over t
more hundreds. "Let's play some pool," he said.

This was it. We had Tony in action getting the se
someone to whom he could give the seven pretty ea
could probably beat Potier straight up and Potier gav

the six and the l
the memory of
wasn't exactly sa
The match s
four, but Tony
then ran out
I got the scar
He sidled
nia? I played
"Is that r
ing focuse
"Yeah, I
Cole Dic
shots I n
Oh fu
I whisp
"Ho
there?
"Ye
back
cou
lon
I a

hell, we're all older. I can't believe he's getting the seven from this kid, it's robbery," Waterdog whispered and limped away. I walked back to the table, and watched Tony make a nice combination on a nine ball to go two up. Saez shook his head and racked.

Tony came over to me. "What's up with Waterdog?" he whispered.

"He made you."

"Fuck, we're done, man, we may not get out of here."

"Don't worry, it's cool, I'm gonna gap him," I whispered in his ear. "He wants you to take these guys off."

Tony just shook his head. "Fuckin amazin," he said, and made two balls on the break.

"Sweet Jesus!" the black guy with the porkpie hat swore in a low groan. He had fifty on the set with me, and he wasn't liking what he was seeing. "Where the fuck did this guy come from?"

"He says he's a businessman," whined Peter Lorre with a sidelong glare at me.

"He *doin* some fuckin business," Porkpie Hat growled. "That's one businessman with some motherfuckin *stroke*. Shit. He get his motherfuckin thumbs broken, comin with that shit in here."

It took Tony only nine games to get to five ahead and the money. He was trying not to show too much, but he wasn't taking any chances with the cash, either.

"You got to give me a chance to get my money back, man, you came off the stall big time," Saez said, rolling the balls around the table. He wasn't happy but he wasn't that angry, either. He understood the game. So did the railbirds, now, though, and they were very pissed off. "Okay, give me the eight and I'll try you like that," Tony said.

"No." Saez shook his head, hard. "Even." He looked over at

his backers, who were gathered in a downcast little knot at the end of the next table. They nodded vigorously. "Don't give him shit, man, make him step up and play you even," one of them said.

"Shit, you should probably give me weight," Saez said. He bent down and fired in a couple of banks.

"Play him even, Tony, let's see if these guys want to gamble some more." I turned to the rail.

"Fuck you," Peter Lorre said.

"Come on, man, he lost five straight to Eddie last night, he might shoot straight up in the air in this set."

"He lost to Eddie, he did it on purpose," Porkpie Hat rumbled. "I don't want no more of it." I was only able to get a hundred out of the rail for the second set, but that wasn't too surprising. These guys weren't here to get beat, and they knew they'd been scammed the first time.

It took a little longer, about an hour and a half, to knock down the second set. Tony had to play very well to beat Saez, who was playing even better than he had against Potier. "You guys fucked up," Robert Saez said cheerfully when it was over. "You showed too much speed."

He was right, in a way, but we were handicapped by our circumstances. Saez and his backers didn't have huge money. If we could have hung around there for two or three weeks and waited, somebody with some real money might have stepped up to play, and we could have made ten thousand or more.

But so what? It was an interesting intellectual exercise. We probably wouldn't do it again; most of the time, these days, good players are too well known, and the risks of hustling are too great. It's easier to simply match up with another good player, perhaps even one who doesn't have a high regard for your game, such as Billy Cress, and take the money. But when

Saez's stakehorse, the small, dark guy who had looked so familiar, said, "I'll play you some, man, straight up for two hundred a game, same way," Tony passed.

"No thanks, Ginky," he said. "You're too fast for me. I saw your picture on the wall at Amsterdam, run a hundred twenty fuckin balls, and I don't need to play you."

It was a pity to pass up another high-stakes game. We were fairly confident the room still had Tony's game underrated by a ball, maybe two, but matching up with Ginky would be no picnic. We didn't know exactly how strong he was, but Tony had heard enough to know it would be a tough game. We had worked hard for almost a week for this payday, and there was no reason to risk losing it all in a game that tough.

Anyway, we got the money that night, what there was of it: twenty-seven hundred and change. I gapped Waterdog a hundred and he was thrilled. He told Tony he was on a methadone program, and doing pretty well. "My biggest problem is this gout," he said, pointing to his leg. "It's a bitch."

"Hey, we heard there's some action up in Harlem," I said to him. "You ever play up there?"

Waterdog snorted. "Are you fuckin crazy, man? They'll cut off your nuts before they'll let you out of there with any of their money. Those rooms up there make this place look like the Waldorf. Speaking of that, I'd get out of here pretty quick if I was you." We took his advice.

OCTOBER 20—ON TUESDAYS, WE HAD HEARD, THERE WAS A TOURNA-ment in Jersey—week in, week out, probably the toughest weekly tournament in the country. Why not? We probably weren't going to make any more money in Chelsea, or anywhere else in the city for that matter. Tony and I had slept most of the day on Monday. Now, we were ready to move.

We paid the tab at the San Carlos out of our winnings, and I called around to find a decent car to rent. Alamo had a special deal on Cadillac Sevilles—unlimited miles, two hundred bucks a week flat. I had to take a shuttle out to Newark Airport to pick it up, but it seemed like a good idea. And it beat the hell out of Amtrak.

The great thing, though, was that the car was brand-new, just delivered that morning: white with a red interior, ugly as a scratch on the break but extremely comfortable for the road. The stakehorse special. When I wheeled it out of the lot into the damp gray decay of an October morning in Newark and gunned it up onto the Turnpike, headed back into the city, it had three and seven-tenths miles on it.

WEST END BILLIARDS IN ELIZABETH, N.J., IS A POOL PLAYER'S SHRINE. Some of the game's true greats play there often: Steve Mizerak, Allen Hopkins, Pat Fleming, "Neptune Joey" Fratte, the Philadelphia players including Jimmy and Petey Fusco, women's tour star Loree Jon Jones, and all the New York City players.

The Tuesday night tournament at West End is known all over the East Coast for a consistently strong field, approaching the level of competition at a pro tour stop. It's a good place to play, and a good place to clock other good players, and maybe to make a game. We showed up at 5 P.M., two and a half hours before tournament time, to sign Tony up. "We have one spot left," the guy said, and so I paid him twenty dollars and Tony was in. We got a table for some practice.

Tony proposed a game of nine-ball. What he suggested seemed like a huge spot: I got the three out, but he got the breaks. That meant that if I legally made the three or any ball after the three—any of the four through nine—I would win the rack; he could only win by legally making the nine.

Sounds ridiculous, doesn't it? After all, I could play a little. But first of all, he was breaking, and maybe 40 percent of the time he would make a ball and run the table, winning without my getting a shot. So in order to come out ahead, I had to win *almost every one* of the remaining 60 percent of the games. And that, I found out, was next to impossible. Sometimes he broke, made nothing, but hooked me. Other times he broke and made a ball but didn't leave himself a shot, so he simply hooked me and waited for a ball in hand, or at worst a better-looking shot than he had just passed up. And of course if I missed a ball or misplayed a safety at any time after the break, chances were maybe 75–25 in favor of him getting out. Basically, it came down to this: For me to win at this game, he had to miss, which he was not in the habit of doing, and I then *could not miss a shot.* That's pressure. Also, it was hard for me to get in stroke playing this game, because I never got a chance to make more than one or two balls in a rack.

The game did afford me the opportunity to consider the psychological aspects of losing. I thought about Moro, how he seemed almost to like losing. I thought about Billy Cress. I thought about our experience in Toronto. And I learned first-hand how it felt, and I will be happy to share that with you now: It felt like being hit in the nuts with a hot steam iron. At the same time, though, I thought it was a valuable thing, knowing how to lose, because it seemed to me that only in that frame of reference could the sweetness of winning be fully appreciated.

I was certainly ready for a little sweetness. By tournament time my tab with Tony was up to $450.

"What kind of an asshole would rob his own stakehorse like this?"

"We've already been through all that. If you don't like the game don't gamble with me anymore."

"I'm stuck like a pig, and you advise me to quit."

"Hey, there's stuck and then there's stuck. It could get a lot worse."

"You're a real beauty, you know that? I should have left you in Toronto to play Insect Man for the rest of your life."

"Oh, now we're coming with the real low shots."

"Talk about low shots, let's talk about my four-fifty."

"Yeah, let's. Let's go over exactly how you lost all of it."

"Go over this."

He laughed. I actually considered our little gambling series an entertaining diversion. Mind you, I wanted to win. And I knew I'd get my opening, sooner or later. The truth was, I was learning a lot about gambling. And about pool. Each day that I woke up, took my bankroll from under my pillow and padded into the bathroom past the snoring machine in the other bed to brush my teeth, I was slipping deeper and deeper into this milieu, as exotic and unforgiving as a tropical rainforest. As I gained understanding, I appreciated my player and the way he handled himself under pressure. This boy had a few moves. Each new challenge we faced helped me understand him a little more. Horrible contretemps between road partners are legendary in pool, but we were actually becoming more comfortable with each other as we went. The interdependence we felt on the road was profound. It certainly lessened the strain of walking into hostile places. The Chelsea success was a measure of our growing ability to work together.

Not that we verbalized any of this. Despite his salesman's ability to articulate, Tony wasn't much for long, serious discussion. He was much more comfortable with the needling, bantering exchange that we had fallen into, and it worked for me as well. We used it to prop each other up when we were discouraged, and to punctuate the highs as well.

After my latest thrashing, we went upstairs to the tournament room. It was beautifully equipped, with a tournament board, six tight, well-lit black Gold Crowns in perfect shape, spectator seating on one side, and a couple of card tables in the back. It was not in any way fancy, though; it had a blue-collar Jersey feel about it, with painted paneling, a few beer signs, and about a hundred men and maybe half a dozen women sitting around waiting for something to happen.

It turned out that Hopkins and Mizerak and Fleming and a few others were at a tournament in Memphis, but the field was plenty strong nevertheless: Neptune Joey, Tony Robles, Frankie Hernandez, and quite a few others. It was single-elimination, race to five, with five hundred for the winner, half that much for second.

Tony drew a local player I'd never heard of in the first round, but when the announcer called his match, Tony wasn't around. He had five minutes to avoid a forfeit. Panicked, I rushed downstairs with Waterdog, who had materialized at the tournament along with a few other rail types from Chelsea. We scoured the poolroom and then, in desperation, dashed outside. Waterdog finally spotted Tony in a restaurant across the street, calmly buying a cup of soup, and I ran in to get him.

"Are you nuts? You've got two minutes."

"That's okay, I've already won enough off you to make my daily nut."

He made it, barely, and more important, won his match. Now he had to play Frankie Hernandez, a top New York player with an attitude to match. A big, muscular twenty-five-year-old known for his loud mouth, he was fresh from a couple of big tournament upsets, and was regarded as one of the best players on the East Coast right now. Tony, unimpressed, drilled him, 5–0.

"I'll play you for money any time, asshole," Hernandez told Tony. "I'll kick your ass." We were going to Philly the next day, and not planning to return to New York, so Tony said, "Let's play tonight. But I know how good you are, I've heard of you. I got lucky here. You've got to give me a ball."

"Fuck you, you just beat me five to nothing. Get a fuckin heart transplant and come back and play me."

"Get a cash transplant and we'll play tonight," Tony said. "But I'm not playing you any two-hundred sets. Let's play some for five hundred a game."

Hernandez left, sneering.

Next, Tony had to play Tony Robles, whose quiet courtesy provided a striking contrast to Hernandez. Tony won that match, too, 5–1, and Robles simply shook his hand, smiled, and walked out.

Porkpie Hat, the guy who had grumbled about losing the fifty dollars to me at Chelsea, was sitting in front of me for that match. When it was over, he turned around to me and shook his head in disgust. "Businessman," he snorted. Tony won two more matches to end up in the finals.

Now all the tables save one in the center were idle, and all the lights in the place were turned off except for the single table's overhead lights. Tony's opponent was a local player named Don Henderson, an enormous fellow with a beefy face and a white work shirt, straining over a huge belly. Despite his size, Henderson played delicately and stylishly, controlling the cue ball beautifully. As I watched him warm up for the final, I couldn't help but admire him. He was not a "name" player. According to the patch on the shoulder of his shirt, he was a municipal bus driver, but he had beaten five good players, including Neptune Joey, to get to this point.

It was the match of the night. He and Tony were an odd pair of combatants; he must have outweighed Tony by 150 pounds. Both men played beautiful position and defense, both made tough shots when the game was on the line, and both made very few errors.

Tony won the first rack to take the lead, but Henderson ran three straight to take a 3–1 lead. Tony then ran three racks right back to take a 4–3 lead in the race to five. He made nothing on the ensuing break, and Henderson played a fine hook shot, curling the cue ball into a corner hard behind two balls. Tony was unable to hit the one, and his opponent calmly took cue ball in hand and ran two racks and out. Tony collected $250, but it seemed like a Pyrrhic victory. There would be no more easy gambling money to be had around here. Word would spread—about Chelsea, and about how Tony came within one game of winning this tournament. Still, it felt good to cash another little ticket.

VIII

The City of Brotherly Love

"I spent a month in Philadelphia last night."
— W. C. Fields

OCTOBER 22—NOW, I THOUGHT, SHOULD COME SOME REAL ACTION. Philadelphia—hometown of the incomparable Willie Mosconi, and of W. C. Fields, who was himself a decent player, probably a hundred-ball runner—has always been a pool town. And we had been hearing repeatedly that they were playing high in Philly.

Jimmy Fusco is one of the best one-pocket players in the country, and a very strong nine-ball player as well. He owns the pro shop at South Philly Billiards. His cousin, Petey, is not as good, but he gambles, and could be a good game. Anticipating another good situation, Bucktooth flew out to meet us.

South Philly Billiards is near Veterans Stadium. It's in a strip shopping area, in more ways than one—there is a topless joint across the street. Walking in the door, it's not hard to tell that this is a players' room: The equipment is excellent, mostly Brunswick $4\frac{1}{2}$-by-9s, with one nice Anniversary 5-by-10 and a couple of billiard tables as well. But when it came time to make a game, things got weird.

Our first bad roll: Cornflakes was out on the road. Second, Jimmy Fusco was very careful, not to say suspicious. "I don't know how either one of you guys play," he told Tony and the Tooth. "I want to make some calls."

Who was he going to call? None other than his old friend, Paul Brienza, in San Francisco.

"We're cooked," Tony said. "Paulie will knock our game, guaranteed."

Sure enough, when Fusco returned from the telephone, he was not dying to make a game. To Tony he said, "I hear you're playing nine-ball as good as anyone in the country, and I'm not supposed to spot you. We're supposed to play even." Tony could do nothing. Playing Jimmy Fusco even in his poolroom was ludicrous.

Jimmy then turned to the Tooth and said, "I heard about Seattle. I'll give you ten to eight." That would be a suicidal one-pocket game and the Tooth knew it. Petey then offered to play the Tooth even.

"That's a heist," the Tooth snorted. "You guys ain't got no fuckin gamble. I'm an old man, but I'm rich. I can't believe you don't want to make a fair game. You beat me, you could retire." Those tactics may have helped get Harry Platis to the table, but they were not destined to succeed with these guys. Even worse, the owner of South Philly Billiards didn't like road players taking his action, and he didn't like anybody coming in giving the Fuscos any lip.

"Listen, you mouthy bastard, if you don't want ten to eight, get the fuck out of my poolroom," he told the Tooth. "You're the one without any gamble. You don't want a game, you want a stickup. If there's a stickup in here, you're going to be the ones with your hands up."

Bucktooth could see he wasn't going to get anywhere, but he wasn't going to get tush-hogged out of a poolroom without getting the last word. "Hey, I got more gamble than any of you bums. I don't need this action. I'll go down to Atlantic City and play some blackjack for a thousand a hand." There was silence for a few moments, broken by a new voice. "Hey, you want to play blackjack? We'll make a blackjack game right here." The speaker was a guy named Ashes, a well-known South Philly habitue. He was in his mid-fifties, gray, and prosperous-looking, and he was a known high-rolling gambler.

"What kind of rules?"

"What do you want?"

The Tooth, of course, wanted everything. "Split aces all the way. Early surrender. Double down on any two. No limit up or down on any hand." In other words, every rule most favorable to the player.

"You've got it. I'll bank, and I'll bust you." We moved into a small back room, maybe nine by twelve, with a table in the middle and four chairs.

One door, no windows.

"I don't want you dealing," the Tooth said.

"Have your guy deal, I don't care."

"Tony, deal the cards." The Tooth was agitated, nervous, excited. He was a spectacular card counter and with the rules as arranged, he smelled a huge score.

I was nervous, too, for a different reason: It was clearly a hostile situation. As play began, Ashes, Tony, the Tooth, and I were joined in the tiny room by maybe ten other local characters, most of them young and muscled. They said nothing, jostling for position around the table. It was a clear effort at intimidation, and it worked.

After a few hands they realized the Tooth was counting cards, and so they started yelling at him, trying to distract him: "Hey, fucker, where are you staying tonight? What are you looking for, some easy money, asshole? What do you think, you can come in here and rob us?" I could see that Tony was getting hot, and suddenly I flashed on him losing his temper with the cab driver in Oakland. If he or Bucktooth pops somebody, I thought to myself, we're done. They'll whack all of us.

The Tooth won a few hands, and got close to a thousand dollars ahead, and it got progressively uglier. Two or three more men crowded in. The airless little room suddenly felt like the trunk of a car. A short, burly guy wearing a black leather jacket and several gold chains shoved his way in front of me, stepping on my toe. An overpowering mélange of Brylcreem and Brut reached my nostrils, and I almost gagged. "Watch it," I hissed, and he turned and glared at me.

Finally, one of the watchers, someone Tony knew, winked at him and shook his head. It was an unequivocal signal: Get out while you can. Tony stood up, put the cards down, and whispered to the Tooth, who for once did not argue. He had won his plane fare plus a couple hundred. There was little question he could have won more. The question was whether we could have gotten out the door with it. "Fuck you guys, I quit," he said, and we were out of there in a flash.

Later, we heard several things that confirmed that we had made the right move. The guy who gave Tony the high sign told us he had overheard one of the observers give the order: "Find their fuckin money." Second, we found out that Ashes had lost maybe $300,000 in that poolroom over the past few months, playing pool, staking other players, on cards, sports, everything. That was okay with the guys who ran the joint, except for one thing: They wanted their cut. He was their pigeon and whoever beat him was expected to pony up 30 percent. That's why they were muscling us: They didn't want anybody to get to him and get out of there with his money without them getting their piece.

We rocketed out of there in the Cadillac. We stopped at a joint called the Philladium, where I talked Tony into coming off his diet and having one of their incredible Philadelphia cheese steak sandwiches. The Tooth didn't need any persuading. We sat and chomped our cholesterol bombs and guzzled Rolling Rock and congratulated one another on being alive.

IX

Chinn Music

"I still believe in a town called Hope."

—Bill Clinton

NOVEMBER 3—BILL WASN'T TALKING ABOUT THIS TOWN, NOT TODAY. It was Election Day, and we were in the southern suburbs of Washington, D.C., which had turned gray and greasy with the fear of soon-to-be-fired bureaucrats. FOR SALE signs lined the streets of Vienna and Alexandria and Springfield like white flags. This place had almost never needed the formality of voting results to know which way the wind blew, and today the wind was blowing in from Arkansas. It was a good day to buy a cheap brick imitation colonial townhouse, two bedrooms up, one down, from a midlevel Republican.

We were not in the market, of course, and our business prospects were not nearly so good. We were in an even bleaker part of the suburbs—just across the bridge from D.C., in Arlington, where the Union vindictively decided to bury its honored war dead in Robert E. Lee's front yard. Our white Caddy was parked in front of another shitty motel room, maybe the worst yet. Here in this dump on Glebe Road, the grayness and greasiness were permanent fixtures.

The motel featured a barbecue restaurant called Hogs, apparently a reference both to the bill of fare and to the sportswriters' sobriquet for the Washington Redskins' offensive line, a few years ago when they had a decent team. Every day from 10 A.M. on, the eye-watering stench of vaporized pork fat emanated from the vent on the outside wall, directly in front of our window. Years of this—the Reagan and Bush years, by some metaphorical accident of history—had coated the wall with a revolting swatch of black grease and smoke. The afternoon's spitting drizzle did nothing to cleanse the air, or the wall.

We had been brought here by a cruel but commonplace twist of fate—bad pool information. In Chicago and New York we got reports about the D.C. area. There was action downtown, we heard, but it carried an unacceptable level of risk. A month previously San Francisco hustler Jack Cooney had gone into a poolroom in D.C. and won three grand. He gave the money to his wife on the way out, thinking that if he got mugged she could get away with the cash. Instead the thugs waiting outside simply shot his wife twice and took the money.

Forget it, we were told. There's a lot of gambling going on in the suburbs. One player singled out Champion Billiards, right there on Glebe Road. But we could now see that the information was either very dated or an intentional double steer. Pool players will always steer you somewhere; nobody wants to admit they don't know. Champion was a nice enough poolroom, but we hadn't seen anybody in the place playing for ten cents.

Nevertheless, we were going back. We were headed for a tournament in Akron, Ohio, in a couple of days, and Tony needed some practice. He was no longer anywhere near the dead stroke he had found in Gotham.

We decided to walk over to Champion, despite the damp, to get some exercise. We passed an incredibly narrow two-story building with a redbrick false front and stucco sides, cheap aluminum window frames with yellowed curtains pulled across each one. A rust-stained black and white sign said succinctly, CHINN FUNERAL DIRECTOR. The building was shaped like a burial plot and looked wide enough for maybe three customers. The rain came down harder as we walked.

Close by Chinn's, probably in more ways than one, was a Weenie Beanie hot-dog stand. Bill Staton, aka Weenie Beanie, was the owner of this modest, elderly fast-food chain. Now a septuagenarian, Staton was still a world-class one-pocket player and a high-rolling gambler. Wouldn't it be great, I thought, if he were here, inspecting the Glebe Road outlet.

We would walk in and order a couple of hot dogs, presumably without danger of being instant Chinn-bait since the boss was on the premises.

The dapper, courtly Staton would be bustling around behind the counter, checking to make sure there were no cockroaches in the toothpick holder or whatever a fast-food-chain owner does when he comes to inspect.

"Hey, Weenie."

"Hello, Tony, my boy, how are you? My Lord, I had no idea you were out here. And who's this? Your stakehorse, you say? It's a pleasure to meet you, too, sir. Well, well, Tony, you're carrying your cue case. You must be ready, heh heh. How about slipping over to Champion and playing a few racks of one-pocket? I'll give you whatever you think is fair, say, nine to seven and the breaks?"

"How about ten to six?" Tony would respond, for the sake of form, and instead of dickering, Staton would simply agree. "Why, surely.

That sounds on the square to me. Say, two thousand a game?" He would turn to his fat, subservient hot-dog chef who was looking at him adoringly with spaniel eyes. "Hey, Sam, you big rascal, you got those dogs for these boys ready?" He'd turn back to us and shove them across the counter. "On the house, on the house, fellows, and how about some beans on those puppies?"

LATER THAT DAY, MY FATHER CAME DOWN TO THE POOLROOM TO meet us. I had seen my father only five or six times since my parents divorced when I was twelve. After years of almost no contact, we had more recently become sporadic letter writers, and whenever I was in the Washington area we would usually have dinner. I admired his intellect and his humor, and he had followed my newspaper and literary career with some degree of pride. But there were too many intervening years and experiences, too much yawning emptiness between us. Our relationship, at least our conversations, would forever be limited to the banal: sports, books, my relatives on his side of the family, only occasionally politics, which was dangerous ground because we were both passionate about it, and our views differed greatly.

It occurred to me that we were both fearful that we would see our own flaws in each other upon deeper inspection; or that we would somehow be forced into a conversation about the disintegration of our family, and how we had both fallen short, in our respective father-and-son roles. But that would not happen today; pool provided another acceptable superficial meeting ground. My father was a devotee of sorts, and he was interested in our trip. So he was there, watching Tony practice and admiring his skill.

Suddenly, I blurted out an invitation to my father to play. I could tell he was pleased, but his male competitiveness made him wary. He had not played in a very long time. He was a successful minor-league baseball player in his day and had been an accomplished pool player as well. But now, in his seventies, the enfeeblements of age did not sit well with him. Nevertheless he agreed, and my heart suddenly pounded as I assembled my cue.

It was the first sporting thing we had done together that I could remember since we had played Monopoly for blood when I was a kid. I racked the balls for nine-ball, suddenly wanting to play very well, and at the same time not wanting to beat my father too badly. I didn't. My nerves betrayed me, and I played poorly. He won his share of games. Even though his eyesight betrayed him, there was much about the game he remembered.

I could neither learn from him nor show him my skill, and I did not have the option of being merciful to him. Instead, we both played half-well and with self-conscious pain. What a tragedy, I thought, that we could not have done this twenty years earlier. We had played out our lives on separate tables, so that when we finally shared this game it felt like a weird coincidence instead of a familial sacrament.

We pushed the balls around in our diminishment as awkwardly as we had the intervening years of our guilt and anger and sorrow, able to feel at ease with neither our achievement nor our failing. The last nine ball jawed in the pocket, and I swore at it with the venom of loss. My father made it, and scratched, and did the same.

JUST FOR THE HELL OF IT, SINCE THERE WAS NO ACTION TO QUEER, Tony entered Champion's weekly tournament, which happened to be that night. It was a piss-ant tournament, twenty bucks to buy in, race to five, single elimination, all of a dozen players. Tony first drew an amiable, pudgy fellow in blue jeans who never really got a chance to play. He got a total of three shots in the process of losing five straight racks.

Next up was a tall, bespectacled Asian guy in white shirt and suit pants. He was a handsome enough fellow, but as a player he was a little goofy looking. Elbows and knees stuck out at weird angles when he got down to shoot, and as he peered through the tops of his lenses at the shot his mouth invariably opened and his tongue stuck out. Tony was in trouble almost from the first shot.

In the first game he hooked Tony half a dozen times. Tony would kick at the ball, hit it but not make it, and Goofy would then try to make it, miss, and hook Tony again. Finally Tony kicked the length of the table at a ball, hit it, and billiarded in the nine ball with the cue ball. Despite this little piece of poetic justice, the match seemed to slip away. Tony couldn't seem to catch a gear. He had little or no incentive to play well, of course. His position play was just off, and he became more and more irritated at himself. Shades of Napoleon. At least this time we had only twenty dollars at stake.

With Goofy leading 3–2, a critical shot came up for Tony. The nine was deep in the jaw of the corner pocket. After breaking, Goofy had missed an easy combo and left it there. The object ball, the one, was all the way down the table, and the cue ball was right on the nine, so Tony was jacked up over it. Tony could not make the one, and from where he was he couldn't even play a decent safety. He tried a two-rail billiard at the nine with the cue ball and just missed, and Goofy was out again. So instead of a 3–3 tie, the match score was 4–2 and Tony had to win three in a row, which he didn't.

In a few days Tony had gone from running 126 balls to losing in the early rounds of a nickel-ante amateur tournament, which forcefully illustrated the ephemeral nature of being in stroke, and the random nature of the game itself. Mind you, talent will almost always prevail, but the fact is that anybody can step up and lose, anytime.

Goofy's next match was a perfect illustration of two other pool axioms that are as constant as anything can be in a game of such infinite dynamics: One, a player who takes the heat will lose; and two, an amateur player who underestimates his opponent will lose.

Goofy's opponent was short, bald, thirtyish, muscular, and borderline psychotic. He was wearing a T-shirt bearing a GLAS-NOST legend, which was sort of like Gary Gilmore wearing a T-shirt advocating gun control.

Goofy's big talent was cutting balls, and after he made a vicious cut down the rail on the first nine ball, Shorty went off the air. "You fucking idiot, you can't make that shot twice in a hundred tries," he screamed. He threw the balls into the rack, still sputtering and shaking his head violently. When he removed the rack he slung it under the table with terrific force, and it made a startling crack that turned every head in the room.

Shorty's preshot routine was quite a production. He would pick up a piece of chalk and scrub his tip savagely in a mastur-batory motion, so hard and fast that it seemed certain he was rubbing the chalk right off the tip. Then he would slam the chalk down, move around the table fast and jerky like an Olympic walker; line up the shot; pick up another piece of chalk and jack off again; get down over the shot; and fire. If he missed, he would swear and shake his head, spittle flying. Shorty was actually the better shotmaker, but his anger made him very likely to lose, and lose he did.

Now, suddenly, Goofy was in the finals—against an excellent player named Jim McAdam, known as "Jimmy Mac." Tony knew of him; he had won some regional tournaments, matched up with some road players and done well, even played some on the road himself.

He was a trim, muscular six-footer, handsome in an Irish way, wearing sweat pants and a rugby shirt. "He's won this tournament three times in a row," one of the railbirds muttered to me. Tonight McAdam had glided into the finals, winning every match easily. But he was not prepared for Goofy, the juju king. Goofy was missing a lot of shots, but typically, just about every time he missed, McAdam found himself peering around two or three balls to get a glimpse of the object ball. Goofy broke on top 4–1, getting roll after roll. Now he needed only one more game to wrap it up. McAdam, on the other hand, needed to win four straight.

Suddenly, Goofy seemed to wake up and realize he was on the brink of winning the tournament, and he froze up like a possum caught in the headlights. With the score tied 4–4, he somehow got a shot at the seven ball, missed it, but left it tough. McAdam looked at the shot for a long time, and made it, but couldn't hold position on the eight. He tried to cut it down the rail. "That's an easy shot to jar," Tony whispered in my ear, and sure enough, McAdam left it in the pocket. Now Goofy was straight in on a hanging eight ball, with the nine out in the middle of the table, for the tournament.

He made the eight but hit it about twice as hard as he should have and nearly scratched, leaving himself a very difficult shot on the nine, which he missed. Predictably, though, he left McAdam rough—the cue ball on the side rail about a foot from the corner pocket, the nine hugging the opposite rail almost in the same position, but a little nearer the side. The one-rail bank looked like a double kiss, which would almost certainly leave the nine easily makeable; and the cut down the rail was even tougher than the one Jimmy had just missed a few minutes earlier on the eight ball. McAdam looked at the shot for what seemed like two full minutes, then got down and hit the bank dead perfect, just missing the kiss, slamming the nine into the side pocket.

Afterward McAdam steered us to a couple of poolrooms in Baltimore. "Come on back after Akron," he said. "You'll find some action over there."

We'd heard that one before.

X

In from the Cold

"I guess it's on you, whether my kids eat this week or
not."

—Jack Hynes

NOVEMBER 5—IN THE GAME OF ONE-POCKET, A PLAYER WHO KNOWS
all the defensive maneuvers is said to "move like a ghost."
Today we were gliding like ectoplasm in our Caddy with the
Uncle Fester color scheme—white on the outside, bloodred
on the inside—through the horrifyingly dull suburbs of D.C.
and Baltimore, then northwest into the strange nozone where
Maryland, Pennsylvania, and West Virginia intersect. This
country *is* haunted, hallowed in the Lincolnesque sense, and
I felt it strongly as we reached Hancock, Maryland, where
Stonewall Jackson's boys bedeviled the Union Army in 1862.
It is a desolate and impoverished corner of the country, and it
gets even more so across the border into West Virginia.

The winter we had seen gathering itself on the plains of
North Dakota a month earlier was now hard upon Hazelton,
West Virginia. The miners gathered in the Bronco Bar were
buttressed scruffily against the threat of snow with denim jackets and greasy hunters' caps and shots of schnapps, and the

sunset was flat and brown and comfortless on the cold, old hills north of town. Perhaps it was all of that, perhaps it was the high-test thirst of the Seville that had to be slaked in Hazelton, but I couldn't help but think of our shrinking bankroll. We had been on the road for six weeks plus. We'd won a little more than seven thousand dollars, but we'd lost three, and we'd spent five, give or take a dollar or two, so we were definitely digging into our original stake now for expenses.

We badly needed a payday, but I knew any money we made in Akron would be hard-earned. We would no longer be incognito. Our cover would be blown; we would be in from the cold, in among our own voracious kind, back in the club. A hundred or so of the best players anywhere were waiting for us. Waiting for our money, even as we coveted theirs.

Still, our mood was not one of desperation. We were still reasonably supplied with Cecils, and even though all that talent awaited, at least this tournament meant a chance to win, a return to the arena, and that lifted our spirits immensely. Tony whistled softly along with McCoy Tyner as we whooshed along, and we joked and talked. I could tell that his basic confidence was unshaken, and that, I thought, was all we needed.

By nightfall, the snow was not a threat but a fact. The big flakes whirled around the stately, massive stone courthouse and wide-hipped old wood-frame houses of Cadiz, Ohio, and the two lanes of Highway 250 were soon coated with packed snow and ice.

As we pulled into Akron, we remembered what winter felt like. It was November, it was northern Ohio, and it was as cold as a hustler's smile. The nearest cheap hotel to the poolroom was the Red Roof Inn, which had made a deal with the tournament, making it even cheaper, thirty-five bucks a night. It was a relief, actually; spartan but clean and quiet. At least it would have been quiet, if Tony hadn't started the needle job immediately.

"Try not to get your shit all over the place immediately, OK?"

"Listen, you fuckin hairy Italian, I'd appreciate it, myself, if you didn't leave long black hairs all over the sink and the shower. You know, you're just like a poodle. I swear, you're all hair. If you shaved all the hair off your body, you'd weigh sixty-five pounds."

"At least I have hair on my head, you frog-faced, bald-domed, four-eyed fuckin nit."

"You have hair in your *eyes,* the way you played in D.C."

FROM THE OUTSIDE, STARCHER'S BILLIARDS LOOKED MORE LIKE A chop shop than a poolroom. The lot was fenced with a seven-foot-high chain link, and the building was as fine an example of central Ohio prefabricated warehouse architecture as you could find. The Q Club, it was not.

Cultural niceties aside, it was doing quite nicely, thank you, and it was actually quite a cozy atmosphere for a tournament. A long, narrow, rectangular building with the entrance at the end of one of the long sides, it was barely wide enough for two rows of tables, but long enough for ten tables in each row. Tonight, though, one whole row of tables had been removed, the lights tied up in the rafters, and eight rows of old wooden folding chairs set down, maybe fifty in each row. Starcher's was ready for the Akron Open.

The dim, smoky light cast a yellow glow upon a battalion of slouching flat-gazed pool hustlers of every physical type, including half a dozen or so of the best players in the world. After having been out on the road, playing locals, I got a funny feeling in my stomach seeing these guys all in one place. This dingy little poolroom was tonight the nerve center of the game, the Pentagon, the Langley, the War Room. It was as though we had been called in to headquarters. Enough, for now, of covert work: We had come in from the cold, but in the best tradition of LeCarré, or Deighton, we were not exactly surrounded with allies.

Tony elbowed me and pointed. Sitting at a table in front, powering through a plate of Dottie Starcher's redolent barbecued chicken, was a chubby little black-haired guy in an embroidered road jacket bearing the legend ZIZI'S CUE BALL BILLIARDS, LAKE WORTH, FLORIDA. It was José Parica, one of the feared Filipino contingent: Parica, Bustamante, Efren Reyes. All of them extraordinary nine-ball players. Parica was widely known as a consummate money player. Some said that when the cash was posted he was the best in the world.

Standing watchfully nearby was Larry Novitsky, owner of the establishment touted on the back of Parica's jacket. Novitsky was a New Yorker who had made a good living in international trade. He also loved pool and loved to stake Parica.

Rolling some balls on the front table, wisecracking, catching up on the gossip, were three formidable pros: Dave Bollman, a former professional golfer, tall, tan, flat-bellied; Tony Ellin, the physical opposite, pale and paunchy, but an explosive player and the defending champion here; and "Spanish Mike" Lebron, still one of the toughest competitors on tour, number ten on the money list the previous season.

"Hey, Tony, great to see you." The warm greeting came from tournament director Joe Kerr, "Joker," a pleasant, rotund, quietly authoritative man who had directed more than a hundred tournaments all over the country. A former pro player, he'd started the Akron Open in 1980 and had run it ever since. He was obviously well known and respected by all the players—Tony had met him when Kerr was directing the Glass City Open in Toledo several years earlier—and he seemed to be enjoying the bustle of Starcher's on the eve of the tournament.

I paid the $125 entry fee. Tony Annigoni was the seventy-fifth player registered; another twenty or so were expected before the opening round the next day. "Tony, we're going to have a little minitournament tonight, starting right away," Kerr said. "Single elim, race to six. Want in?" Yes, of course.

Only eight players opted for this little warm-up event, entry fee $28, payout $150 for first, $50 for second. One of them happened to be José Parica. Tony, battling a cold earned by walking past Chinn Funeral Director in the rain, left his jacket on as he screwed his cue together and began to warm up.

His first opponent was a sour-faced guy in his fifties named Eschenmann, who played accurately but stiffly. Tony, too, seemed uncomfortable, and I was less than thrilled to see that his play seemed nearly as uninspired as it had been in Arlington. They went hill-hill, five games apiece, and Eschenmann broke and ran the first four. He got straight in on the five, on a diagonal line from the center of the table to the corner pocket. He decided to power the ball in and spin the cue back on to the six, a tough shot. He hit it perfectly straight but a little harder than necessary, and somehow the five hit the back of the pocket liner and spun out. He slammed his cue down in disgust, and Tony calmly ran the five balls out.

In the second round, which was the semifinals of the eight-man tournament, Tony played a young poolroom owner from West Virginia. Tony was now striking the balls a little better, but his cold was clearly bothering his concentration. Even so, he played well enough to win, and suddenly, without even taking his coat off, he was in the finals of this little event. Against—who else?—José Parica.

I knew this match would tell us a lot about the weekend. Would Tony continue to play sporadic, second-level pool? Or would he regain the stroke that enabled him to beat champions in New Jersey? He won the flip and ran the first two racks. Perhaps it was the pleasure of having a world-class opponent, but suddenly his intensity was back. He was snapping the balls into the pockets and keeping the cue ball under much better control. On rack three, Tony hooked Parica off the break and got ball in hand, which was actually no bargain. The best he had was a tough little draw shot to get an angle on the four. He made it, but scratched in the side. Parica ran out effortlessly but scratched on the break, and Tony ran it right back to lead 3–1. Tony then scratched on the break, and sat down, and that was that.

José Parica, all five-two of him, ran five racks and out. The cue ball was like a leashed pit bull, prowling from shot to shot with almost total precision. On the few occasions he got out of line, Parica made a pouty little moue, scratched his head, studied the shot, and made it anyway. He never looked remotely like missing.

As we headed back to the Red Roof, I said, "You played damned well against Parica."

"Fat fuckin lot of good it did me. That little fucker's a *machine.*"

"Yeah, but look at the bright side. We're twenty-two ahead on the night."

"It won't take you long to eat your way through that."

NOVEMBER 6—BY 11 A.M. THE NEXT MORNING THEY WERE THERE. Not the rest of the tour champions, such as Buddy Hall, Johnny Archer, Kim Davenport, Efren Reyes, and Earl Strickland, but, befitting Akron, the blue-collar players, capable of beating anyone in the world: Fix, McAninch, Vickery, Hynes, Spaeth, Garrison, Roget. And Annigoni.

I was beginning to understand, though, that luck was highly overrated. If José Parica kept playing the way he had the night before, I thought, the only luck that would matter was the luck of the draw. The players who drew him in the early rounds would likely face a long, uphill hump through the losers' bracket to get into the money.

Tony Ellin was an affable defending champion, meeting and greeting many of the players who hoped to dethrone him. He was startlingly dressed to match his nickname, "Tony the Tiger," in a wacky polyester electric rust-brown warm-up suit with faux tiger fur inserts across the yoke and down the legs. It was the only time this weekend that would truly be social—before the bloodletting began. Players sipped coffee, rolled balls around, made quiet jokes, and caught up on the gossip.

"They say Billy Cress came into some money."

"Yeah, I hear he's playin high out on the coast, he's beating Harry out of some dough regular."

"Hey, you hear about Richie Florence, had a stroke?"

"Yeah, it's too bad, Richie's a great guy, he was a fabulous player, too, I seen him beat Ed Kelly for a lot of money."

"Yeah, and I heard Ronnie Allen moved out of his house, livin in his car or some shit."

"No, not Ronnie Allen!"

"Yeah, he's tryin to get off the booze and the nags, is what Jack told me."

Some of this was true, but none of it was new. I strolled over to the board where the pairings were going up and surveyed the field. One of the entrants, Rick Garrison, had been a friend of Tony's for twenty years. He was slim, dark, bearded, about forty-five, formerly an accomplished gymnast, still in great shape. He had been living in San Mateo when Tony was starting to play, and Tony had always respected Rick's ability and class.

Years later, Rick was the player Tony ran into in Tucson, the one who had set him up in the game with the old man at the truck stop. It was nearly fifteen years before they met again, at another Ohio tournament. They had stayed close—and, as often happens in tournaments, were also close in the bracket. If they won their first-round matches, they would have to play each other.

Tony and Rick sat in the bleachers, watching a surprisingly even match between Mike Lebron and a scrappy player named Antonelli. Garrison got up to get a Coke, and I asked Tony, "How do you feel about playing Rick?"

"He's tough," Tony said quietly, eyes never leaving the table. Antonelli had just made a nice bank on the eight and had the nine straight in. He made it to tie the match at ten games apiece—hill-hill in the race to eleven. "I don't think I've ever matched up with him, either gambling or in a tournament. We were always friends. I've been in some payball games with him. He used to beat a lot of players in San Francisco, and he still beats a lot of players. I think a lot of people underrate his game—maybe including himself. I'm going to have to play great to beat him, but I don't know if he thinks that."

Antonelli clearly had Lebron rattled, but the old pro's stroke smoothed out nicely with the match on the line. He ran the three out for the win.

"What about the mental aspect of playing a friend?" I asked Tony as he stood up and took off his jacket to play his first-round match.

"It doesn't make much difference. You can't really focus too much on your opponent anyway. That stuff used to bother me. Now it doesn't. It's just the luck of the draw. Look at it this way: I'd rather play him than Parica." With a chuckle, he cut over to the aisle and went down to the table. He won easily, against a local player, and Garrison did the same. The two friends would play later in the evening. The winner would have pretty bright prospects in the winner's bracket, and the loser would be halfway to elimination.

After dinner, Joe Kerr introduced the players for the evening matches.

"On Table Ten, from Philadelphia, a tour mainstay, winner of the Challenge of Champions in Las Vegas last year and a consistent money leader on tour, Mike Lebron." Lebron, a crowd favorite, smiled into the middle distance at the applause. "His opponent, a flashy young player with tremendous firepower, nicknamed 'Jumpin' Jack Flash,' Jack Hynes." Hynes was a tall, powerful, cocky-looking kid with a UCLA baseball cap perched on the back of his head. "A real headcase, that boy," the guy next to me whispered. "I'm surprised they let him in. He threw a real fit here once before."

"On Table Eleven, a familiar competitor here in Ohio, now living in Cincinnati, the always-tough Rick Garrison." And after the polite applause faded: "All the way from San Francisco, one of the nicest guys in the game, unless you have to play against him, Tony Annigoni."

"Who the hell is Annigoni?" a guy in front of me muttered.

"He's a good player," the guy in the next seat whispered back. "He'll give Rick all he wants."

"Ahhh, sure. Whoever heard of him? I'll take Garrison for fifty," the first guy said.

"Sure."

Affronted, I reached forward and tapped the guy on the shoulder. "You want another fifty?" I asked. He peered at me suspiciously. "You got fifty? Let's see it."

I palmed my bankroll and peeled three twenties from the

middle. "Okay," he said. "You going to be here for the whole match?"

"Yep."

The friends shook hands and lagged for break. Tony won, broke, and made nothing, but left the one unmakeable. Rick pushed out on to the end rail, and Tony elected to shoot, then made a picture-perfect one-rail bank with position on the two. He made the two through five just right, the cue ball rolling sweet, getting the great angle on everything. Then he missed the six straight in. I saw him glance at his tip, as though the cue had skidded on the stroke, and he shook his head once, sat down, and watched Garrison make the easy run. The guy in front of me couldn't resist a triumphant glance over his shoulder.

Garrison broke, making the five, then ran the one through four, but he got bad on the six, tried a very tough cut and whiffed it, missing the ball completely and giving Tony a ball in hand and the rack. A mistake apiece, a rack apiece.

The next rack turned on a terrific shot, and Tony made it. Garrison had left him on the rail, but he jacked up and speared the four, making it down the rail, the length of the table, and drawing the cue ball back onto the five. *Perfect*. He ran the rest to lead 2–1.

The dynamic between the two players was fascinating. It was as though they both wanted to play well, to be a worthy opponent, to honor their meeting by making a good game. Whenever Garrison missed, he cocked his head at the table and shook it, as if to apologize for spoiling the symmetry of the match. Neither player was missing very often. They were barely off their best games, but still trading racks, making flashy shots, and very rarely making unforced errors. After Garrison made a beautiful bank billiard on the nine and then rolled in the nine on the following break, Tony was suddenly down 7–4.

Rick made nothing on the break, and Tony studied the table carefully. He made a nice shot on the one and then hooked Garrison dead behind the nine. Somehow, Garrison hit it, but couldn't make it. Tony made the two left-handed, grinding now, perfect on the three through seven, which he also made left-handed, and ran the last two out. As he switched hands for the second time in the rack, the guy in front of me muttered, "Shit, I can't believe he plays with either hand." He didn't look so sanguine now, I thought.

Tony ran the next rack, then left the nine in the hole on the following break, which Rick made, to run his lead back to two games. But again, he could make nothing on the break, and Tony ran them out smoothly. He had caught another gear now, playing calmly and relentlessly, playing better nine-ball than he had since Seattle, I thought. He hit it on the sweet spot the next rack, making two balls, and never looked like missing the whole rack, tying the match at 8–8.

Then, after three flawless racks in the last four, another mistake: a cornered deuce. Rick went back on top, 9–8.

"Attaway, Rick, you got him," the guy in front of me yelled hoarsely. But Garrison seemed a little rattled, and gave Tony an opportunity to tie, which he did. Tony took a deep breath, and broke well again, making the three. He ran through the six, but got too tight on the seven, but had a chance to play a good hook and got it. Incredibly, Garrison hit it and hooked Tony right back. Tony kicked and hit the ball, but left Garrison a shot—which he missed. Then Tony made a terrific cut, but the cue ball rolled neatly off the top rail and right into the opposite side pocket for a scratch that put Garrison on the hill, ahead 10–9.

Again, Rick made nothing on the break. Tony had no shot

on the one, so he played another dazzling defensive shot, spinning the cue ball back into a corner, behind no less than three balls. Rick missed and Tony ran out to tie the match at ten games apiece.

The match came down to this. Tony broke and made the eight in the side, but was tough on the one. He missed it and Rick made it, but let the cue ball loose, kissed off the seven, and got tough on the two. Also, the seven rolled down the table and tied up the three. There was an audible groan from the crowd. The way the balls lay now meant it would be a long, agonizing rack.

The two players traded safeties, and then Rick left a shot that tempted Tony sorely: a sharp cut into the corner and a chance to break the three out with a two-rail billiard. He tried it, and two bad things happened: He overcut the two and scratched. One good thing happened, though: He didn't break out the three.

Rick elected for caution over aggression, leaving the two close to the pocket but breaking out the three and leaving the cue ball tough. Tony tried to reverse the defensive maneuver by hooking Rick right back, but barely missed, leaving the two even closer to the corner pocket. That looked like the match. Rick made the two and the three, but he hit the three too hard, and it looked as if the cue ball, sliding down toward the four, which was dead on the rail near the left bottom pocket, would scratch.

It stopped on the lip of the pocket. But it was so deep in the jaw that Rick was corner-hooked on the four—the edge of the rail was between cue and object ball. He tried the only shot he had, spinning the ball around the corner to hit the four, but couldn't pull it off, and Tony calmly ran the balls out and escaped with an 11–10 victory.

Rick bounded over to shake Tony's hand, and Tony's usual

reserve evaporated as he grabbed Rick's shoulder and gave him a hug. "Ahh, your guy shit out," the guy in front of me snarled, handing me a Ulysses S. Grant. To some degree, I thought, he was right. Either player could have won, and Rick did have some bad luck in the last rack. But Tony showed great heart getting back in it, I thought, down by three racks late in the match.

Another tense drama was being played out on the next table. Jack Hynes was putting on quite a show, breaking with tremendous power, running racks, spinning the cue ball around the table for position and safeties, completely controlling the tempo of the match. Next to Hynes's bubbling, kinetic play, Mike Lebron seemed a little tentative.

Hynes got to the hill, leading 10–7, but couldn't quite put Lebron away. He cornered an eight ball, and Lebron took the easy out, then ran two key racks, showing the smoothness that made him so consistent, running the match to hill-hill. Starting the case rack, Lebron made the five on the break, then drew applause by hitting a beautiful spinning safety, hooking Hynes deep in a corner pocket, two balls between him and the one, which was about two inches out from the left-hand side pocket.

But Hynes wasn't done. He made a spectacular one-rail kick, not only hitting the one but *making* it, with position on the two. He ran the balls through the four, but got terrible on the six. He was jacked up, on the end rail, and the six was two thirds of the way down the table. Hynes scowled at the shot for at least two minutes, stalking around the table, looking at it from every angle. Then he stepped up and made a beauty— banging the six into the corner and force-following the cue ball so that it got straight in on the seven. The crowd roared with surprise. It was similar to the shot Tony had made early in his match with Garrison, and it was a remarkable thing to see, particularly with the match at hill-hill.

Now Hynes was precisely straight in on the seven, about eight inches from the ball. The eight was all the way down the table on the end rail, and the nine was hanging in the corner pocket close to it. Hynes looked the shot over for a long time, again, and this time it was a little harder to see what he was thinking about. It seemed like he should simply knock the seven in and draw his rock down the table toward the eight. There weren't too many places on the bottom third of the table where he would be in trouble, as long as he didn't scratch.

But unaccountably, instead of drawing the ball low, he got on top of the shot and addressed the cue ball almost as he would for a massé. A murmur ran through the crowd as he took a few practice strokes. Apparently he was going to try to stun the ball, hitting it way on top and spinning it back. It was a showy, risky shot. He stopped, and looked at it again, then got back over in the same position and hit it.

The stroke had to be hard, but he dug it a little too much. The seven flew into the pocket, but the cue ball jumped off the surface, came down and spun right into the same pocket, right behind the seven, like a trick shot. He threw his cue aside savagely and swept the other balls into the corner pocket as the crowd's roar hit a crescendo. For the second straight night, Lebron had escaped.

Hynes stayed at the table as the spectators milled out. I watched him set the shot up again, hit it again—with exactly the same result. He shook his head, then set it up a third time. This time he drew the cue ball back down the table, the way everybody in the place had expected him to, and it stopped right in front of the eight. That seemed to enrage him even more, and he slammed his cue down on the table, turned, and sat down, staring dazedly at the table. I could almost see George C. Scott telling Paul Newman, "You're a loser, Eddie."

NOVEMBER 7—TONY'S NEXT OPPONENT WAS A YOUNG PLAYER named Kevin England. Maybe six-three, muscular, with red-brown hair, he was a smart, hardworking Ohioan, twenty-five years old. He had some presence and a pretty good stroke, but he was obviously nervous, playing in front of the home folks, this far into the winner's side.

He showed a couple of flashes of talent, but Tony's game was back, and he never gave England a chance to get into the match, winning nine of the first ten racks, eventually winning 11–2. The match didn't take much more than half an hour, and when it was over, Tony was in the top sixteen. Afterward, he came up and sat next to me in the stands. He was quiet, but I could tell he was pleased. To start playing this well again couldn't have happened at a better time, and he knew it.

"Pretty pure," I said.

"The kid was nervous."

"Break's going good, though."

"Fuck, don't say that. Let's sweat this match. Gary Spaeth's the son of a great player, a Bucktooth type, but he died young. And Gary is a great player in his own right. He may be the best bank-pool player short of Bugs. Hell, he's beaten Bugs a few times, playing banks. Not many can say that." Tony paused, remembering. "I first saw him when I was on the road in Burlington, Iowa, must have been in seventy-five. He gave me the eight and beat me."

"Jesus."

"No, his name's Spaeth, Gary Spaeth, he just banks like Jesus."

Spaeth was just back from Germany, where his longtime stakehorse, David Myerson, had put him in action quite successfully. I watched with new interest. Gary Spaeth wasn't much to look at this Saturday afternoon, as he screwed his cue together and got ready to shoot a practice rack before his match. He was about five-eight, wearing baggy, faded jeans and a sweatshirt, with a sandy beard and unkempt hair. But then he broke the balls, and ran them—banking every shot.

"My God," I breathed. "Did you see that?"

"I told you," Tony said quietly. "He'd rather bank a ball than shoot it straight in, and he doesn't miss too often."

I remembered, a few years back, interviewing the fabulous professional golfer Rod Funseth, a year or so before his death. When I talked to him, he had just hit a tremendous sand shot, blasting out of a trap to within inches of the cup, and I asked him about sand play. "If I'm going to miss a green, I'd really rather be in the sand than on the short grass, as long as the ball is sitting up good. I can control the ball better," he told me. For most golfers, such a thing is beyond comprehension. For most pool players, the concept of *preferring* to bank a ball is similarly outlandish.

Today, though, Spaeth had left a few angles unfigured. Joe Kerr came up to him as he was reracking the balls and said, quietly, "Gary, remember, I told you and everybody else at the players' meeting, no jeans, and shirts must have collars. You'll have to change before your match." Spaeth fussed and stormed, but Joe was obdurate. Pool had never been more conscious of its image, and dress codes were being enforced at all the major tournaments. Spaeth stormed out and returned a few minutes later in khakis and a collared shirt. But he left his game in the pocket of his jeans. The contretemps with Kerr seemed to have cost him his focus, and he lost his match to a much less talented player. Tony shook his head. "A good lesson there. You can't let any of the other stuff that goes on affect how you play. It's brutal, but you just can't. You know, the Tooth always looks down his nose at tournaments, but one thing about it, in a tournament there's no time to waste, you've got to come with the great stroke right now, or you're dead. You can't get behind and then grind on somebody and come out okay. You lose, you're out."

ONE SOFT SPOT WAS ALL TONY WAS GOING TO GET. HIS NEXT OPPO- nent was Mike Lebron.

"Well, Lebron hasn't been sharp," I said.

"Yeah, but he'll play when he has to," Tony said. "He's tough, a real clutch player. Don't worry, he'll give me all I want."

Mike Lebron hadn't had many soft spots in his life. He grew up in Puerto Rico, emigrating to Philadelphia as an adult. He was working in a dry cleaners' when he saw a pool tourna- ment on TV. He had played and hustled all his life in Puerto Rico and he had no concept of a professional tour, but when he watched the tournament he said to himself, "I can beat them." It turned out that he could—at least enough of them to be a consistent top-ten finisher on the tour. Now sixty, his eyes, stroke, heart, and stamina were still a lot more than most pros could handle.

Tony won the lag, made the one on the break, and ran the table out like silk. Lebron racked, and this time Tony made the six on the break, made the one, a nice two-seven billiard, then the two through five, and Lebron raked the eight and nine irritably with his cue and racked. He had not yet shot, and he was down 2–0.

Tony really nailed the next break, making the one, six, and eight, all in the same side pocket. He made the two in the corner, playing for position on the three in the side, and somehow the cue ball found a slot between two balls, hit the end rail and scratched in the opposite side. It made a big difference. Lebron had an easy run, and instead of 3–0 the score was 2–1.

It got much worse very quickly. Lebron ran three more racks without a miss, to lead 4–2. Finally, he caught a bad roll on the fourth break, leaving himself no shot on the one. He pushed out, and Tony hooked him. He missed, and Tony got out to make it 4–3. He then made nothing on the break, and Mike made the one through four, but missed his position on the five. He played a safety, but Tony made the shot anyway, and struggled his way through a tough table to tie the match at 4–4.

Then Tony played one of the gutsiest racks of nine-ball I'd seen on the trip. He made the one-eight on the break, leaving himself straight in on the two. He left himself a nasty little cut on the three, but made it with position, and despite how tough they lay, ran through the rest to retake the lead by one.

In the next rack, the two players traded safeties before Tony tried a swerve shot, "bending" the cue ball just a little to get it around an intervening ball, then driving it down the table on to the one. He hit it well, but the one cornered and hung, and Lebron ran that rack and the next to go up 6–5.

Lebron made three balls on the next break, leaving himself perfect position to run the rest. He made it to the nine and then hit his first really bad shot of the match, leaving the ball in the hole for Tony to tie the match.

Lebron's street experience showed up in the next rack. Tony made the one and a great shot on the two to set himself up perfectly on the rest of the rack. Lebron could see that Tony was in great stroke, and the balls were sitting perfectly, so he reached over with his cue and raked the remaining seven balls, conceding the rack. He didn't want Tony to gain even more confidence and momentum shooting them down. It was actually a violation of tournament rules to concede any shot, much less seven balls in one rack, but Tony didn't call him on it.

The stratagem was effective; it broke Tony's concentration. Lebron won the next two racks to take a one-game lead, 8–7. He made the one-eight on the subsequent break, but couldn't see the two, and pushed out. Tony elected to shoot and played a beautiful safety. Lebron hit the two but could do nothing with it, and Tony ran the rest of the rack. But on the nine ball, he hit the cue ball a fraction hard, and somehow it rolled the length of the table, looking like every inch would be its last but still continuing to roll, until it barely dropped into the corner pocket.

That killed the match for Tony. Instead of being tied at eight, he was down 9–7 with Lebron breaking. And of course Lebron made the one-five on the break and left himself a perfect two-nine combination, putting himself just one game short of victory.

Tony had one more chance. Lebron missed the six ball in the next rack, and Tony made it, but again, unbelievably, he scratched, and that was it—another escape for Mike Lebron and a tough loss for Tony Annigoni. He had to play right back in the loser's bracket. The problem with reaching the loser's side so late in the tournament was that there were no easy spots over there, either. All the players who were still alive had beaten a lot of people to get where they were.

Certainly, Tony's first opponent on the loser's side was a force to be reckoned with—Howard Vickery. Howard, who looked a little like Homer Simpson with a ponytail, was as nice a guy as you can find over a pool table. But tonight, he was in a tough spot. Tony was motivated to avenge his loss to

Lebron—and an earlier loss to Vickery. The two had only met once before, back in the early eighties. Tony had been poised to win the McDermott Masters, a major tournament, but lost to Vickery, 11–3, and eventually finished fifth. On this night, Howard would pay.

Tony was hitting the break lights-out, making two or three balls every time, and he was also making all the shots he should make, playing under control, fighting for his payday. He beat Vickery, in front of Howard's home-state fans, by the historically significant score of 11–3.

NOVEMBER 8—IT WAS SUNDAY, DAY OF RECKONING, AND THE RECK-oning started early. Tony's first match was against a Pittsburgh player named Steve McAninch, young, dark-haired, and very similar in style to Tony—lots of firepower, clever defensively, capable of getting very hot and running multiple racks. This race to eleven would be worth three hundred dollars, the difference between the prize money for fifth and sixth places.

Both players were sharp, and both had three-rack runs during the match, but Tony was playing nearly flawlessly and he slowly wore McAninch down, taking a hard-fought 11–9 victory. That put him into the match for fourth place against the mercurial Jack Hynes, who had beaten three players since his loss to Lebron. The loser would finish fifth. The winner would be guaranteed no lower than fourth.

Hynes played his usual flashy but erratic game, playing "football field" position, with the cue ball often on the other end of the table from the next object ball, often making the tough shots anyway. Hynes's reckless play was fun to watch, but no match for Tony's deliberate, steady, heady game. Tony charged him for each error, converting those mistakes into games won, giving Hynes very few openings to strike back.

Down 6–3, Hynes got petulant, flouncing around the table after a missed shot, waving his cue at errant balls. The histrionics seemed to be calculated, as if the whole act were a shark tactic. A couple of times, as Tony prepared to shoot nine balls, Hynes got up and walked up to the table, as if he were going to concede the rack, but not actually doing so.

As Tony ran a rack, Hynes committed a heinous breach of etiquette: He began whistling loudly through his teeth, causing a slapstick chain reaction. At the next table, Dave Bollman, who had knocked out Lebron, was in the process of getting barbecued by José Parica. That had put him in an agitated frame of mind, to say the least. When the whistling started, he was losing 6–0, and just getting down over a shot. He shot upright at the noise and glared at Tony, who was getting ready to shoot the eight.

Tony pulled up and did a double take, listening to Hynes, looking at Bollman. He walked over and whispered, "Dave, it's not me, it's Hynes." Bollman turned his outraged gaze to Hynes, who grinned back at him.

Bollman snarled, "My God, will you shut up," and turned back to his lost cause. Tony got down and made the eight-nine to lead 10–7.

But Hynes had saved the best shark for last. In the next rack, Tony was addressing a difficult but makeable shot on the eight. If he made it, he would almost certainly win; the nine was easily makeable near a corner pocket. Hynes was sitting at the end of the table where Tony stood as he got down over the shot. At the last moment, Hynes said, "I guess it's on you, whether my kids eat this week or not. Go ahead."

Tony stopped, looked at him disgustedly for a moment, then bore down and drilled the eight and nine to win the match. Steaming, he said absolutely nothing when Hynes halfheartedly shook his hand. It was an important victory. From the original ninety-six players, there were now but four: José Parica, Tony Ellin, Tony Annigoni, and a rather colorless but very efficient player named Greg Fix—Tony's next opponent. Fix's style made him a very tough challenger. He didn't make a lot of flashy shots, but the way he played, he didn't have to. As steadily as Tony played, Fix was like a robot by comparison.

The winner would play Ellin to see who had the pleasure of playing Mr. Parica in the final. Parica had played like a deity all week. He won his first four matches by a combined score of 44–2. For the entire tournament, it had seemed as if everyone else was playing for second place.

Three days of brilliant play seemed to have left Tony with little left in the tank. Perhaps it was Fix's style, perhaps the residual effect of the Hynes match, perhaps fatigue, but Tony played erratically and it cost him dearly. Each time he left Fix a shot, Fix got out. Period. Still, Tony was trailing by only one game at 9–8 when he missed a key shot on the five, by the closest of margins, the ball wobbling and hanging. Fix, relentless, got out and then ran the case rack to win the match 11–8.

Even though the loss was a big disappointment to Tony, it had been a good week. Considering the strength of the field, fourth place was a big accomplishment, and there was a large consolation. Joe Kerr handed him a thick envelope, and Tony handed it to me. It contained $1,200 in cash, which covered our tab at the Red Roof Inn, with a little to spare.

Later, Tony Ellin defeated Fix—and finally, impressively, beat Parica twice, to defend his title successfully. But by then we were already zooming southeastward in the Cadillac, back toward the underbelly of the game.

XI

The Dew Factor

Hard times in the city in a hard town by the sea
Ain't nowhere to run to, ain't nothin here for me
Oh, Baltimore
Man it's hard, just to live
　　　　　　　　　　—Randy Newman, "Baltimore"

NOVEMBER 13—JIM MCADAM TOLD US TO GO TO BALTIMORE. LARRY Novitsky said he'd heard of good action in Baltimore. Paul Potier told us to look for a kid named Danny Green in Baltimore. "He's a good, aggressive young player but he doesn't have to win playing you," Potier said. "He's got quite a bit of gamble and I heard he has some cash, too."

We'd been on the road long enough to know what all that advice was worth, but we had a few days before our Miami-to-L.A. plane reservations, and Baltimore was vaguely in the right direction, which was close enough for us. Neither of us had any better ideas.

Potier had told us about two gambling rooms: a new joint named Greenie's out on Reistertown Road, northwest of the city; and a place called Jack and Jill Billiards, south of town in Glen Burnie.

Reistertown Road runs from one circle of hell to another, from serious projects to a particularly bleak suburban sprawl just south of Towson. As the bail bondsmen and boarded-up windows fade into a tired gaggle of shopping centers, it loses whatever identity it ever had and becomes another strip of motels, gas stations, chain stores, and cheap apartments. Right in the middle of that miasma was Greenie's, in the basement of a faceless new building a couple of miles in from the freeway. We checked into a fifty-dollar-a-night shitbox right across the parking lot from a Bob's Big Boy and went over to clock Greenie's.

As we descended the concrete stairs, we could hear a big sound system blaring. It was a cavernous room, featuring thirty-plus Gold Crowns, one six-by-twelve, and two old Ohlhausens converted from pocket to three-rail billiards, along with table tennis in the back, the requisite video games, a snack bar, and a few card tables constantly clustered with backgammon freaks. In its four-month existence, we had been told, Greenie's had acquired a reputation for serious action. It didn't take long to see that it had also gathered an impressive collection of players, rail sitters, scufflers, hustlers, and thieves. In short, it was an attractive, promising poolroom.

We scanned the room for familiar faces, and finally Tony found one. He nudged me and pointed to a dark-haired man about thirty with a nervous, engaging smile and a formidable stroke. "That's Junior Harris," Tony whispered. "He's a little crazy but a player for sure. I heard he was out here somewhere. I've seen him on the road before, at one of the Reno tournaments and then in San Diego. He offered me the eight then."

"What happened?"

"He was playing McCready first and McCready busted him so our match never came off. He might not remember me."

Now, Junior Harris was playing a stocky young kid with a beard who couldn't make a ball, giving him the seven and robbing him for five dollars a game. In between shots, Harris walked over and stood beside a woman sitting primly next to the table and looking completely out of place in Greenie's. She was blonde, almost professorial, maybe ten years older than he was, very self-possessed in a neat little collared white blouse and a blue sweater. While he was waiting for the kid to rack, he put his arm around her.

"He's on the lemon," Tony whispered, "but he still can't prop this guy up. The kid's got to quit him soon."

Sure enough, a hundred was the guy's limit and after a dozen games it was gone and so was he. Harris and his lady strolled out arm in arm with the kid's money. "There's a good match for us," Tony said.

It was 2 A.M. I looked around the room again. Three railbirds were dozing. Other than a couple of old men playing ten-dollar one-pocket, it looked like Greenie's was tucked in for the evening, so we cruised back to the motel, much heartened.

NOVEMBER 15—OVER A COUPLE OF DAYS WE GOT TO KNOW GREENIE, a fleshy, likable blond-haired guy in his forties who favored dark green sweat suits and described himself as "the biggest gambler in Maryland, no shit."

"Sounds like the ponies to me," Tony said.

"Yeah, I've lost eight million at the track and two mil, I'm talkin *cash*, not paper, in the sporting goods business," he said. "So I thought I'd try this for a while." Greenie talked like a big sport, but I wasn't seeing him doing any gambling in his own place. Unfortunately, nobody else was doing anything too exciting either, if you didn't find ten-dollar one-pocket exciting, which I didn't particularly when it wasn't my ten dollars.

Patience, I had learned, was the toughest thing about being

on the road. You're watching your bankroll shrink, eating in restaurants, living in motels, burning the gas, and you want to make something happen. *Now.* The sense of urgency we'd felt in Akron was back. It had been too long since we'd done any serious gambling. "I can't believe how hard it is to find anybody playing high," Tony said, and it was true. Still, the place felt pretty good, and so we hung out, and ate crummy food, and waited, and practiced, and ate more crummy food. We sent word to Junior Harris that he had a game if he wanted it, and he said he did, but was vague about when he might be back in. And we kept an eye out for Danny Green.

NOVEMBER 16—ON OUR THIRD AFTERNOON AT GREENIE'S WE finally saw a halfway decent money game, hundred-dollar one-pocket between an older player named Jake and the cook in Greenie's coffee shop, a tall, wisecracking Chinese guy who played relatively well.

"They do this two or three times a week," Greenie said. "Jake loses and loses, but he gets even every time playing one-handed. Watch for this guy one-handed, he plays great."

On this day Jake dropped five hundred before quitting, and the cook strolled back to the coffee shop, folding his money and grinning.

"Hey, why don't you play me some?" Tony asked him.

"Give me ten to six," the cook said.

"Fuck you," Tony said, and that was that.

Tony had to settle for giving me the three out for ten bucks a rack. He was sixty ahead and running out when a squint-eyed blond guy about thirty-five years old, bowlegged, in painter's jeans and an Orioles cap, came up and asked, "You all gambling?"

"Yeah," Tony said shortly. "Why? What do you want to do?"

"You play one-pocket?"

"Not if I don't have to."

He walked a few feet away and watched us hit a few more balls, then came back and said, "Twenty-dollar nine-ball?"

"Rack 'em." The rail materialized, as if by magic. I asked a couple of people for side action but got no takers. Hanging around for a few days, looking for action, is not a good way to engage the rail—unless you're laying down a larcenous riff like at Chelsea Billiards. These fellows wanted to see Tony play before they risked a dime.

The blond guy played well, cutting balls particularly impressively, but his game lacked consistency. His position play was theoretically sound, but he wasn't executing the way he should and he knew it. I thought perhaps he hadn't been playing much lately, because he had an impressive stroke but just didn't always get out when he should. Tony tried not to show too much, but this player didn't seem like a real long-term prospect, so he showed enough to win. After an hour, Tony was a hundred dollars ahead and his opponent nodded pleasantly and said, "That's enough. I only had five bullets. I just can't get it going." He turned out to be Larry Neudecker, certainly one of the best players in the area. Even though he had indeed not been playing much and was demonstrably out of stroke, it was a serious knock to beat him.

The hundred dollars would take care of expenses for a day or two, but we worried that the easy win might make action even tougher to come by. That did not turn out to be the case. We spent that evening right there in Greenie's, having heard that Junior Harris might come down. We'd met a big, long-haired kid named Mike who managed a poolroom in nearby Rosedale and wanted to hang around Tony in hopes of seeing a big money game. He was a friendly, genuinely pleasant guy, and he was fascinated with Tony's game. "Jesus," he whispered to me, watching Tony practice. "Your player will crush these local guys. He plays strong."

"Yeah, well, I don't know," I said. "It's not that easy." Tony gave Mike a few lessons, and then I put him on to finding Danny Green for us. We waited for several hours. No Junior. Finally, at midnight, Tony stopped his desultory practice and said, "Fuck it, let's go get some rest. We'll give this another day and then blow."

At that moment Mike came loping across the room like a frightened mule deer. "I just called Jack and Jill's and Danny Green answered the phone," he said breathlessly. "And he said, yeah, he wants to play, bring the guy over."

"Does he have any money?"

"You'll like this part," Mike said. "Yesterday I heard that he beat somebody in New York City out of five grand last week."

It was midnight. Tony looked at me, eyes red and irritated, the lines around them carved deep by grimy vacant nights on the road. I knew what he really wanted was a good night's sleep, but it didn't work that way, and he knew it. We'd been looking for Danny Green and we'd finally found him, ready to play and very likely carrying some cash. "Let's go," Tony said finally, the weariness like sand in his throat.

We made the forty-minute haul down to Glen Burnie, then along Route 3, a blue-collar street of plumbing-supply outlets and storage buildings and body shops. We followed as Mike turned into a warehouse complex and drove around back. The place was seedy and weird and very dark. "What a five-star place for a heist," Tony said. "Carjacking, mugging, robbery, fuckin homicide, you name it, what a sweet spot."

There it was, on the ass end of a warehouse, the only sign of life for blocks: JACK AND JILL'S CUE CLUB, a little sixties-style sign, light spilling out from a swinging glass door. We walked in and immediately a kid hitting balls on the back table straightened up, came up to me, grinning, and said, "You must be the road player. Want to play some nine-ball for a hundred?"

"Not me," I said. "Him."

"Sure, let's play. My name is Tony."

"Danny Green, nice to meet you." He was a strong, handsome kid, maybe eighteen or nineteen, the hipster model, featuring stylishly long sandy hair, a tie-dyed Grateful Dead T-shirt, and pupils the size of nickels.

"Let's play five ahead, freeze up five hundred," Tony said. That's good, I thought. It effectively raised the stake to five hundred dollars; nothing happened until somebody gained a five-game advantage.

"Sure, fine by me."

If this kid were any more agreeable, he'd just hand us the money and leave. He was grinning nonstop, chattering like a baboon. It was unnerving. What did he know that we didn't?

It took only a few minutes to see that young Danny Green was obviously possessed of a terrific stroke, but he was missing a hell of a lot of shots. That combination usually means a player on the stall, but in this case I thought maybe his problem was chemical.

He certainly was frisky. The house man was playing chess with a quiet, white-haired man of about sixty. They were deep into the game, the position close to even, when the older guy, playing the white pieces, made a move and then went to the john. When the house man stepped away from the board to ring up somebody's pool time, Danny stepped over and swept a white rook off the board and into his pocket. When he saw me watching him, he put a finger to his lips and glided back to the table.

Down by four games, in grave danger of losing the bet, Danny Green was still as loose and talkative as he'd been in the first rack. "Yeah, I got busted for pot two days ago," he jabbered to me as Tony broke. "It was a drag. I'd just scammed a little cash and I had to give most of it to my lawyer right on the spot." *Fuck,* I thought, so much for his bankroll.

The chess players returned to the board and immersed themselves in the game once again. A frown crossed the house man's face for a moment, but he said nothing.

Back at the pool table, Tony missed a long cut on the four ball and Danny won a rack, but Tony got the next two to go five ahead and win the set—five hundred dollars up. "Go again," the kid said, still grinning. He turned around and walked to the counter. "Hey, you guys need this? I found it on the floor." He produced the white rook.

"No, just put it down," the house man said at the same time that the other guy said, "Yes, hell, yes, I need that, I wondered what the fuck happened to my position, Jesus, did you knock that off the board while I was in the head?" he glared at the house man.

Danny turned around quickly and said to Tony, "This time I need some weight. You kicked my ass."

"Bullshit," Tony said.

"Come on, man, I won two out of nine fucking games."

"I'll give you the eight but let's play for a thousand, five ahead."

"Five ahead, eight hundred."

"Rack 'em."

"This is bullshit, I ain't payin on this game," the older guy said, knocking the rest of the pieces off the chessboard.

"Danny, you're a fuckhead," the house man said, shaking his head, setting up the pieces for a new game. Danny Green giggled and broke the first rack, and made the two, four, and nine. He was playing two balls better immediately. He got three games ahead and I said to him, "Jesus, Danny, you need to work on your routine. You're way too fuckin obvious." He just grinned, but Tony sobered him up soon enough, running three racks, losing one then running two more to go one game ahead.

For the next two hours nobody won more than two games straight. The kid was playing better and better. He knew the table well, and that was a big help. It was tricky. The pocket falls were cut very deep, and the corners, particularly, spit balls out a lot. Somehow, though, despite having been awake for about twenty hours, Tony was holding his own, taking advantage of every mistake, playing all-world defense. He got up to four games ahead, and the kid ran two racks to cut his lead in half. It was almost four o'clock when he got four up again, and this time he didn't leave the door open, breaking and running out to win the set.

That took part of the smile off the kid's face. He was down $1,300 now. "Fuck, I got one more bullet," he said. "Same way."

He started out hot, winning the first two. He was beautiful to watch now, hitting full-table draws, fancy force-follows, playing spectacular position. He still scratched too much, because he was throwing the cue ball all over the table, but most of the time it was working fine. Tony was really torturing him on defense, hooking him time and again, but he managed to shoot his way out of almost every one. He was sober and sharp, accurate as a smart bomb.

Mike leaned over and whispered into my ear. "An old player told me once that in long sessions, the momentum usually shifts at around this time," he said. "It's the dew. It forms on the cloth about dawn and the table begins to play different."

I looked at him hard to see if he was serious. "The *dew?*" I said. "Fuck. It's seventy degrees in this joint, I don't think we got a whole lot of condensation happening."

"All right man, but *something's* changing this game," he said sulkily, and turned his back. As it usually was, that something was fatigue, not dew. The kid was playing like Luther Lassiter now, and Tony was reeling around the table, eyes red and swollen, on the defensive, clawing to keep the set within reach. He got it to one game on his side, but then the kid ran three. They traded games for forty minutes before the kid won two straight to get it to four. Tony won the next but the kid won two more to close out the set at precisely 8 A.M.

"That's it, I'm done," Tony said. "You're five hundred stuck, and I'll give you another chance for it, but I got to get some rest now."

"Okay," Danny chirped, obviously pleased to have won back his eight hundred dollars. "I'll be in here at eleven tonight. Let's play some more. You play good, man. I'll see if I can get staked some, too, so we can take the bet upstairs if you want."

The time cost thirty dollars, so we left a hard-won $470 to the good and with some hope of more to come. "I'll play better tonight, with some rest," Tony said softly to me as we walked toward the door, but I wasn't so sure. Tired or not, he had played extremely well but still just managed to break even after giving up the eight.

The sun felt like an angry scratch across the cornea when we stepped outside, but at least the air smelled better than the stale smoke of the Jack and Jill. I ached all over and my eyes felt like they were going to swell shut. It was all I could do to pilot the Caddy up the freeway through commuter traffic toward the Reistertown exit.

I'd been looking forward to a greasy omelet at Bob's Big Boy, but the place was closed for remodeling. "Fuck it," Tony said. "I need sleep, not food." That sounded right so I drove around to our shitty little room and we went in and collapsed.

But the rest of the world doesn't work in the pool time zone. At 9:30 hard pounding on the door woke me up. Tony groaned and buried his head under the pillow. At the door I found a grim-faced Nordic-looking maid who probably outweighed me by eighty pounds. The fact that I was naked made no impression on her whatsoever. "Maid service," she said forcefully.

"No, that's okay, just give me some fresh towels," I croaked.

"Okay, I'll be right back," she said, but it was forty minutes later when she woke me again. I threw the towels across the room and slammed the door. I didn't get back to sleep until noon.

NOVEMBER 17—SIX HOURS LATER, I AWOKE TO TONY'S CHAINSAW snoring with a horrible headache from sleep, caffeine, and food deprivation.

I walked across the street to the Hilton. The coffee shop was closed, so I went into the bar and ordered a double espresso. The bartender disappeared—I was the only soul in the place—only to reappear fifteen agonizing minutes later with the news that the espresso machine was broken. Bitterly, I accepted a cup of rancid bar coffee and returned to the room.

Tony was awake. "Thanks for the coffee, prick."

"Oh, fuck you. Have this. It tastes like goat piss anyway. Get your ass up, I need some food."

"Easy, killer, you'll be all right."

"Oh, I'll be fine. I can't wait to sweat your action all night again. Watch out for the dew factor, though."

"You need to relax. You're a brutal sweater, man. Watching you watching me makes me laugh so hard I can't concentrate on the game."

"You'd sweat too if you had your bankroll riding on a shifty little Italian pool hustler."

"Oh, now we're coming with the ethnic jokes. You're a little hot about the seventy I won yesterday, aren't you?"

"What joke? Anyway, it was fifty."

"Come on, man, it was sixty at least, I was sixty ahead and had a road map out when we quit."

"You forfeited the last rack."

"Forfeit this."

"Come on, you robbing little bastard, I've got to eat."

We ate a pizza and rolled some balls around at Greenie's. There was no sign of Junior Harris, but he had left word that he'd be in the next night. "He said he's got a thousand bucks worth of action if you want it," Greenie said, "but I don't think he's giving anything up."

"He offered me the eight once," Tony said.

"Yeah, that's what he told me, but then he said he heard you're playin jam up and he says he's off his game."

"Fuck that," the cook said. "Off his game. Shit. Junior Harris got a heart the size of a fuckin Raisinet."

"Let's play some nine-ball," Tony said to the cook. "I'll give you the last two, hundred a rack, let's go."

"I want the last four and the breaks."

"Of course you do."

At eleven we drove back down to Glen Burnie. Word of our arrival had preceded us. The place was full of sweaters, maybe fifty people waiting for the big match.

There was a different house man this night, tall, sepulchral, about fifty, with an Adam's apple the size of a grapefruit. "You the road player?" he asked.

"Yep," Tony said. "Is Danny here?"

"He'll be here," the guy said. "He told me to call him, wake him up at midnight."

"Wake him up? Hell, that's when we're supposed to play."

The house man shrugged. "He'll be here," he said.

Everybody in the place was watching Tony. As he took his cue out of his case, a fat guy with a greasy pompadour and bad teeth said, "Hey, road man, give me eight to six and I'll play you some one-pocket for five hundred."

"Stay away from him," Mike whispered. "That's Geese. He's crazy and he used to be the best one-pocket player in Maryland, one of the best anywhere on the coast. He gave Weenie Beanie all he wanted."

"Hee hee, where's your heart, road man?" Geese cackled. "Come on, one-pocket, one-pocket, eight to six, hee hee hee hee."

"Save it, buddy, I know who you are," Tony said. "I can see why he's called Geese," he added quietly to me.

"Come on, man, let's play," Geese piped again, and this time the house man turned on him. "Shut up, Geese, the man has a game." He turned to Tony. "If you'd like, sir, I'll clean that table up and you can hit some balls."

"That'd be great, thanks."

I looked at the table dubiously. It was obviously filthy. How clean could he get it?

The house man took his job seriously. I thought he must be a carryover from Jack and Jill's glory days as one of the hottest action spots around. The poolroom was in decay now, but he was still the house man, and by God he wasn't going to have his A table dirty for a big money game. He got two brushes from beneath the counter and descended on the table like an avenging angel. He started working with the larger brush, center outward, first one way then the other, and the dirt and chalk rose like a thunderstorm off the Gulf, great green and brown billows diffusing the overhead light, flowing higher and farther outward as he brushed.

Tony coughed. "God, this is awful," he said. "This table hasn't been cleaned in a year."

Now the house man curled sheets of paper into the pockets and began brushing down the rails with his smaller brush, getting into the little crevice under the rail, pushing the dirt toward the paper cones inside the pockets.

When he was done, he removed the dust-filled cones of paper, threw them away, then turned to Tony and said, "See how that plays, partner."

Tony was touched. "Thanks, thanks a lot for your trouble, man," he said.

Tony began to hit balls, slowly lengthening his stroke, hitting the balls a little harder as he warmed up. I watched him perform one of his favorite practice rituals. He spread all fifteen balls in the center of the table, between the second diamond from the end of each rail, and began to make them without touching the cue ball to a cushion. It didn't look fancy but it was a terrific exercise, great for timing, finding the correct pocket speed for the table, keeping the cue ball tight, sometimes drawing it with low English, sometimes hitting slow center-ball and letting the ball roll a few inches forward, sometimes killing it with a perfect stun stroke, always making sure of the favorable angle on the next shot. As the crowd watched I realized most of them had no idea how demanding that drill really was. I heard a guy behind Mike say, "Why does he practice those shots? I can make those in my sleep."

"He doesn't want to show too much," his partner whispered back knowingly.

"Hey," Mike whispered in my ear. "You wouldn't stake me to a little game, would you? I got a guy over there I know I can beat." He motioned with his head toward a player hitting balls on one of the back tables.

"What sort of a game did you make?"

"He's giving me the seven, ten a game."

I held out three twenties. "Here's six bullets. I get half of whatever you win."

"Thanks, man, I really appreciate it," he said.

Tony began work on the break, popping the cue ball back into the center of the table. The table was tough to break on, as he had discovered the night before. He played a couple of racks of rotation, the balls snapping into the pockets, the cue ball floating obediently around the table. He looked as sharp as I'd ever seen him.

It took Mike about an hour to lose the sixty. Meanwhile, about twenty-five sweaters were gathered around the table where Tony was practicing. The only problem was, none of them was Danny Green.

At 2 A.M. I asked the house man, "Hey, can you give Danny a call?"

"I just did, man, no answer, he must be on the way."

After another few minutes, Tony unscrewed his cue. "How much is the time?" he asked.

"On the house. I don't know where that Danny is."

"We'll wait a few more minutes."

Tony came over and sat down next to me. "I don't like the look of this," he said quietly. "Even if Danny isn't setting us up, too many of these guys know we've got cash. This crowd is not pretty."

He was right about that.

The pay phone rang, and a kid lounging near it picked it up. "Is Danny Green here?" he called, and the crowd broke into laughter. "Oh, wait, wait," he said, holding the phone out. "This *is* Danny Green . . . is the road toad here?" More laughter. The guy grinned and handed the phone to Tony. "He sounds real *stoned*," he said, milking it for one more laugh.

"Yeah?" Tony took the phone. "No shit. How long will it take you? Never mind that, we'll talk about that when you get here.

sed, and as soon as he missed turned from the table, talk-
to himself, more agitated than I had seen him since
onto. Junior could not believe his good fortune. He had
n one shot away from being closed out—maybe a thirty-
nd of an inch away when the nine ball hung—and
ugh luck and clutch shooting managed to pull out a
ory. He shook his head, as if to clear it, walked slowly to the
e, and ran the balls out.

watched, in shock, as Harris pulled the thousand dollars
the light. It was clear Tony wanted no more. He jammed
ue into the case, shook hands quickly with Junior, with
, with Greenie, and we were out of the room in less than
nute.

was only a five-hundred-dollar set, but psychologically, it
y far the worst loss of the trip. It was a thousand-dollar
, and it made the difference between almost breaking
after expenses in Baltimore (we did) and actually win-
money (we didn't).

ove back to the motel in complete silence. We went into
om and sat in more silence.

lly, Tony spoke. "No fuckin excuse for that. Losing like
tough to fade."

got some bad rolls."

h, horseshit, I should have beaten him easy. I can't
that combo didn't go down. That son of a bitch started
, did you see it?"

,

s cooked after he shit out leaving me that shot on the
was so pissed at myself for letting it get to me that I
even worse."

t shit yourself, that boy's a smart gambler. But he was
pretty fuckin sad when it was ten to seven. Right now

I'll wait another hour, and that's it." He hung up and looked
at me exasperatedly. "He says he has a flat tire, and he'll be
here in forty-five minutes. Little fucker's high as a monkey."

"I'll bet you fifty he doesn't show in an hour."

"No bet."

We finally left at 3:15. Just another fuckaround, waiting all
night for no action. The warehouse parking lot was dark and
ugly. I hit the lock and Tony said as he got in, "Haul ass, man,
there's nothing good that can happen out here." But we got
back to the motel just fine, a little after four. I'd left word at
the desk that we didn't require maid service, but of course
they forgot to tell Brunhilde, who rousted us at 8:45.

NOVEMBER 18—ONLY ONE ITEM OF BUSINESS REMAINED ON THE
Baltimore agenda: Mr. Junior Harris. We had a game set for 9
P.M. at Greenie's, although after the Danny fiasco, I had no
confidence it would come off. When we walked in, Mike came
up and said, "Hey, you guys, you should of stuck around.
Danny Green came in about 4:30 and played some guy for a
hundred a game, ended up winning about six hundred."

My fears about this night were unfounded. At 8:45, here
was Harris, coming over with his girlfriend, shaking hands
politely, and saying, "Let's play a race to eleven for five
hundred."

"Let's play by the game instead," Tony said. "And you were
going to give me the eight in San Diego."

"No, I'd rather play sets," Harris said, firmly, "and we'll play
straight up." So there we were. I knew this was the only game
we could make this night, unless Danny Green should miraculously appear, which seemed doubtful. Tony looked at me
and nodded, then said, "All right, Junior, let's post the money.
Flip for break?"

Junior Harris won the flip, and Tony racked. He looked determined, if not thrilled with the game. Junior Harris was a recognized player, and Tony knew this match would not be easy. But this was what we had come for, and he wasn't about to turn down the game because he couldn't get spotted.

Junior looked a little nervous. He made the three on the break, ran the one, two, and four, but left himself a tough angle on the five and missed it. Tony ran out, then ran the next rack to jump out to a 2–0 lead. Tony made nothing on the next break, though, and even worse left Junior an easy two-nine combination, which he drilled to make it 2–1.

Junior didn't make another ball for twenty minutes. Tony ran three racks without getting in the slightest bit of trouble. Suddenly, his break was perfect. He made two balls, three balls, and two balls on the breaks. It looked like he would get the fourth rack, but he jawed a long six ball and let Junior Harris back into the match.

Harris made the nine on the next break, then ran a rack out to pull within a game. They traded mistakes, and racks, to take the score to 6–5. But Tony, showing some brilliant play now, making long draw shots, delicate position plays, and sharp cuts with cue control, ran two more racks to lead 8–5. Harris looked to me to be a careful player, with a strong, precise stroke, but I thought Tony had more firepower, more defense, and played better position.

Still, Harris refused to crumble. He got a break when Tony hooked himself on a break, then made a nice shot to get out after Tony elected to push out. Junior won a rack and then gave one away to bring it to 9–7. Tony methodically ran out then, to get to the hill, 10–7. Junior looked agitated now, shaking his head, muttering to himself, banging the butt of his cue angrily. And well he might. Tony was breaking, and he

had to win only one game. Junior had to w
take the set.

Tony broke and nearly made the nine, bu
He left Junior a decent shot on the one,
Junior then took a Billy Cress baseball swir
he'd left Tony a three-ball combination on
match. It wasn't an easy shot, but Tony ha
try it. He had no other clear-cut shot to r
nine was pretty near the corner pocket; it
Harris a shot at the combination. So he
combo down the rail for the match and i
one hit the six, and the six hit the nine,
and the nine shot toward the pocket. It
started to fall, but hung on the lip, an
roar of surprise. Tony twisted his bod
drop, but it wouldn't, and he let his h
disappointment.

Harris took the gift, making it 10–8
rack seemed to give him hope where
none. He made several nice shots
missed an eight ball, but the ball
halfway along the end rail, the cue ba
the other end of the table. Tony didr
long one-rail bank on the eight, a
another gift rack to pull within one,

Junior then proceeded to break
match, hill-hill. Where he had be
whelming superiority, now Tony
momentum, and shocked at the p
seemed such a sure thing.

Harris missed the four ball, bu
tough. Tony tried a very hard

he can't believe it. I've never seen anything like it and I bet he hasn't either."

"Fuck it, let's get some sleep and head south."

"Junior Harris. Goddamn."

XII

Southbound

Lord, I was born a ramblin' man,
Tryin' to make a livin' and doin' the best I can.
                                        —The Allman Brothers

NOVEMBER 19—IN THE MORNING I WAS HAPPY, AT LEAST, TO SEE THE last of the shitbox and 695. Now we turned south for real, circumnavigating D.C., and cruising deep into Virginia by noon. We did not stop until we arrived in Henderson, North Carolina. It was a sunny afternoon, shockingly warm compared with Baltimore, and it felt like a foreign country. We pulled the Caddy to a stop on Main Street and strolled down a block to an old bar and poolroom. The tables were ancient scarred Brunswicks, dark and vacant. The three men at the bar turned and looked at us, their stony expressions giving nothing away—neither courtesy nor invitation.

The bartender, jowly, suspicious, took the initiative. "Hep you boys with somethin?"

"Cup of coffee?" I asked.

"Nope. Try the lunchroom across the street," he said. One of the men at the bar sniggered and swigged his draft beer. The place felt hopeless. This guy wouldn't bet ten cents out of

I'll wait another hour, and that's it." He hung up and looked at me exasperatedly. "He says he has a flat tire, and he'll be here in forty-five minutes. Little fucker's high as a monkey."

"I'll bet you fifty he doesn't show in an hour."

"No bet."

We finally left at 3:15. Just another fuckaround, waiting all night for no action. The warehouse parking lot was dark and ugly. I hit the lock and Tony said as he got in, "Haul ass, man, there's nothing good that can happen out here." But we got back to the motel just fine, a little after four. I'd left word at the desk that we didn't require maid service, but of course they forgot to tell Brunhilde, who rousted us at 8:45.

NOVEMBER 18—ONLY ONE ITEM OF BUSINESS REMAINED ON THE Baltimore agenda: Mr. Junior Harris. We had a game set for 9 P.M. at Greenie's, although after the Danny fiasco, I had no confidence it would come off. When we walked in, Mike came up and said, "Hey, you guys, you should of stuck around. Danny Green came in about 4:30 and played some guy for a hundred a game, ended up winning about six hundred."

My fears about this night were unfounded. At 8:45, here was Harris, coming over with his girlfriend, shaking hands politely, and saying, "Let's play a race to eleven for five hundred."

"Let's play by the game instead," Tony said. "And you were going to give me the eight in San Diego."

"No, I'd rather play sets," Harris said, firmly, "and we'll play straight up." So there we were. I knew this was the only game we could make this night, unless Danny Green should miraculously appear, which seemed doubtful. Tony looked at me and nodded, then said, "All right, Junior, let's post the money. Flip for break?"

Junior Harris won the flip, and Tony racked. He looked determined, if not thrilled with the game. Junior Harris was a recognized player, and Tony knew this match would not be easy. But this was what we had come for, and he wasn't about to turn down the game because he couldn't get spotted.

Junior looked a little nervous. He made the three on the break, ran the one, two, and four, but left himself a tough angle on the five and missed it. Tony ran out, then ran the next rack to jump out to a 2–0 lead. Tony made nothing on the next break, though, and even worse left Junior an easy two-nine combination, which he drilled to make it 2–1.

Junior didn't make another ball for twenty minutes. Tony ran three racks without getting in the slightest bit of trouble. Suddenly, his break was perfect. He made two balls, three balls, and two balls on the breaks. It looked like he would get the fourth rack, but he jawed a long six ball and let Junior Harris back into the match.

Harris made the nine on the next break, then ran a rack out to pull within a game. They traded mistakes, and racks, to take the score to 6–5. But Tony, showing some brilliant play now, making long draw shots, delicate position plays, and sharp cuts with cue control, ran two more racks to lead 8–5. Harris looked to me to be a careful player, with a strong, precise stroke, but I thought Tony had more firepower, more defense, and played better position.

Still, Harris refused to crumble. He got a break when Tony hooked himself on a break, then made a nice shot to get out after Tony elected to push out. Junior won a rack and then gave one away to bring it to 9–7. Tony methodically ran out then, to get to the hill, 10–7. Junior looked agitated now, shaking his head, muttering to himself, banging the butt of his cue angrily. And well he might. Tony was breaking, and he had to win only one game. Junior had to win four straight to take the set.

Tony broke and nearly made the nine, but nothing went in. He left Junior a decent shot on the one, which he missed. Junior then took a Billy Cress baseball swing when he realized he'd left Tony a three-ball combination on the nine to win the match. It wasn't an easy shot, but Tony had little choice but to try it. He had no other clear-cut shot to make a ball, and the nine was pretty near the corner pocket; it wouldn't do to leave Harris a shot at the combination. So he shot the three-ball combo down the rail for the match and it looked perfect. The one hit the six, and the six hit the nine, as it was supposed to, and the nine shot toward the pocket. It wobbled and actually started to fall, but hung on the lip, and the crowd let out a roar of surprise. Tony twisted his body, urging the ball to drop, but it wouldn't, and he let his head fall to his chest in disappointment.

Harris took the gift, making it 10–8. The surprisingly easy rack seemed to give him hope where moments ago there was none. He made several nice shots in the next rack, then missed an eight ball, but the ball bounced out and died halfway along the end rail, the cue ball on the opposite rail on the other end of the table. Tony didn't have much. He tried a long one-rail bank on the eight, and it hung; Harris had another gift rack to pull within one, 10–9.

Junior then proceeded to break and run a rack to tie the match, hill-hill. Where he had been in a position of overwhelming superiority, now Tony was rattled, devoid of momentum, and shocked at the prospect of losing what had seemed such a sure thing.

Harris missed the four ball, but got lucky again and left it tough. Tony tried a very hard cut in the side pocket but

missed, and as soon as he missed turned from the table, talking to himself, more agitated than I had seen him since
Toronto. Junior could not believe his good fortune. He had
been one shot away from being closed out—maybe a thirty-
second of an inch away when the nine ball hung—and
through luck and clutch shooting managed to pull out a
victory. He shook his head, as if to clear it, walked slowly to the
table, and ran the balls out.

I watched, in shock, as Harris pulled the thousand dollars
from the light. It was clear Tony wanted no more. He jammed
his cue into the case, shook hands quickly with Junior, with
Mike, with Greenie, and we were out of the room in less than
a minute.

It was only a five-hundred-dollar set, but psychologically, it
was by far the worst loss of the trip. It was a thousand-dollar
swing, and it made the difference between almost breaking
even after expenses in Baltimore (we did) and actually winning money (we didn't).

I drove back to the motel in complete silence. We went into
the room and sat in more silence.

Finally, Tony spoke. "No fuckin excuse for that. Losing like
that is tough to fade."

"You got some bad rolls."

"Yeah, horseshit, I should have beaten him easy. I can't
believe that combo didn't go down. That son of a bitch started
to drop, did you see it?"

"Yes."

"I was cooked after he shit out leaving me that shot on the
eight. I was so pissed at myself for letting it get to me that I
made it even worse."

"Don't shit yourself, that boy's a smart gambler. But he was
looking pretty fuckin sad when it was ten to seven. Right now

he can't believe it. I've never seen anything like it and I bet he hasn't either."

"Fuck it, let's get some sleep and head south."

"Junior Harris. Goddamn."

XII

Southbound

Lord, I was born a ramblin' man,
Tryin' to make a livin' and doin' the best I can.
—The Allman Brothers

NOVEMBER 19—IN THE MORNING I WAS HAPPY, AT LEAST, TO SEE THE last of the shitbox and 695. Now we turned south for real, circumnavigating D.C., and cruising deep into Virginia by noon. We did not stop until we arrived in Henderson, North Carolina. It was a sunny afternoon, shockingly warm compared with Baltimore, and it felt like a foreign country. We pulled the Caddy to a stop on Main Street and strolled down a block to an old bar and poolroom. The tables were ancient scarred Brunswicks, dark and vacant. The three men at the bar turned and looked at us, their stony expressions giving nothing away—neither courtesy nor invitation.

The bartender, jowly, suspicious, took the initiative. "Hep you boys with somethin?"

"Cup of coffee?" I asked.

"Nope. Try the lunchroom across the street," he said. One of the men at the bar sniggered and swigged his draft beer. The place felt hopeless. This guy wouldn't bet ten cents out of the till that water was wet, especially against some Yankee stranger pool-shooting asshole.

We gassed up and pointed it south again, looking for that sweet spot, that game we couldn't lose. We stopped in Charlotte, at a well-known poolroom called Mother's, a pleasant, modern place, built in two halves—one side for the apple-heads, the ball-slamming public, with juke and bar and a lot of smoke and chatter; and one side for the players, with a pro shop and nice tables in great shape.

Tony immediately zeroed in on a game of one-pocket in the corner of the room. "See that Asian guy?" he asked me in a whisper. "That's Wesley Oyama. I can't believe he's here. He plays real high from time to time. This may be our spot."

Tony didn't want to interrupt Oyama's game, but he sure wanted to clock it, so he got some balls to practice. I wandered back over to the other side of the room, lured by the wail of the Marshall Tucker Band coming from the Rock-Ola: "Gonna ride me a southbound, all the way to Georgia, till the train run out of track . . ." I struck up a game of five-dollar nine-ball with a tall, thin guy, maybe twenty, with shoulder-length blond hair. Suddenly, for the first time in weeks, I was playing someone who didn't run out every time I made a mistake. The difference was refreshing, and I won thirty dollars in an hour.

By then the clock was breaking up Oyama's game, and he finally came over and chatted some with Tony. Oyama was suspicious of Tony's claim that he didn't play much one-pocket. He had been beaten often in the past, with two results: His game had improved, and he had become a lot more cautious. He demanded ten to six and the break—a ludicrous spot. Tony offered him a ball, but it was clear that they were too far apart. There was money there, but we weren't going to get it. I said: Let's head south. *Gonna ride me a southbound, all the way to Georgia* . . . It was 2 A.M. and 77 degrees, far too nice to sleep. It was a perfect highway night.

Dickie Betts's guitar filled the car, sweet and heavy as night-blooming jasmine, and Gregg Allman's voice suffused me with manic Cadillac energy as we whooshed across the state line at ninety-plus. By dawn the adrenaline, or L-dopamine, or whatever the hell the music released into my brain and my accelerator foot, carried us right through to Savannah. We were driven by a strange water-mania; we thought we must see the Atlantic Ocean at sunup, so we went on through to Tybee Island, where the train really does run out of track. But we were destined to be disappointed once again. The refineries and factories splotched along the mouth of the Savannah River and the Intracoastal Waterway churned foul vapor into the red delta sunrise, turning it the color of tobacco juice. The air was gravid, painful to breathe, heavy with acidic waste chemicals and squandered beauty.

We retreated to downtown Savannah, indolent and lyrical as ever, so strongly reminiscent of New Orleans, with its profusion of parks and squares and big old clapboards and elegant colonnaded piles of brick. We even found passable beignets and *café au lait* at a tourist joint on the river. Tony spotted a fancy old billiards sign, but on closer inspection the poolroom was just a faded neon dream, the building for lease.

NOVEMBER 20—THE SMELL OF MONEY WAS STILL IN MY NOSE WHEN we woke up, and I stubbornly suggested that we poke around Savannah for a game.

Tony just wanted to get to Florida as soon as possible. We had entered him in a tournament in L.A. in a week, and the quicker we got down to Miami the more chance we would have to play there. Finally Tony agreed to indulge me, to go take a look around. We headed down Abercorn, away from the city's historic district, and quickly encountered first tenements and then suburban sprawl.

The good old yellow pages sent us to the two major poolrooms in town. It was Friday night and both were doing a good trade, but they seemed overwhelmingly recreational in nature. Probably a money game or two could be found, but it would take a few days to sniff out. We went for the direct approach in the second place, and talked to the house man. He told us, nope, not too much here, just those boys—he pointed to a table of loutish types playing for two bucks a rack—but you might try the Office, they have three or four tables over there.

The Office turned out to be a bar. Other than our little Everett escapade we had carefully avoided bar pool on this trip. The stakes are typically tiny, the risk of complications disproportionately great. People get drunk, they get crazy, and it's not worth it. Nevertheless, when some people get drunk, they get a little careless, and all that naked machismo can be useful. So we decided to stop in at the Office. Great name for a bar. ("Honey, I'm tied up at the Office, I'll be late.")

For once our timing was right: We walked in just as an eight-ball tournament had ended. A couple of guys were playing nine-ball on a front table, and at a little card table near the bar they were whacking up the prize money. A couple of people looked a little sharply at us as we walked over to the pool area.

"So who won the tournament?" I asked.

"Ah did," said one of the nine-ball players, proudly and a bit unsteadily. He was about six-two, thirtyish, handsome, dapper in suit pants and white shirt, tie askew, with dark curly hair and mustache and the beginnings of a beer belly.

"How much did you win?" Tony asked, a little rudely.

The player turned his head toward the table where the figuring was being done. "Hunnert and fifty, Russell," a guy at the table said.

"Thanks," Russell said, and looked at Tony.

"You want to play a game for it?" Tony asked.

He gazed at Tony a little more intently for a few seconds, and for that time I couldn't tell how he was going to take it, but then a smile appeared beneath the mustache and he said, "Sure. Let's play—say, a race to five for the buck and a half?"

"No, a *game* for it," Tony said. "That way, if you beat me we can play another one, right after."

"Play him, Russell," one of the other men said. "Kick his *ass.*"

Russell was getting high-rolled in his own bar. A few hours ago, he would have been more careful, but a few hours ago he hadn't won a tournament, and a few hours ago he hadn't had a six-pack of Budweiser, either. "Look, pal, whoevah the *fuck* you are," he said. "Ah don't like your style much, but ah like mah chances. Let's play five ahead for five hundred."

I posted the money without another word, and so did Russell. Tony looked at me with a smile. "I don't think it's a good idea to go get the cue out of the car," he whispered. "They might not take kindly to it." While he looked for a decent house cue, I was offered side action—a hundred and thirty in all.

My God, I thought. This is just a crummy little bar. It took us three days to get this kind of action in New York City. And here we didn't lay down a spread, we didn't do anything but ask this guy to play. Russell, whoevah the fuck *he* was, played with a cheap Meucci cue, but he handled it well enough to win a lot of tournaments. He was used to the big bar-table cue ball, and he broke well. But not as well as Tony, and he didn't get out every time he should have. Tony got out every time. In an hour, it was over. "Again?" Tony asked.

"Ah've seen enough, podna," Russell said pleasantly. He took the money off the light and handed it to Tony, who handed it to me. Thanks, I thought to myself, looking at the array of sullen faces around us.

"Get to fuck out of here," somebody said.

"Easy, Jackie," Russell said quietly. "He beat us on the square, there was no hustlin to it. He just shoots too fuckin straight." He forced a little smile in our direction. "Darlene, another Bud, please, hon?" I slapped a twenty on the bar on the way out and told Darlene to take care of Russell and herself with it, and in ten minutes we were back on U.S. 95, rejuvenated, the money we'd lost to Junior Harris back in the poke.

NOVEMBER 21—AT DAYTONA, WE DECIDED TO CUT OVER TO U.S. 1 to follow the coast.

Which would have been fine if we could have *seen* the coast, or even the Intracoastal, but most of the time all we saw were cheesy decaying 1950s tourist traps. By the time we crawled down to West Palm, I was overwhelmed with disgust at what has been done to this spectacular state in the euphemistic name of progress. Even John D. MacDonald and Charles Willeford and Carl Hiassen had not prepared me for the soul-stomping squalor of it all.

Fortunately for our purposes, none of this prevented the proliferation of poolrooms. We hit Zizi's Cue Room, Larry Novitsky's place in Lake Worth. Nothing was happening there, but we got a steer to a place in West Palm. "The owner, Grover, is usually there, and he'll give anybody who comes in some action," Larry's house man told us. "He's not afraid to play anyone."

When we walked in, Grover was playing in a ring nine-ball game: The winner stayed on the table, the loser paid and relinquished his spot to the next player. Grover looked smart and careful, an athletic forty-plus. When the ring game broke up, Tony introduced himself and asked if there was a game anywhere around. "Sure," Grover said. "I'll play you a race to five for fifty dollars."

He didn't play badly, but Tony won, and Grover asked for the eight, got it, and lost that way, too. Grover then suggested some even one-pocket, and it didn't take long to see that one-pocket was his game. Tony gave him a good game, but Grover's one-pocket experience and his home-table advantage were too tough to overcome. After Tony had lost Grover's hundred back to him, they agreed to break even and quit.

While they were playing I had walked around the pool-room, which was clean and cozy, looking at the pictures of players on the wall, stars such as Mizerak and Sigel and Hopkins. In the backroom I was surprised to see a magnificent old table. The slate and rails were obscured with a cover but I recognized the ornate wrought-iron legs of a Brunswick Monarch, circa 1880, worth perhaps $50,000. When I came back into the main room I noticed a guy sitting at the bar who looked familiar, and it took me a minute or two to realize that he was in one of the framed pictures I'd seen a few minutes ago. I'd been surprised then because I'd never heard of the name and never seen the face. I was about to tell Tony about this when the guy walked up and asked Tony, "Would you care to play a game of straight pool, sir?"

"Sure," Tony said. "What did you have in mind?"

"We could play to a hundred, say, for fifty dollars."

"Let's go."

I caught Tony's arm and whispered to him, "I don't know who the fuck he is but his picture's on the wall with all the Hall of Famers."

"Great," Tony said. He shook his head and reassembled his cue.

I sat down at the bar to watch the match, and Grover came up to me and said softly, "The dumb shit. He can't come close to your buddy. I told him that. But he doesn't care. He just likes to play champions."

"Is that why his picture's on the wall?" I asked skeptically. I thought Grover was setting us up, big time.

Grover knew it, and smiled. "Shit. He brought it in, frame and all, and asked me if I'd hang it. He's a good customer and a really nice guy. . . ." He shrugged.

Grover was accurate. The fellow was several notches shy of being a great player, and Tony won easily, then spotted him twenty to a hundred and beat him again, running sixty and out to finish it.

During the bloodletting Grover got a phone call. "Hey, Miz!" he said. It was the great Mizerak himself, Hall of Fame player, star of the Miller Lite commercials, enormously fat now but still one of the toughest competitors in the game. It turned out he and Grover had a date on the links the next morning, and he was calling to confirm the tee time. Tony broke away from his game for a moment to pay his respects and Mizerak told him, "Listen to Grover's advice; he'll steer you straight." Mizerak was not a game for us; he just didn't gamble that much anymore. He didn't need to; he made a handsome living from tournaments, endorsements, and commercials. Of course, he was also very tough to beat. I'd seen Tony play him in the '92 L.A. Open and lose, 13–12, in a great match.

Grover steered us to a couple more places, then offered to

go with us for a night, and tell us about the players, who played well, who'd go off. It was a valuable offer, but we couldn't take advantage. It would be three days before he could go, and we had nonrefundable tickets to L.A. and a tournament to play in. We'd managed to be successful despite our tight schedule, but in other spots it had been a real handicap. For us, Miami became a hundred dollars here, a hundred there, instead of the payday it could have been.

XIII

Hard Times

"It is a game of infinite variables. . . . True excellence is rare and vanities are punished."
—Jim Harrison, *Just Before Dark*

NOVEMBER 24—FOR MOST POOL PLAYERS, MORNINGS ARE RIGHT UP there with paying table time and shooting over a ball: things to be avoided if at all possible. But we had no such option on this day. Instead, we had a morning that lasted about nine hours.

At 6:30 A.M. we left our no-longer-new Cadillac at the Miami International return lot, showing every one of its 5,321 free miles. I hoped Alamo wouldn't mind the dark spot on the otherwise bright red carpet where I spilled coffee when Tony fishtailed to a stop at the Pennsylvania Turnpike tollbooth. Or the chip on the driver's door incurred in the parking lot of South Philly Billiards. I didn't figure they'd have to deal with the odd ratcheting noise the car was making when you jammed the throttle down and tried to force the bugger into passing gear at 85 m.p.h. Whatever the ads tell you, believe this: Cadillacs aren't what they used to be. And this one would never be young again.

Within the hour we were airborne on a nonstop to L.A.,

and we had traveled across the continent, eaten a crummy in-flight breakfast, and collected our mound of luggage by 10 A.M. Pacific time.

It was time, once again, to take stock. We sat in the Delta terminal at LAX and discussed our options. We'd been on the road for nine weeks. We were a few thousand dollars winner, but expenses continued to eat up the profits.

Our next two stops were pretty much set. We were in Los Angeles for the Southern California Open, a healthy $10,000-added tournament to be contested at Hard Times, a hard-edged gamblers' room in Bellflower, right after Thanksgiving. Then, along with forty or fifty of the other top players in the world, Tony would play in the Sands Regency tournament in Reno. After that, prospects were a little murkier. Originally, we'd planned to take the train east out of Reno, through the midwest to Omaha, then south to Memphis, on to New Orleans, then finish up here in L.A. But neither of us had much desire to resume our train torture. And in six weeks' time pool hustler and entrepreneur Grady Mathews was hosting what promised to be the best one-pocket tournament in years, also in Reno, and it wasn't an event to be missed. What would we do in the days between Reno I and Reno II? It wasn't enough time to make the southern loop by train, and anyway we had no indi-cation of any particularly good action on that route.

Tony yawned as we walked out to hail a cab. "Whatever happens, we've got to make Grady's tournament. One way or the other we'll have big action there."

"Besides, I want to see all those one-pocket players."

"A beady-eyed, ball-bunting old fart like yourself would."

"Give me ten to three and the breaks, and we'll see who gets bunted."

"Ten to three? Why don't I just *give* you the money?"

"OK."

. . .

BELLFLOWER, CALIFORNIA, IS A DREARY BLUE-COLLAR TOWN WITH AN oft-forgotten favorite son—Indy 500 champion turned tire huckster Parnelli Jones—and it gives off the sour halitosis of urban decay, the bitterness of late middle age spent in the lower middle class.

Our motel was not the garden spot of Bellflower, if there was such a thing. But it was cheap, and only a couple of blocks from Hard Times, and so for the next week it would be full of pool players. As I finished moving bags in from our new road vehicle—my own middle-aged Land Cruiser—I saw Mike Lebron unpacking his car and Billy Incardona coming down the steps from the second floor.

"Hey, Billy, how you hittin 'em?"

"Pretty straight," Billy said, and flashed the grin that changed him in an instant from Omar Sharif to Jack Nicholson. The years have been kind to Billy Incardona. He's still movie-star handsome in his mid-forties, and his eyes are still sharp. He is still a flashy dresser and his sense of humor still sneaks up on you, just like his pool game.

That game may not be quite as sharp as it was in the seventies, when he was known to be one of the very best, but it's a lot closer to that speed than most people know, which is fine with him. He plays mostly one-pocket now, but if the money is right, he'll bring his nine-ball game out. Discreetly, efficiently, showing no more speed than necessary, he'll take the money. He doesn't book too many losers.

NOVEMBER 26—HOLIDAYS HAVE LITTLE RELEVANCE TO POOL PLAYERS' lives. They tend to be, if anything, a minor inconvenience affecting travel, poolroom and cafe hours, and small-time marks' disposable income level. Nevertheless, Tony would have preferred to spend Thanksgiving with his sons in San Francisco. Instead, he spent it crouched over a Gold Crown in the dim, smoky back row at Hard Times, working on his break, time after time: rack, break, rack, break, rack, break: charting balls made, rack distribution, and most important cue ball position after the break.

He tried hard to forget about the mess four hundred miles north, at the Q Club. The fight had been on his mind constantly for the past month. He had an attorney or two on the case, but they were not optimistic. It looked as though he would lose most or all of his investment—the money, the time, the dreams of stability and success, most of all the vindication of his own history in the place. He tried to forget the disappointment of not seeing his kids. He used his martial arts training, his understanding of Eastern philosophy, his training in computer logic, most of all his innate toughness, to block out everything but the memory of Bucktooth's voice, repetitive, nasal, annoying, ever-demanding, never completely satisfied: *"You're not quite hitting the contact point. You need to turn the hips into the break more. Get the power into it. That cue ball should jump back and kill. If it doesn't you're not hitting it right. You'll never make a dime that way."*

"Fuck you, Tooie," he muttered under his breath, but he kept setting them up and swinging at them, punching wearily like a club fighter in the ninth round, late into the evening, until hunger and muscle fatigue reduced his effectiveness. He had practiced for more than nine hours, and the work had grudgingly yielded a dividend: By the end of the night he was hitting the break much more consistently.

The following day, the tournament would begin. The ten thousand dollars added to the purse and the proximity in time and geography to the Reno tournament the next week made for an illustrious field that included most of the game's top stars: Johnny Archer, the slick young Georgian who was nine-ball's reigning world champion; Earl Strickland, one of the most talented and explosive tour performers, with a stunning break and the ability to get out from anywhere; Buddy Hall, the slow-talking, slow-moving "Rifleman" who was the calmest and steadiest of the top rank, and therefore often the most dangerous; Keith McCready, swaggering hard-living bantam rooster, spectacular and streaky; Billy Incardona; and maybe a dozen more with a legitimate chance to win—including, of course, Tony.

His first opponent would be Ernesto Dominguez, a hard-working part-time player who doubled as a table mechanic, working on pool tables all over the L.A. area. He'd put the Hard Times tables together, and took care of them. He was a meticulous, hard-nosed player who was at his best in that poolroom.

"Tough draw," Tony sighed as we walked from the nearly deserted poolroom. It was about sixty degrees, but the smog was bad; the air had an acrid scent, and my eyes were watering by the time we reached the car. "Tough on Ernesto, too," I said. "Anyhow, it could have been Earl or Buddy."

"True. Don't worry, Ernesto's plenty tough."

NOVEMBER 27—HARD TIMES, LIKE MOTHER'S IN SOUTH CAROLINA and a growing number of other poolrooms, was split into two areas, not counting the private room upstairs. One side had video games, juke, and tables that showed a little more wear. Just to your left was a six-by-twelve with tiny pockets, which most days from 10 A.M. to 2 A.M. was monopolized by a vicious golf game. The table was so tight, the players so tough, that anybody not of the first rank was guaranteed to get cut up immediately. I was drawn to this table, fascinated by its slick roll and tiny pockets, but today my business was on the other side of the room. It featured a dozen Gold Crowns, just re-covered with beautiful quick Simonis, the Belgian cloth so superior to any other; banked spectator seating on each side; and a big backlit tournament bracket on the far end of the room. The Southern California Open Nine-Ball tournament was about to begin.

I looked around at the players getting in some last-minute practice on the tables to which they were assigned, alternating racks politely with their opponents. There was Howard Vick-ery, looking like an Ohioan, Homer Simpsonish as ever, shooting as smooth and straight as ever, too. A table over, Johnny Archer stroked balls effortlessly into the pockets. Quick, slim, focused, he was the picture of efficiency as he moved around the table. On his shirt was printed a stylized map of the world—a not-so-subtle reminder of his status as world champion. He looked like the fine little athlete he was. I had heard recently that somebody had challenged Johnny Archer to a free-throw-shooting contest, best of a hundred, for a thousand bucks. The challenger had made ninety-one— and lost. It was another testimonial to Johnny Archer's great hand-eye coordination and clutch toughness.

Buddy Hall, by contrast, looked sluggish and ungainly as he lumbered around Table Eight, his big bear's belly stretching his corny red polo shirt to the limit. But when he addressed the cue ball, he looked like the champion he was, with his great head, complete with leonine thatch of brown hair and beard, bent low over the cue, his eyes sharp and every bit as intense as Archer's.

Earl Strickland wasn't slim like Archer—he actually had a bit of a paunch going, along with his polyesterish shirt and gold chain—but nothing like Buddy, either. Earl simply

looked faultless, coolly rocketing balls into the pockets, floating the cue ball a few inches here, a few there, just enough to
get perfect on the next shot—with an angle for the one after
that.

At one table, I noticed, only one player was warming up—a
veteran California player, Frank "the Barber" Almanza. As
time for the first matches drew near, I thought maybe Frank
would coast into the second round with a forfeit. But no. With
a couple of minutes to spare, Frank's opponent sauntered in.
It was Keith McCready, looking like the pool hustler from
central casting, with tennis shoes, a pair of black chinos, and a
white T-shirt, cigs rolled up in one sleeve. He had made it to
the table in time, but he had one problem: No cue. He
scanned the stands for likely prospects, and his eyes fell on
me. "Hey! You got that Robinson you were playing with
earlier? Does it have a flat tip? I like a flat tip."

Keith McCready grew up in Orange County. His mother
and father were divorced when he was a young boy. His father
had custody of the kids on weekends. He would give Keith,
then about eight, and his brothers twenty dollars each for a
weekend allowance. Then he would take them to the bowling
alley, or the pool hall, or the miniature golf course, and he
would force them to gamble their twenties with him, usually
until he had won it back.

Keith's mother died when he was twelve, and by then his
father was nowhere to be found. An aunt came out from Indi-
ana and gave each child fifty dollars to take a bus back to Indi-
ana to live with her, but Keith headed straight for the
poolroom and put his fifty in action.

A local poolroom owner adopted little Keith, and he lived
right there in the room, sleeping under tables. Just as Tony
Annigoni did when he fell asleep at Cochran's as a kid, Keith
had his pockets slit with a razor blade and his money stolen

while he slept. A lot of the time he didn't bother to go to school; he just played pool. His guardian would match him up with the players who came in, and stake him to play. Keith would win and get some of the winnings for himself, then bet his winnings in the next match. But the room owner would match him with tougher and tougher players, every once in a while making a game for Keith with someone he couldn't beat, cutting a private deal with the other player to get a piece of Keith's money.

By the time he was sixteen, Keith knew all the moves; he'd been chopped up every which way and he understood all the ways you could lose. But he was losing less and less often; he showed prodigious talent for the game, and he had nerve and incredible heart. He was small in stature, but he was a battler and an athlete. He was an exercise boy at Santa Anita and Hollywood Park when he wasn't playing pool, which helped toughen him, and also gave him an incurable jones for pari-mutuel wagering.

By the time he was nineteen there was certainly no one in Orange County who could beat him playing nine-ball. He was truly a world-class player, in terms of talent and heart probably in the top five. He earned the nickname "Keither with the Ether," administering quick paralysis to opponent after opponent. He made some enormous pool scores, but not much of the money ever stuck to the inside of his pockets. It was not unusual for him to win ten thousand dollars in a night playing pool, and lose it all on one equine nose the next day.

Now Keith was in his thirties, and his odometer had been turned over a few times. He offered the world a cocky grin and a fuck-you attitude; he had a street urchin's face with a fifty-year-old drinking man's nose, making him look like a cross between Alfred E. Neumann and W. C. Fields. He was smart in that abstract, dangerous way that rarely translated into success. He was loud and obnoxious and funny and full of confidence, and watching him play, whatever the outcome, was entertaining in the extreme. For Keith, the trick was getting the right chemical balance; he didn't play at his best "on the natch," or, conversely, if he was too lit up.

He had a weird sidesaddle stance. He one-stroked every ball, lining up the shot, getting down on it for no more than a second, and bang! The object ball disappeared. Lights out. At least that was the theory. The ball hadn't been disappearing quite as often of late, but he was still capable of playing all-world at any time. You never knew.

About a minute from disqualification, he took my cue, won the flip, and attacked the balls in characteristic fashion, chattering to himself as he speared shot after shot. "Yeah, that's it, come on, whitey, jump back, *yeah*." He ran the first three racks of the match before he missed, and somebody yelled from the stands, "Hey, you got that ether flowin good now, Keith." He grinned, and shot back, "I'm puttin a package on him, ain't I?" Twenty minutes later he had drilled Frank Almanza, 9–1.

Tony, too, had a great opening match. His rest and practice showed up well. He played almost faultlessly. Even so, I thought he was going to lose. He got out to a 6–3 lead, but it turned into a hook-and-safety contest and he had to scrap for every ball, winning only three of the next seven racks, but it was just barely enough for a 9–7 win. Tony had been right about how tough Ernesto would be on this equipment.

KEITH MCCREADY'S PRIMARY STAKEHORSE WAS A GUY NAMED FAT Tony who had made a lot of money in the carnival business, not as a corpulent freak-show attraction but as a shrewd manager. Quite a few pool players have worked the carnival circuit; one of them who had worked for Fat Tony was Keith's girlfriend, Nancy Anne Shine, a pretty, large-boned blonde with a degree in English from the University of Michigan— and a mouth as loud as Keith's. Maybe louder. She was a fine athlete herself, an accomplished gymnast and a very good pool player.

Today, Nancy Shine was pissed off at Fat Tony. That was because Fat Tony was pissed off at Keith. That was because Keith had not looked good at all in losing his second-round match to Earl Strickland, 9–3. Fat Tony had staked Keith in the tournament, and also bought him in the Calcutta, and now his chances looked slim indeed.

"What the fuck does he expect?" Nancy fumed. "Sure, Keith can beat Earl, has before, but Earl can beat Keith, too. He can beat anyone in the fucking *world*. I mean, get mad at Keith for losing to some piece of meat, okay, but *Earl Strickland*?" Tears sprang to her eyes. "Fuckin Tony's a tom motherfucker. He won't even give us hotel money for tonight."

Such were the stressful moments in the life of a pool player's girlfriend. Nancy had fallen in love with this skinny, mouthy little hustler, and although she didn't know where the thirty-five dollars for the night's lodging was going to come from, she did know they would be there together when they finally raised it. Either one of them was capable of beating almost anybody they encountered on a bar table for five dollars a game, and if that didn't happen maybe someone would come along and put Keith in action against a player at the tournament. Someone like me.

Keith came up to Nancy and me, the crooked grin still on his face, and said, "That miserable fuckin Strickland. Come on, let's go burn one."

"What the fuck are you talking about?" Nancy said. "We don't have any weed."

"Shit, one of the guys working security's got some great

reefer," Keith said. "He gave me a sample, and it's only forty a quarter."

"You must have had the sample before you played Earl," Nancy snorted. "Anyway, we don't even have a motel room, much less forty bucks."

"David, lend me forty, I got a good game, I can't miss, I'll pay you back tonight."

"Wait a minute, what game?"

"Cecil, man, *Cecil.* He shoots straight up in the air, I can't help but beat him. Hell, you've seen him play, you know I'll beat him."

"Who's staking you?"

"Fat Tony, he'll stake me anytime to play Cecil. Come on, Cecil wants to play pretty soon, give me that forty, let's get stoned now."

"Tony wouldn't stake you to play me right now," Nancy interjected. "He's really pissed."

"Fuck him!" Keith said angrily. "What, he's pissed that Earl beat me? Well, shit. I can't beat Earl every time, fuck, did you see it, he got every fuckin roll."

"I know, baby, he did, and I couldn't believe that six ball hung." Nancy's momentary irritation with Keith was gone. "You win the first couple, it's a different match."

"Fuckin A," Keith said, then switched gears with remarkable alacrity. "Come on, David, let's go get some of Cecil's fuckin money. He wants to play one-pocket. Back me for two, we'll play a set to three."

I considered this. I appreciated Keith's confidence. If he was right, he should win, but he didn't have to. Cecil Tugwell moved like a ghost. He was an excellent one-pocket player, a slim, handsome, gray-haired black man, somewhere between forty and fifty, and he was famous for being slippery, hence his nickname, Cecil the Serpent. I had only seen him play left-handed; apparently, he was even better right-handed until somebody broke his right arm in an Eddie Felson–like pool incident. Of course, the concept of Keith doing some business, that is, dumping to Cecil to split my stake, did cross my mind.

All in all, it didn't seem like a great investment, but it did seem like a great game to watch—and to hear. Both Keith and Cecil loved to talk, preferably to their opponent, Dennis Rodman–style. They were sharking, jawing, whining pool players. It would be worth the money, I thought, just to hear them yap at each other. So I agreed to put up two hundred for Keith and he said, "That's george! Okay, now! Let's go! Bring that Robinson! Come on, before he loses his stakehorse or his balls!" Keith scuttled eagerly up the stairs to the private room. As I followed him into the room I saw that Cecil, resplendent in a Giorgio of Beverly Hills sweatshirt and white jeans, was already rolling some balls, prowling around the table like a caged panther. Watching him were his stakehorses—three sharply dressed, bejeweled black men. We exchanged polite, professional greetings, posted the money, and let Keith and Cecil take over.

Keith broke well, pushing several balls to his side and leaving Cecil no shot at his hole. The match was only one shot old, but Keith was declaring victory. "There you are, I'm Keither with the Ether, and that break leaves 'em paralyzed."

Cecil started to walk around and look at the table. "Oh, Keith, I've got you now, I'm—"

"You've got *shit*."

"—I'm going to, let's see, I can snap that combo out of the rack, it goes, hell, yes, it goes, I can pick off that fifteen and—"

"If it goes, *shoot* the motherfucker. Go on, *shoot* it. Pig's ass it goes. *Shoot* the fuckin thing. It'll be your last shot this rack." Cecil was still walking around, looking at the table. He bent over the combination, stroked at it a couple of times with his cue, got up, and looked at another shot up the table. Keith circled too, looking at the layout, smiling broadly.

Cecil reacted irritably. "Be still, motherfucker, don't be walkin around when I'm getting ready to shoot. You sharkin me, you distractin me, I don't need you doin that."

"I'm not sharkin you, you aren't ready to shoot yet, you take *forever* to shoot. *Shoot,* for God's sake, let's play."

The break and the shot after the break are the two most important shots in a one-pocket game, and Cecil would not be hurried. Finally, he apparently concurred with Keith's analysis of the combination. He eschewed it, instead playing a brilliant safety, pushing three balls out of the rack toward his pocket and killing the cue ball on the lip of Keith's pocket.

"There!" he said. "How's *that,* baby? How's *that* feel? You can jam that one right up your ass. Keither with the Ether. *Shit.*" His stakehorses grinned at one another, and two of them touched fingertips, briefly.

For ten minutes both players played safety after safety, not giving up anything. Then Keith lagged the thirteen with a two-rail bank to his hole and it hung there, in perfect position, but it looked as though he might leave Cecil an open shot, which could result in him running eight and out, the way the balls were positioned.

"You done it now, baby, you done it now," Cecil chortled as the cue ball rolled down the table.

"You *bet* I did," Keith said, watching the ball in the final few inches of its roll, "and if I did it the way I meant to . . . you should be . . . *dead snooked* . . . YES!!" he shouted, coming over and high-fiving me as Cecil stared balefully at the cue ball, which had stopped behind—and frozen to—a ball that blocked the shot he thought he would have.

Cecil, left with precious few options, made a nice kick-shot safety. "That'll make you a lot of money," Keith scoffed. "Watch this shot."

"Watch *what?* You ain't got no shot there, you crazy motherfucker."

"Watch *this*," Keith said, and he cut-banked a ball the length of the table, from Cecil's side toward his hole. It was an audacious, dangerous shot. "WATCH THIS!!!" he screamed, as the ball rolled down and knocked the hanging thirteen into his hole. He danced around the table then, waving my Robinson precariously close to the ceiling and table lights like a drum-major's baton, and lined up his next shot, a straight-in draw with position. He made it and got right on the next, and the next, weaving whitey in and out of the rack.

"Damn it, quit hovering my hole," he barked at Cecil, who had camped rather close to the table, right in Keith's line. "You're hovering my hole while I'm shooting, right in front of me. I don't do that to you."

"Fuck you don't," muttered Cecil, backing up maybe a foot.

"All right, motherfucker," Keith warned, "you watch what I do to you, *if* you ever shoot again."

It looked as if he wouldn't, this rack, but Keith jawed a long cut on his seventh ball and suddenly it was Cecil's turn. He bent over the table, then yelled "Get away!" at Keith, who was squatting, hands on knees, right over Cecil's pocket.

"I told you, what you do to me, I'll do to you," Keith said righteously, but in a few seconds he backed off, his point made.

Cecil made the four, and five more balls after that. Then he ducked, knocking the ball Keith had jawed out of his pocket and getting a safety. There were three balls left on the table. Each player needed two to win. As Keith surveyed the table, Cecil said, "Now if you leave me down *here*, I could bank the ten, kill the rock on the rail, and if you leave me up *there*, I could—"

"You'll do *this*, from *here*," Keith said, leaving Cecil frozen on the end rail by his pocket, the three balls uptable, on Keith's side.

"I can do that," said Cecil, undaunted, and hit an all-world shot, banking one of the balls two rails into his pocket. He never looked like missing. Now he needed only one ball, and Keith needed both. He banked another ball one rail, and it looked as if it was all over, but the ball wobbled and hung.

"That's okay, what you gonna do now? You ain't gonna do nothin 'cause there ain't nothin you *can* do but give me the cheese," Cecil said triumphantly.

Keith deliberately made the ball in Cecil's pocket and just as deliberately followed it in with the cue ball, so that the ball came back out on the spot—along with a penalty ball for Keith—and Cecil got ball in hand behind the line. It was a desperation shot. It meant that Keith now needed all three balls and Cecil only one, but he had averted—for the moment—what appeared to be a sure loss.

Cecil tried a dangerous shot, cross-banking the one loose ball toward his pocket. He didn't hit it as well as he had the last two and the ball stopped up the rail two inches from the pocket.

"That shot will get you broke," Keith said delightedly. "Broke, I tell you! BROKE! You just got busted!" He hit a picture-perfect cross-bank, making the ball in his pocket, the cue ball powering through the spot balls, leaving him straight in on one of them.

"Yeah! Give me the *money!*"

"Shit, you lucky."

Perhaps, but Cecil hit a horrible break on the next rack and

Keith ran eight and out. Half an hour later, he had won the third straight rack, 8–6, and the set was over.

"I've got a match downstairs in half an hour," Keith said. "We'll play more later if you want."

"Fuckin right, I want to, let's play tomorrow," Cecil said cheerfully. His backers looked less sanguine, but we shook hands all around. I picked up the four hundreds, put three of them in my pocket and one into Keith's right hand, and followed him downstairs. "I got to go find that guy with the smoke," Keith said, and drifted out into the Bellflower evening.

NOVEMBER 28—EARLY IN THE MORNING, TONY EASILY BEAT A FINE young L.A. player named Tang Hoa, which guaranteed us some prize money. I was much heartened.

As he had in Akron, Tony seemed to have drawn into the most promising side of the bracket, and caught a break or two besides. Earl Strickland, probably the most dangerous player on Tony's side of the chart, had been upset in shocking fashion last night by George Michaels. The match had been close all the way, but Strickland, leading 8–6 and needing only one more game to win, missed a tough cut-shot. Michaels ran the balls out, then, improbably and miraculously, made the nine ball on two straight breaks to win the match. Strickland was stunned and angry, but the damage had been done. He was in the loser's bracket.

TONY WAS SITTING PRETTY. HE COULD FINISH NO WORSE THAN eighth, and his next opponent was a player he should beat consistently, a California transplant from Oklahoma named, improbably, Jeremiah Johnson. Suddenly Tony's game collapsed. He was just off, but off just the same. Balls jawed and hung. The cue ball rolled just too far or not quite far enough for optimum position. Each time, Tony made the little sucking sound through his mustache that he made when he was angry, and stared off into the middle distance, obviously fighting for control. It was a flashback to Mario, to Goofy, to Junior Harris. When he was down 6–3 in the match, I said to him, "Tony, chill out. You're not that far out of line. When you just barely miss position, think of it like this: If the other guy had missed and left you that shot, you'd be pleased, and you'd step up and run the rack. You're just such a fucking perfectionist that you can't stand being a couple of inches out of line from the perfect angle. Fuck that. Just loosen up and play." He nodded and said, "I should be able to give this guy two balls and barbecue him. I'm playing like shit, and that's what's bothering me."

I knew that as long as he was thinking that way, there was nothing to be done, and the match played itself out depressingly. Johnson won 9–6, dumping Tony into the losers' bracket.

That was bad enough, but it wasn't the worst of it. His first opponent in the losers' bracket would be Johnny Archer, the nine-ball champion of the world. I stood up wearily from the stands and walked toward Tony, who was stabbing his cue back into the case. He just shook his head, said, "I'll see you in a couple of hours," and walked out the door.

In a couple of hours, he had to play Johnny Archer. Until this last match he'd been playing very well, but given his state of mind I didn't see that he had much of a shot, which meant he'd finish eighth, earn maybe four hundred dollars, and we'd be in the hole for this leg of the trip, unless somehow we could make a game on the side with someone—and win.

I picked a seat high in the stands, away from Tony's field of vision. I figured he didn't need the added pressure of seeing me sweating his match. Still, my seat up in the rafters was a good enough vantage point from which to witness a mugging. It was like gazing down at the Little Bighorn from a nearby hillside.

Tony strode to the table about five minutes before the match. "You want to hit some balls?" Archer asked.

"No, that's okay, I'm ready," Tony said.

Archer broke and ran the rack, broke again, and made nothing. He shook his head as if to indicate disbelief that some moving part in the machine had let him down, produced a momentary failure.

Tony stepped up, looked at the table carefully, and began to run the balls. Good, he's staying down much better, I thought, and his rhythm seems to be back. At least he'll make a good account of himself. He ran the table out, slowly, methodically, with no drama or flash, just solid position play, easy angles, nothing rushed, no desperation force-follows or draws or banks or combinations. It made me think of that first game with Billy Cress, and I edged forward a little in my seat.

Tony broke, and made two balls, and I could see the table unfold in my mind, and I knew he could see it even better, and would run it. As he made the shots I was overpowered by the beauty of this game, at once immutably logical, governed by physical inevitabilities, and at the same time infinitely poetic and varied. This game at its best, as it was being played before me, had the transcendent power of a Handel chorus.

I thought about what an impressive mental exercise it was for Tony, after a miserable session against an unremarkable player two hours earlier, to reinvent himself so completely. It was a question of heart, a gathering of everything stored inside a man, a refusal to fall after stumbling. It was a very rare thing for a player to take such advantage of the game's intrinsic quality of renewal, the fresh start with each match, each rack, each shot. Nothing pharmaceutical could ever exceed the jolt of bliss that comes with the self-mastery that sort of play entails: *knowing* the ball is going in, *knowing* the cue ball is going to stop precisely where you willed it to, *knowing* that the next shot is going in too. I thought of Willie Hoppe, running an astonishing twenty-five billiards in an exhibition in 1918, seeing all those rails and angles and spins and caroms in his head like presents waiting to be opened. It was no accident that Hoppe was the most disciplined and controlled player of his era. Power over the cue ball, over the object ball, is power over ourselves. It is the sweetest irony that pool has gathered the reputation of being a game for louts and idlers, when, to be played well, it demands such incredible discipline of movement, of thinking, of emotion.

Tony was playing the same way against Archer as he had against me the day in New York when he had run 126 balls. One of the astonishing things about this game, in the hands of a world-class talent, is that it is possible, for some periods, to play not just very well, but *perfectly.*

To his credit, Tony was just as likely—maybe more likely— to get into dead stroke against the world champion, or for a thousand bucks a rack, as he was clowning around with me, because he was really playing against himself, against his own emotions, his own power of concentration. It certainly must have seemed to Johnny Archer that Tony was playing solitaire. It was twenty minutes and five racks later when he finally stepped up to the table again, behind 5–1, looking at a brutal hook, which he missed.

Tony's intensity and concentration never faded. To beat a champion you must play very close to that level of perfection, and sometimes even that won't be enough, but this time it was plenty. I'd watched Tony play almost every day for the past ninety days, and I'd never seen him any better. When it was over he had drilled the world champion at his own game, 9–3. The spectators applauded enthusiastically when it was over; they had just seen a nine-ball masterpiece, and they knew it. Archer smiled, albeit a little tightly—he had, after all, just been knocked out of the tournament—and shook Tony's hand.

I went down to meet Tony. "Hey, wherever you went for those two hours, you should go there more often."

"Yeah?" He smiled. "Hey, man I just walked around, trying to get a grip."

"You got it."

"I analyzed what I was doing wrong physically—not staying down well enough, not finishing right, you know—and also the mental stuff. I'd let the Q Club creep into my mind during that last match. And I just couldn't shake the feeling that I should be beating the hell out of him and I wasn't, and I got angrier and angrier at not playing right, and I realized that's what beat me. I thought about what you said, too, about not getting down on myself when I left myself a little out of line, just step up and hit it like I would if the other guy left me the shot. I was in a total trance, walking around. I'm lucky I didn't get hit by a truck."

"Johnny must feel like he just did."

"Hey, we should go down to Hollywood Billiards tonight to see if we can get a game. Morro might be down there. But first, you want to get something to eat? I'm really hungry."

"Thought you'd never ask."

HOLLYWOOD BOULEVARD WASN'T AS GLITZY AS IT USED TO BE, BUT IT had its moments. You might get hassled by a pimp or a panhandler or both on the way in or out, but you could still get a terrific meal at Musso & Frank's, an old-timey Hollywood fixture. Tony had a plate of correct, vegetarian pasta while I indulged myself with veal marsala, mushrooms, and enough garlic to ward off a covey of vampires, which I thought was prudent considering what some of the people strolling down the boulevard looked like.

Farther down, past the famous Pantages Theater, past an elaborately garish sex shop called The Cave, past most of the tourist venues, was a ratty-looking, Deco-era pile at the corner of Hollywood and Western. Downstairs was Hollywood Billiards, one of the best action poolrooms on the West Coast. It was open all night, staffed not only by the efficient counter-men but also by equally efficient hustlers of all descriptions. The club had two rooms, one on each side of the wide stairs. "Take a left," Tony said as we went down. "The first Gold Crown you'll run into is one of the toughest—and best, I think—in California. Ernesto put it together for Morro, and that's where he likes to play, but I like it too. The tougher the box the better—especially with Morro, because he shits out more than any player I've ever seen."

I had seen evidence of this. I remembered watching Ismael "Morro" Paez "shit out," as Tony put it, at the Los Angeles Open the previous year. He was playing Jimmy Rempe, and the match was tied at 10. Rempe left Morro in jail—cue ball frozen on the head rail, seven ball two thirds of the way down the table. There was no such thing as trying to play safe against a champion in that situation. Morro did all he could— he took a stab at making the seven in the nearest corner. He missed by two inches, but the seven turned two rails and slid the length of the table into the opposite corner pocket, and Morro was straight in on the eight. He ran out, then ran the next two racks and it was over. Rempe never made a mistake, and he never had a chance.

There was no question: Morro Paez was a great player. He could make all the shots, and he did not choke for the money. He was also magnificently confident—a bouncing, bubbling player, hopping from shot to shot like a robin going from worm to worm. He was a natty dresser, favoring Palm Beach suits and silk shirts, and he was almost always smiling. Also, astonishingly often, he shit out. All of which made him one of the most dangerous pool players in the world.

He had assembled a gaudy retinue of stakehorses, including cue maker (and himself a terrific player) Jerry McWhorter; singer Jude Cole; and actor Keifer Sutherland.

Sure enough, there was Morro, doing his hip-hop act around his favorite table. Sutherland was sitting nearby, and I realized there was a serious game going on. Sitting by the table, cue in hand, glowering, was one of the top players on the tour, Californian Kim Davenport.

Just then, Morro made a cross-table bank on the eight, and when it went in Davenport shook his head once and moved up to rack the balls.

"Looks like we're late," I said to Tony. "And looks like Kim's giving him the eight."

"He's got to, to get the game," he whispered back. "Kim's a great player, one of the very best. He's used to giving weight, but I don't like his chances with Morro."

Davenport's status as one of the world's best players was undeniable. But tonight that ranking proved expensive. Paez was playing at least as well as Kim; the spot created a mismatch, and Kim knew it, and he quit, but not before he'd lost five thousand dollars.

Just then Morro saw us and came over, beaming. "Hey, I saw you beat Johnny," he said.

"I saw you beat Kim," Tony retorted, wolfishly. "I need the seven ball."

Paez threw back his head and laughed, then stared at Tony, wide-eyed, one hand splayed across his chest, parodying a heart attack. "The seven? You beat the world champion, man."

"Your town, your equipment," Tony said, pointing to the table where Paez had just won.

"I should get weight from you," Morro said. "But I'll play you even. I can't play tonight, but maybe tomorrow or—you going to Reno?"

"Yep."

"Maybe there."

"Maybe," Tony said. "But not even."

"Where are you going after that?"

"I don't know yet."

"Come on back here and we'll get a liability game going," Morro said. "Ernesto, Francisco, you, me, Parica, whoever."

"At Hard Times, where you guys rob everybody?"

"Hey, I lose in that game, man. But we might play at Jerry Jamgotchian's new place. You know? South Beach Billiards? We're setting up a six-by-twelve in the back and it ought to be ready by then."

"Yeah, that sounds good, Morro."

Paez turned to me, interested, checking me out with his bright accountant's eyes. "You staking Tony?"

"Sometimes."

Tony performed the introductions, and Morro asked, "You play too?"

"No," Tony and I said together, but Tony said it more emphatically.

"Fuck you," I said to Tony, and Morro Paez laughed.

NOVEMBER 29—IT WAS SUNDAY AFTERNOON, AND IN A FEW HOURS one of six remaining players would win. Tony was one of them, but to advance beyond sixth place, he had to beat someone he'd played several times but never beaten, veteran San Diego pro Jay Swanson.

This match, too, started badly. Tony hung a tough combination in the first rack, and Swanson went up 1–0, and then caught some great rolls in the second rack. He broke in the five, then missed his shot on the one but sent it two rails, Morro-style, toward the corner pocket where it knocked in the eight. He made the one through four, then tried a break-out shot on the six and missed it but left Tony hooked.

Tony missed a one-rail kick shot, leaving the six for Swanson. The seven and nine were lined up perfectly near the corner pocket, but Swanny got a bad angle on the combination and missed it. He left the cue ball on the end rail, though, and when Tony tried an eight-nine combo, he jawed it for the second straight rack, and Swanson went up 2–0. Then Tony missed an easy billiard, and found himself three games down.

But he refused to get down on himself the way he had against Johnson, and when Swanson made a mistake in the next rack, Tony ran four racks to take the lead, looking as tough as he had against Archer. From there, the match seesawed, neither player getting more than a game ahead. It was tied at five, at six, and at seven.

Along the way, Tony made the shot of the tournament, certainly the shot of the trip, and probably the most spectacular shot he'd ever made in tournament play. Trailing 6–5, he had a relatively easy out. The eight and the nine were at opposite ends of the table, the nine about a foot from the right corner pocket, a couple of inches off the end rail. When he made the eight, Tony hit the shot a little too hard, and it looked as though the cue would scratch in the other corner, opposite the one near the nine ball. Instead, the cue ball hung on the lip of the pocket, just inside the edge of the rail. Tony had escaped a scratch, and a sure loss, but he was so deep in the pocket he was corner-hooked on the nine—the edge of the rail was between the cue ball and the nine, making a straight shot at the nine impossible. The spectators had buzzed, louder and louder, as the cue ball headed for the pocket, and when it hung the buzz turned into a roar, which faded quickly into a groan as they realized he was hooked.

He looked at the situation for a full minute, then addressed the shot with the butt of his cue high in the air. I realized that he meant to hit a massé, which imparts terrific sideways spin to the cue ball, to get it to curve in midpath.

The crowd was hushed as Tony struck the cue ball sharply. It squirted out from the rail a few inches, then made a dramatic ninety-degree turn and rolled straight at the nine. It made contact at exactly the right point, and the nine rolled into the heart of the corner pocket. The crowd roared, then clapped. Tony shook his head and smiled, and Swanson did the same. To massé around the rail was one thing, but to hit the shot so that the spin caught at the right moment and made the cue turn exactly at the nine, was another entirely. To *make* the nine—well, it was simply a shot for the ages.

Unfortunately, Swanny was not awed. After the match was tied at seven, Swanson broke and ran two racks, and that was that. Tony had come back strong several times after falling behind and had made that great shot, but you don't win matches just because you play well. Sometimes, the other guy plays better. Great thrills, a win over the world's champion, a terrific shot, but sixth place. A thousand dollars. Better than losing. Next case.

XIV

Nit, Nevada

"Somebody's trying to kill me."
　　　　　　—Bucktooth, upon finding bones
　　　　　　　　　　in his salmon entrée

DECEMBER 2—THE L.A.-TO-RENO FLIGHT TOOK ONLY AN HOUR, BUT
it was an hour that Mike Lebron would have liked to spend in
any other way imaginable. Like a surprising number of pool
players, so fearless in other ways, Lebron was scared shitless of
flying. He had little choice, though. A nasty snowstorm had
turned much of Interstate 80, including Donner Pass, into a
ski slope, and the road had been closed. The Reno airport was
still open—barely. It looked as if anybody who wanted to get
into the Biggest Little City in the World for the next couple of
days was going to have to drop in from the sky.

　　Mike Lebron was across the aisle from me, and I felt for
him. He was pallid, sweating, gripping his armrest so hard
that the veins on the back of his bridge hand bulged alarm-
ingly. "Two to one Mike uses his barf bag," Tony whispered. I
thought for a moment. It was not a great bet, but I was desperate to cash a ticket. Mike Lebron was a dignified man, and I

knew he would do everything he could to preserve his usual decorum. "Done, my fifty, your hundred."

Meanwhile, Tony and Billy Incardona tried to comfort Mike the only way they knew how, by needling him unmercifully. Lebron could only manage a weak smile or two. Somehow, though, like Larry Mahan making it eight seconds to the buzzer on the back of a Brahma, Spanish Mike Lebron pulled through for me, staggering off the plane with his lunch intact. I felt like high-fiving him.

WHATEVER ELATION I FELT EVAPORATED FAST WHEN WE GOT TO THE Sands Regency. Banks of nickel slots surrounded the front entrance, patronized by legions of retirees—the Slot Zombies: sixtyish women with white curls, costume jewelry, and tubs of nickels, cigarettes clenched grimly in their jaws; their men nearby, wearing cheap windbreakers and off-brand denims and work boots and gimme caps with obscure slogans such as MAGNATude and WILD HORSE CAFE and WHERE THE HELL IS COPPEROPOLIS? The lighting (slot-machine flickers and the background harsh fluorescence); the blare of the slots and resultant squeals and groans; and acres of hideous red and gold carpeting gave the place a Dantean cast. It was a typical casino floor plan, which is to say a weird, disorienting, multi-level layout, so that once you got in, it was hard to find your way out. Exits and cashier windows were about as easy to unearth as truffles. If you did get lost, you'd never starve, although your cholesterol level might jump fifty points or so by the time help arrived: At various strategic points on the main floor were scattered a Baskin-Robbins, a Dunkin' Donuts and a Tony Roma's.

At least the room was clean and cheap—twenty-four dollars

per day for two queen beds, special pool tournament rate. There were locks on the windows, of course, so luckless gamblers wouldn't defenestrate themselves (bad for business). "I'm going to clock the tournament room," Tony said, and I nodded. It was all of 9 P.M., but suddenly I was seized with a deep ennui. "Call me if you get in action," I said, and as the door closed behind him I slipped into a muddy, troubled sleep.

DECEMBER 3—WHEN THE PHONE RANG, IT WASN'T TONY. IT WAS A woman's voice—one I didn't immediately recognize. "Whosis?"

"Nancy."

"Nancy?"

"Yes, Nancy," said Nancy, louder this time, as if the message might better penetrate my semiconscious skull if it were delivered more forcefully. "Nancy Shine. *Keith's* Nancy."

"Oh. Yeah?"

"Keith wants to see you, we just got in, we drove faster than God through the storm, they just opened the pass, I thought we were going to die, Keith wants to gamble."

"Oh, fuck. What time is it, Nancy?"

"Three-twenty."

"Sweet Jesus. Call me back at noon."

Tony stirred fitfully in the other bed as I hung up. "Who was that?" he muttered thickly.

"Don't worry about it," I said. "Wrong number." I put a pillow over my head and tried hard to pick up the threads of my interrupted dream.

I had been playing a lengthy snooker match against somebody—I couldn't remember who—before a motionless crowd in a darkened room, with no lights but those above the table, which was a six-by-

twelve Brunswick Dave Kling model, circa 1909, inlaid with ebony and white holly and mother-of-pearl, big blocky korbels above six massive bell-shaped legs. Like some sort of deep-sea creature, the table seemed to glow with its own light source as though the inlays were iridescent. The flawless green expanse, bathed in the blaze from two huge metal-shaded fixtures, stretched out to the edge of the gloom like a Narnian meadow, beckoning backward into the beginning of myself. The men in rows of old wooden folding chairs around the table were all infinite in their age and discernment, wearing fedoras and pork-pie hats and unfathomable expressions. Their eyes were bottomless, hidden by the black-on-black shadows of their hat brims, and the only ones I could recognize were Freddie Byers and another old man from the Stag Tavern in 1969 whose apologetic emphysemic cough I knew, and I wondered why his throat had not yet died. I was playing super-naturally. My opponent—was it Jimmy Moore?—was leaving me brutal shots, length-of-the-table cuts, long straight drives from the rail, kick shots out of hooks, but I was making *them. I prowled around that massive table, eyeing the shot from every angle, then got down on it feeling the smooth, cool wood of the Willie Hoppe under my chin and made the stroke slowly, precisely, powerfully. With three beautiful crisp clacks—cue on cue ball, cue ball on object ball, object ball on pocket iron—the shot would be made, and the dry grizzled faceless ones would clap, softly and politely. I would run the table then, but they would never clap again until I had made the final black. Then there would be another scratchy patter of applause, like the sound of dead October elm leaves sweeping across an old front porch in Cozad, Nebraska. I'd break, and hit the second-to-last ball of the right side of the rack, and three red balls would float out of formation and brush the rails and burrow back into their impregnable nest. Jimmy—it* was *Jimmy—would glare at me through steel-rimmed glasses, shake his white brush-cut head once, jack up on the rail with his pudgy bridge fingers bowed solid as gravestones, and throw the cue at the ball with his famous slip stroke, getting a terrific safety right back, not quite*

hooking me behind the brown but leaving me ten and a half feet from
the nearest red ball. I'd walk around the table and look at the cluster
of red balls, knowing I was going to make that three-ball combination
out of the rack with position on the pink . . .

The phone rang again. "Dave, it's Keith. Look, man, I'm
busted and I've got a great game here, we can't lose, I tell you
the guy shoots straight up in the air, he's a Canadian, John
Bear, and he can't play nine-ball—"

In my fog I remembered the pictures on the wall of the
Club Dynasty in Vancouver, about a lifetime ago. "John Bear
plays jam-up," I said, sighing, "and you know it. Get me a cup
of coffee. I'll be downstairs in a few minutes."

"Bring your cue."

KEITH MCCREADY JAMMED A STYROFOAM CUP IN MY HAND AS SOON AS
the elevator door opened and tried the little grin on. Here
was the proposition: John Bear wanted the eight. A hundred a
game, five ahead, freeze up five hundred. Impossible to know.
If Keith was right, it should be like bank robbery. If Keith was
not quite right, it could be like handing out twenty-dollar bills
to the busted-out drunks out on Virginia Street. And if Keith
was doing business, of course, I would be just another
dumped stakehorse with a bullet-riddled bankroll.

"No."

"Aw, shit, David, why not?" I said nothing, just looked at him
mournfully, like a man who had been interrupted when he
was on the verge of winning the 1948 United States snooker
championship. He looked at me speculatively. "Awright, let's
go shoot some craps, and if I win you the five hundred, will
you put it in action?"

What else was I going to do in Reno at four in the morning?

"Oh, hell. Sure. But you got one bullet to work with. One hundred."

"No problem." The gap-toothed grin was back in full force: What, me worry? We walked over to the pit. "Cocktails," Keith brayed.

Just before 5 A.M. Keith was down to forty dollars on the come line when he caught a hand, and in twenty more minutes I grabbed the little fucker and made him cash out $920 worth of chips. I gave him $210, took $210 and put it in the left pocket of my jeans, with my bankroll, and put the other $500 in the right-hand pocket. Keith hooked another beer from a passing waitress's tray, and when she started to bitch he tossed her the ten. "Give me some of that," Nancy said to him, "or it'll be fuckin gone."

"Fuck you." But Keith handed her four twenties, and she folded them twice and put them in the left cup of her bra. "Hey, baby, you know I'll find it there." He grinned. "Let's go find John-boy."

That wasn't hard. He was in the practice room, a conference-room-turned-poolroom on the mezzanine. John Bear was big and burly, appropriate to his name, with slicked-back black hair and calculating eyes. He smiled and shook my hand, and I said, "Let's make this game even," and he said shortly, "No chance," and smiled again as I shrugged and posted the five hundred on the light.

That's the last I saw of it. John Bear could have given Keith the six. Not that Keith was playing badly, but Bear started the set by running four racks. "Okay, you got me," I said, and ignored Keith's pleas for "one more bullet," opting instead for a shitty breakfast at the cafe on the mezzanine. By the time I was done the first matches were getting set to start, so I wandered into the tournament room to check the pairings.

Since I'd been asleep when Tony had come back I had no idea who he was playing. His first match was in two hours, I discovered—against Johnny Archer. I groaned. There's nothing like a motivated opponent.

Just then I heard raised voices across the room, right under the noses of the tournament officials, who sat on an elevated scorers' dais. "What's first place in the tournament worth? Ten grand or some shit?" somebody was bellowing. "Here, I'll play you for that. You can win first place right now."

Oh, God, I thought, that has to be the Tooth, and sure enough, there he was, up on his hind legs, woofing at Tony Ellin, doing his Toothasaurus act, spittle flying, waving a huge wad of hundreds above his head, so close one of the scorers could have reached out and grabbed it. "What's the next five places worth?" he roared, pulling out another bale. "WHAT'S *ALL* THE FREAKIN PLACES WORTH???" He pulled out yet another clump of greenbacks and held the whole pile out in front of him like Macbeth's dagger, shoving it with two hands toward Ellin. "You can win every place in this tournament playing me," he screamed.

"Jesus, Rich, easy, easy, you'll get me barred," Ellin said, glancing nervously up at the scorers' table, backing up even more. "I'll talk to you later." He broke into full retreat and hustled away.

The PBTA was taking itself very seriously, and the organization had decided that gambling was Bad for the Image of the Game, which struck me as being rather hypocritical, and also shortsighted from a marketing standpoint. Some of the real outlaws, such as Jimmy Mataya and Keith McCready, even Cole Dickson, were among the most enjoyable players to watch. The pool tour would be in even more trouble than it was already, I thought, if the players were all Fellowship of Christian Athletes types, like so many of the golfers. I could see that they would want to safeguard the integrity of the tour stops, and had to outlaw gambling on those matches. But why act as though gambling didn't exist? Almost all the top players were or had been big gamblers. A case in point was Billy Incardona, one of the tour's media darlings who often did commentary on TV matches. When he wasn't doing that, he was booking action on the tournaments. He was too important to reprimand, so the PBTA just looked the other way.

Anyway, I stepped up to Bucktooth and said hello. "Hey, hey, how are you?" he said, bringing his voice down a couple of notches. "I'm having trouble scaring up a game, all these nits."

"I noticed," I said dryly. Just then somebody from the stands yelled, "Hey, you! You, the loudmouth! I'll try you some right now."

"Get your ass down here!" the Tooth roared back.

"Oh, God, what the fuck is this?" Tony had come up behind us. "Where did you go, by the way?" he said to me.

"You wouldn't believe it, but don't worry, I'm a C-note to the good."

"Wow."

"Fuck you, it wasn't easy."

Just then Bucktooth's challenger got to floor level. He was pretty near floor level himself—about five feet four—with reddish hair and reddish eyes, too. "I'll play you some one-pocket, five hundred a game."

"Let's go." The Tooth led him into the practice room, and Tony and I followed. His name turned out to be Kamikaze Bob. He was flashing serious cash. Somebody said he was a pilot, which, given his name, was too horrible to contemplate. Kamikaze Bob put five hundred on the light with the Tooth's money and won the flip for break.

In one-pocket, the break is a touch shot, soft, precise, careful. It's an effort to steer balls to your side of the table without letting the cue ball free so that your opponent has a shot, even a bank, at his pocket. So it was a real jaw-dropper when Kamikaze Bob smashed the balls wide open like he was playing eight-ball down at the corner tavern. The Tooth couldn't believe his eyes. "Somebody's settin me up," he said to Tony. "This guy can't be real." Even after Bucktooth had won $3,500—which Tony and I did *not* get a piece of—he still couldn't believe it. "Something's not right, this just doesn't happen," he said. So when Kamikaze Bob tried to make a nine-ball game, even, for $500 a game, the Tooth declined despite our urging. "He's gotta be trappin me," he said darkly.

TONY PLAYED WELL, AGAIN, AGAINST JOHNNY ARCHER. WELL ENOUGH to win—except he scratched an astounding five times on the break. Four of those times, the cue ball popped back and killed, but got kicked in by another ball. Archer seemed a little spooked by the previous week's game, and didn't play perfectly, but he had a lot better luck on the breaks than Tony did. The final score was 13–9, which meant that over the past week Tony had outscored Archer in their two tournament meetings, 18–16. But that still spelled an early trip to the losers' bracket here.

COLE DICKSON HAILED ME FROM THE MEZZANINE BAR AS I LEFT THE tournament room. I sat down wearily next to him and ordered a beer. It was barely noon and I'd already put in a long day.

Cole was one of my favorite pool players. He was absolutely terrific when he was on, but any time he was a force to be reckoned with. Cole Dickson was a bit of a throwback, a gunslinger if ever there were one, a tough, cold-blooded hustler who could handle himself in any situation—and would do anything for a friend. He had fought a lot of battles with himself, winning some and losing some, and as a result he was a mass of contradictions. Cole loved the road, the hustle and the high life, but he also loved to hunt and fish and work on his old Victorian house in tiny Davenport, Washington, where he had lived for the past decade. And he adored his wife, Lori, and his two daughters. He'd been a road player, on and off, since he was a long-haired hippie kid from Oakland, California, in the 1970s, when he could hit a baseball into the sky as high and far as you could see, then take off like Rickey Henderson and *catch* the ball when it came down. He was one of the most remarkable players in the game.

Even Bucktooth, who has had his share of contretemps with Cole Dickson, admitted this to me. "Cole, you know, him and Keither, they both had so much talent when they were kids it was pitiful. I wanted to take Cole and make him a champion, but he was always whacked out on them pills and raising hell, I couldn't teach him anything. But when he was right he'd make shots you couldn't imagine anyone making. I mean, you'd be playing one-pocket against him and you knew you had him sewn up tighter than a bull's ass, and then you'd see the shot he was going to try and you'd be so happy that you were jumping out of your skin because you knew nobody could ever make a shot like that, and then he'd *make* it. He's made some of the most amazing shots ever been made on a pool table."

When I asked Cole about this, he snorted. "There's no pills to it. Bucktooth, he couldn't teach me shit, because I was better than he was, and he knows it."

As a kid, Cole ran around the country hustling pool like few other players could, playing in bars, poolrooms, wherever he could make a game. He was just old enough to have been able to attend the Janscos' gambling fests in Johnston City. A program from one of the brothers' gatherings shows Cole, sporting shoulder-length blond curls, smiling insolently at the camera.

Now Cole wanted to talk about one of his compadres from those days. "You hear about Mataya?" he asked. By that I presumed he didn't mean Ewa, but rather her ex, Jimmy Mataya, the Michigan hustler, still one of the most flamboyant players in the game.

"He got here this morning and headed right for the craps table," Cole said. "He hadn't been there twenty minutes before he was a thousand down." I thought about Keith's hand with almost guilty pleasure. "So he asks the pit boss could he have a chit for some breakfast, and the guy says something like, fuck you, what makes you so special, what's a thousand bucks? So Mataya's getting more and more pissed about it, and in the meantime he just keeps losing. Pretty soon he's *five* thousand down, and finally the pit boss figures the Sands can afford the price of some ham and eggs, and gives Jim a breakfast ticket.

"So he stalks into the restaurant, and when they bring him a glass of ice water Jimmy picks it up and throws it through the mirror behind the counter, then turns around and heads up to his room. And it ain't long before about eight security guys come up and collect him and toss him and his bags out in a snowbank. Now he's barred from playing in the tournament, can't even come in the door. He's just *fucked.*" He shook his head. "Poor bastard."

"Hey, Cole, you heard the rest of it?" The growl came from behind us, and I looked over Cole's shoulder. It was Billy Cress. We exchanged hellos. Billy offered me a beer. I bought him one instead, and he turned the talk back to Jimmy Mataya.

"So Mataya is screwed, he can't play in the tournament and he's five thousand stuck. So he just went down a few minutes ago and hocked his jewelry, his cue, and got everything he could off his credit cards, maxed 'em all out . . ."

"Oh, fuck." Cole could see it coming.

"Yeah," Cress said. "He raised like twenty-seven thousand, which was everything he was worth, and he went over to the Cal-Neva sports book and put every friggin penny of it on the Lions against the Browns, giving twelve points."

"No," I said.

"Yep. He's dead busted, and if he loses he'll have no fuckin shot to pay it back. He swears if the Lions don't cover he'll kill himself."

"The *Detroit Lions*," I said. "I can think of other people I'd rather have controlling my fate."

"No shit," Cole Dickson said.

IT WAS 9 P.M. AND I WAS IN THE PRACTICE ROOM WITH TONY AND THE Tooth. I'd been sweating pool matches all day, but this promised to be entertaining. The Tooth was woofing like only he could. It had started at dinner. We'd gone to Tony Roma's, which was awful, but there was no other cuisine in Reno that could persuade us to go outside. It was five above and the wind was blowing. Bucktooth had absolutely tortured the waitress: "I said *ranch,* ma'am, ranch dressing, not this orange shit. Please! Take it away quick!" Followed by, "My God, this salmon's nothing but *bones!* Ma'am!" Snapping fingers. "Somebody's trying to *kill* me! I can't eat this! Bring me something else!"

Now he was playing to the gallery, rolling some balls around, muttering louder and louder as he watched José

Parica giving Keith McCready nine to six on the next table for two hundred a game.

"I been sitting on my ass so long I look like a chair. I'm drunk, I'm old, I've got broken legs, broken shoulder, broken everything, but I want to play. Where are all these champions at? I guess they don't want to play me. Shit, I've emptied more champions than anyone in the history of pool."

"Bucktooth, put a fuckin sock in it," McCready said irritably, watching Parica draw a bead on another ball. Whoever was staking Keith tonight wouldn't be happy. Keith would play great for several shots but then he would try something he couldn't do and Parica would shoot the lights out.

Bucktooth snorted in derision. "These two guys here, these two *champions,* are playing for two hundred dollars. Shit. When's someone going to play for some real money? They're all nits here. This is a town full of nits. Reno, Nevada, gambling central. Shit. They got low limits at all the tables. Every pool player you could ever meet is here and nobody wants to play for anything. They ought to call it Nit City. Nit, Nevada. I been to six county fairs, three goat ropings, and two ape rapings and I never seen nothin like this."

During this lament McCready had quit Parica, and so the Tooth turned both barrels on the little Filipino. "José, if you beat me you'll win so much money you'll be the king of the fucking Philippines. You'll make Marcos look like a two-dollar mooch. Come on, Paprika, what do you say?" Parica grinned, shook his head slightly, and said, "Nine to six and the breaks."

"What? You just gave Keither that game and emptied him, and he's a fuckin champion. I'm an old man. I'm drunk, and I'm rich. Come on, Giant Killer, what are we going to do? Give me a ten to five, and let's play for ten thousand." He fanned a stack of hundreds out on the table.

"Ten to six."

"Shit."

"GREAT, JUST GREAT." I WOKE TO THE SOUND OF TONY, BITCHING about something on the telephone. "I can't believe the Tooth didn't take that game." I knew right then what that meant— somebody had robbed Kamikaze Bob, who had certainly seemed unfazed by his one-pocket lesson and ready to go off for a big number the other night.

Sure enough, Tony hung up and said, "That was Billy. Guess who dropped sixteen grand playing nine-ball last night?"

"Kamikaze Bob."

"You got it. And he lost to a kid."

"Who?"

"Boy George. You remember me telling you about Boy George? He won the AA tournament here a year ago. He's from Stockton, sort of a tough kid, always has money, runs around looking like a gang-banger, L.A. Raiders clothes, cellu- lar phone, enough gold around his neck to finance a Central American revolution. He's not afraid to gamble. He gave Kamikaze Bob the seven. And the Tooth wouldn't play the guy even. Shit, we could have made a ton. Anyway, Boy George could be another Moro, only he probably doesn't have *that* much money. He's been tryin to get me to give him the Orange Crush, the five and the break. He might get that game here."

"That's a lot of weight."

"I can beat him that way."

"Let's make the game, we know he's got plenty of cash."

For the first time in a major tournament since we went on the road Tony had missed the money here. The early loss to

Archer took a toll—but I thought it might be a blessing in disguise. He'd been playing real well, and getting knocked out early might enable him to get a pretty good game.

In the early afternoon I went by to clock the tournament and the practice room, and I saw Jimmy Mataya in a dark corner of the bar, looking reckless and dissolute and not in the least bit worried. Billy Cress was there, too, and he motioned me over to collect a pay-back beer. I talked a little to Mataya, and bought him a cocktail. His buddies were keeping him in food and drinks; he'd literally laid all he had on the line. "You have the balls of a bull moose," I told him. "But why the Lions?"

"Well, I'm from Michigan, of course, although that doesn't really have that much to do with it," he said hurriedly, making the point to me, and maybe to himself, that he wouldn't risk his all on a sucker hometown bet. "I just like the matchup and the spread, that's all."

"Well, it's a few points," I said. "But I'm pulling for you."

"Thanks," he said. "Everybody's been great."

The Bet, as it was now known, was the primary topic of conversation for the tournament. Probably 60 percent of the people I talked to thought the Lions would get their asses kicked. Even those who picked them to cover thought it was a pretty strange game to plunge on. But somehow nobody was surprised. After all, Diamond Jim Mataya, aka Pretty Boy Floyd, was known to be impulsive, and fearless, and crazier than Winnie Ruth Judd. "If he wins," Billy Cress told me, "Sunday night will get pretty much out of hand."

AS I WALKED INTO THE TOURNAMENT ROOM, SOMEBODY CALLED MY name. I looked around and there, a master of understatement in a black fringed buckskin jacket, orange shirt, orange Nikes, and his usual half a dozen diamonds, was Curtis.

"How have you been?" I asked.

"No good, man," he said, his usual deadpan self, but his smile contradicted him. "You wanna play some nine-ball?"

"No, but I'll play you some one-pocket."

"Forget that shit." Curtis shook his head. "I'm gonna go play some blackjack. You wanna come? We gotta go over to the Hilton. Better rules."

A few minutes later, Curtis chose a table. Both of us bet the $5 minimum. I kept betting $5 a hand, slowly getting ground down, but when Curtis liked the deck he jacked up the bet to $20, $50, all the way to the $200 maximum. After half an hour and a couple of favorable decks Curtis had earned $2,000— and a steady glare from the pit boss, stationed directly behind the dealer's left shoulder.

Just then Bucktooth walked up. He knew better than to sit down—he'd been barred from the Hilton for counting cards, which was a fate that seemed likely to befall Curtis at any time, so he just stood behind me and gave advice. I began increasing my bets when he thought the deck was favorable, and I went from $40 down to $150 ahead in fifteen minutes.

"Mr. Cook, we really can't have you doing that," the pit boss said, his attention diverted now from Curtis.

"Why? You sure don't mind when I go over to the craps table and drop a few thousand, do you?"

"No, sir."

"Well then, why shouldn't I be able to stand here and talk to my friend? You guys make me sick."

Uh-oh, I thought. The pit boss turned on his heel, picked up a telephone, and dialed. "The deck is plus ten, bet the farm," the Tooth whispered to me, and I pushed $200 out there. "Cash plays, two hundred," the dealer said, and the pit boss whipped around, phone still in his ear. I got dealt two aces; the dealer had a nine showing. I pushed another $200 forward. The dealer gave me a ten on one side and an eight on the other. Curtis had paint showing and declined another card. He flashed me a look at the jack he had in the hole. The dealer flipped his hole card up and it was a king. A $200 win for Curtis, and $300 for me, plus a push. "Shuffle that deck," the pit boss growled.

"What? There's half the deck left," Curtis said, outraged.

"I can't believe you guys," the Tooth stormed. "If I get terminal cancer and I got nothing to lose I'm gonna come back here and shoot every one of you motherfuckers." He walked away, shaking his head.

"Well, *shit,*" said the dealer, watching the Tooth go. "I haven't heard that one before."

"We better hope he stays healthy," the pit boss said. "That son of a bitch will do exactly what he says he'll do."

DECEMBER 5—BOY GEORGE WAS A REAL BEAUTY, A BABY-FACED KID who was definitely older than he looked, which after you stripped him of the L.A. Raiders warm-up jacket and the L.A. Raiders sweatshirt and the L.A. Raiders baseball cap and more layers of gold than King Tut was buried with was probably about seventeen. In calendar years he was probably twenty-three or twenty-four. In brain years, sort of like dog years, I figured, somewhere around eight—at least in terms of common sense.

Otherwise, why would he be talking about fighting Mitch? Mitch was a pretty good pool player and inveterate boasting ladies' man who hung around the Q Club. He was up for the tournament. Whatever ego forces ruled Mitch in terms of the way he related to women, and in terms of gambling, had also induced him to learn about eight different varieties of martial arts. Mitch was about thirty, six feet even, maybe one-eighty, with the look of an athlete. His straight brown hair was fashionably long, and he wore Levi's, a leather jacket, Nikes, and an open-necked shirt displaying a gold necklace—demure by Curtis or Boy George standards.

He also had Charlie Manson eyes that shone like new pennies when he talked about fucking Boy George up, as he was doing right now, sitting next to me in the bleachers while we watched Paulie Brienza get barbecued by Steve Mizerak.

Boy George and Mitch were negotiating the terms of a prize fight. Each side was talking about putting up ten grand. A bell-hop had been found who would let them into a room for a couple of hundred, so whatever happened the room couldn't be traced to them. Damage. Broken lamps. Bloodstains on the carpet. Crime scene. Whatever.

"Ten grand," Mitch was saying. "He wants to go for five, but I'm not doin it for less than ten. We fight until somebody can't go anymore." He laughed. "Which ain't gonna be *me*. I don't want to kill the kid, that's the only thing I'm worried about here, but it could happen. He has no idea what he's doing, fuckin with me."

Fight until death or disabling injury in a Reno hotel room for ten grand. As an investment vehicle, the Detroit Lions were beginning to look better. "I think we can get side action out of his friends," Mitch was saying. I wasn't interested—in this ridiculous proposed fight, in watching this nine-ball match. Seeing Brienza made me uncomfortable. He was staying, rent-free, in Tony's house and at the same time siding with Tony's opponents in the fight over the Q Club, which was the primary cause of my player's worry, which translated to money out of my pocket. And Tony's. I knew how the match would turn out. I'd seen them play in a tournament a year earlier. Paulie would play Mizzie tough for a few games, and then fold up.

I bailed. I needed to get away from the whole scene for a little while, so I drove over to the Keystone Cue & Cushion, a little poolroom about ten blocks away. It's one of my favorite rooms in the West, run by a friendly couple, Mickey Peele and his girlfriend, Becky. In a town singularly lacking in good food, the Keystone's french fries stood out in sharp relief.

Cole Dickson was practicing at Table Two. He was more comfortable here than over in the practice room; even more than Bucktooth, he'd had serious difficulties with the authorities at various Reno casinos.

"Where are you and Tony going next?" he asked me.

"I don't know, we have a couple of spots in L.A. and then we'll be back here for Grady's one-pocket tournament. Are you going to that?" I asked.

"No, it's at the Hilton and I don't do the Hilton." He smiled.

"Anyway, that's my plan. Why do you ask?"

"Thought you might want to take a quick trip to Seattle in there somewhere. I got a game with Harry any time I want it."

"I'm sure he'd be thrilled to see me again."

"Hell, Harry doesn't mind. He just likes to step up and play."

True enough, I thought. Some people might characterize Harry Platis as a sucker, but you had to admire his guts and his competitiveness. He didn't care if he had the worst of the matchup—he just ground away like a boxer unafraid to take a punch in order to deliver one.

It would be fun to stake Cole. But did I want to return to the scene of the robbery? Well, why not? If Harry could handle it, I sure could.

IT WAS SATURDAY NIGHT, AND MOST OF THE PLAYERS ALREADY ELIMI-nated from the tournament—and, likely as not, eliminated from the craps tables as well—were in the practice room, trying to line up stakehorses, make games, or just watch the action.

Billy Incardona methodically drilled a promising young player named Bobby Wales from Georgia, who was particu-larly well regarded by the other players at the tournament because he was traveling with a stunning blonde who looked like a young Marilyn Monroe. Wales was maybe nineteen, and he had no idea that Incardona was one of the best players ever to pick up a cue. He flummoxed Incardona after the match was over by saying, "Jeez, if an old fart like you beat me I must not be worth a shit."

Meanwhile, the Tooth was at center stage, trying to match up with Bobby Hunter, a top-rated Nevada pro. He wanted nine to six, and Hunter wasn't having any. "I'll play you even," he said.

"You want to play an old man even? All right, put one hand in your pocket and hold on to your dick and I'll play you even, you world champion motherfucker. You can play with yourself while I play you one-handed." Hunter could hardly refuse, and he didn't.

Meanwhile Tony had been trying in his much quieter way to get into action, with little success. Suddenly, though, it seemed like things might be looking up.

Tony had been trying to get a game with a Minnesota player named Louie Lemke. Lemke had a reputation as a tough player, and he hadn't seen Tony play at all recently, so Tony had been asking him for the eight, with no success. But this evening, Lemke walked into the tournament room accompanied by none other than Kamikaze Bob.

Lemke made game with another San Franciscan, Dave Piona, playing a set for a thousand. Piona was not at the top of his game, and Lemke made short work of him, taking the thousand and splitting it with Kamikaze Bob. "Hey, Louie," Tony called. "I want that five hundred you owe me." It was true; he had lent Lemke the money months before. When Lemke demurred, Tony saw his opening, and took a page out of the Tooth's book.

"You're a no-good prick," he said to Lemke in a louder tone. "I want my five hundred and you just won it, and you ain't leaving until I get it."

"Fuck you." Lemke glared at him, embarrassed.

"Hey, you see this motherfucker?" Tony asked loudly, pointing at Lemke. "He's a no-good piece of shit. Don't anybody ever lend him a quarter. He's a nit motherfucker."

"Why don't you get your ass up here and play me some?" Lemke demanded.

"Give me a chance and you can play for ten thousand," Tony retorted. "But I want my money first."

"Fuck you. I'll play you a set even, ten ahead for two thousand."

"Don't play him even, Tony," the Tooth called. "Make him give you something. You ought to get the eight."

"Fuck that, Rich," said Tony, who was into his role with the intensity of a Barrymore. "I don't care if he kicks my ass, I'm going to play this piece of shit no matter what happens." He turned back to Lemke. "I'll play you even right now, ten ahead for five thousand, Louie, but if we're going to make this game you're going to put up fifty-five to my forty-five. I'm not playin against my own money."

Lemke, still furious, turned and whispered to Kamikaze Bob, who nodded vigorously and hauled a roll out of his pocket. "Here's the fifty-five, asshole, get up here and let's play some," Lemke snarled.

I peeled off $4,500 and the battle was joined.

Lemke's anger was barely controlled as he won the flip and broke, making two balls. He ran the balls off smoothly, until he got a little funny on the nine and dogged it, which did nothing to improve his disposition—particularly when Tony made it and immediately ran four more racks before missing.

It never got any better for Louie Lemke. Tony made the nine on the break three times, and Lemke missed shot after shot. He would make the difficult shots—he showed amazing ability to make jump shots, jumping the cue ball over an intervening ball and making the object ball—but he seemed to have a lot more trouble with the routine. By the time Tony got ten games ahead, the time bill was only eight dollars. The match had lasted less than an hour—perhaps the most lucrative fifty minutes of the trip since Seattle.

Bucktooth, meanwhile, had won three hundred dollars from Bobby Hunter playing one-handed before Hunter quit. Immediately after that session a couple of rough-looking young characters started tush-hogging the Tooth.

"Look at that loud old motherfucker. He's got a lot of money. Maybe we ought to take it from him right now," one of the punks said.

Wrong thing to say.

The Tooth grabbed the four and the fourteen off the table in one hand, and the eight in the other hand and glared at the guy who had threatened him. "Hey, you know, when I start chuckin fuckin pool balls your fuckin head is going to look like a sack of shit," he yelled. "You think I won't whack your young ass? I sure as fuck *will*. FUCK IT. I'M JUST GONNA WHACK EVERY-FUCKIN-BODY IN HERE." He drew back his arm to throw and the guy and his friend, horrified, ran like rats.

"Easy, Tooth, easy." Tony was in front of him.

"Easy my ass!" The Tooth bellowed. "I worked too hard for my money to get ripped off by some ignorant country asshole who . . ."

"I know, I know," Tony said. "But they're gone, Rich. They're *gone*. Calm down."

"I'd a whacked every fuckin body in the room," Bucktooth muttered balefully, dropping his hand, still clutching the eight ball. "I'm like Nolan fuckin Ryan with these . . ."

DECEMBER 6—SUNDAY WAS GAME DAY. SWEET REDEMPTION FOR some, the Garden of Agony for (most) others. If the *Reno Gazette* had run a real Sunday box score in agate type on the Monday morning sports scoreboard page, it would have looked like this:

SANDS REGENCY TOURNAMENT

Championship:

Earl Strickland d. Steve Mizerak, 13–9; Strickland +**$10,000,** Mizerak +**$6,000.**

Week's totals (cumulative):

Jim Mataya: +**$19,300.** (Detroit Lions 28, Cleveland Browns 10.)

Kamikaze Bob: −**$50,000** (approx; precise figures unavailable at press time.)

Boy George: **+15,000.** Boy George v. Mitch: No Action (disagreement over purse.)

McCumber/Annigoni: **+$4,800.**
(McCumber v. Annigoni: McCumber wins **$280**; Annigoni is still **+$500** on the season.)

Bucktooth: **+$4,000.**

Almost every other pool player at the tournament: **Busted.**

I showed up at the mezzanine bar outside the tournament room just in time to catch the Detroit score on the TV. A huge cheer went up; even the players who weren't big fans of Mataya, and there were many of those, were impressed with his play. And his close friends were really relieved. There was a real fear that he would, indeed, have done himself harm if he had lost.

All such thoughts were forgotten an hour later when the winner strolled into the mezzanine bar decked out in a silk suit, Italian loafers, snowy white shirt, and silk tie complete with blinking neon tie tack, a gorgeous brunette resting comfortably on his arm. "Party tonight at the Flamingo Hilton, boys, suite 1937. Great eats, all you want to drink. But please"—a big wink—"bring your own ladies."

After that, the championship match between Mizzie and Earl was anticlimactic, but it would have been anyway. Earl had regained his will to win after the L.A. disaster, not to mention his break, and he was way too tough for Mizerak. Buddy Hall, Mr. Consistent, beat Johnny Archer to take third place.

By evening, the players began dispersing, and the true toll of the tournament began to show. For most of the players, trying to win money at a Reno tournament is a Sisyphean proposition. The money they bring, the money they win playing pool, all of it departs via craps, blackjack, the sports book, the slots. They are used to gambling smart, betting on their own abilities and winning, and they tend to think of themselves as smart gamblers no matter what the game; in Nevada that is dangerous thinking.

I asked Mike Lebron how he had done for the week, and he said simply, "Too much casino." A California player named Dickie Renk, who'd won a thousand dollars in prize money, was bumming for gas money to get back home. The thousand plus the three hundred he'd brought with him were gone. For some reason I gave him twenty dollars, and I watched him go downstairs and put it down on the come line.

That night, Tony and I had to make a decision. We had pretty much determined not to make the eastern swing on the train—we wanted to return for Grady's tournament, and prospects for action in Omaha in January weren't nearly as attractive. But that tournament didn't start for more than four weeks. Of course, there was Christmas to consider.

"We can go down to L.A. and get in that liability game," Tony said. "It's a hard dollar, but it's action just the same."

I had something else on my mind. "How do you feel about Cole's spot against Harry Platis?" I asked.

"At nine to six? I like it a lot. Harry's playing a lot better, and Cole doesn't have to win, but I like his chances."

"Why don't I go up there and do that, and meet you back in L.A.? At least then I could get a decent night's sleep."

"That's a good idea," said Tony seriously. "You're getting to be quite the traveling stakehorse, eh?"

"I figure it increases our reach a little bit."

"I think it makes sense, buddy, I really do," Tony said. "I like the game and with you around to watch Cole he might not pull some of his crazier moves." He smiled. "I'd be happy to get rid of you for a day or two. In fact, you could stay the whole week."

"Thanks, I love you too, but dealing with Cole and Harry, I think a quick hit probably is the way to go."

"Yeah, well you put a quick hit on me this afternoon."

"A hundred and eighty bucks. Big deal. I can't help it you gave me a game I could finally beat you at." At the Keystone Cue & Cushion, Tony had given me the three out, with him breaking again.

Somehow, this time I had managed to win a set for eighty and one for a hundred that way.

"With that and the hundred you won on Lebron, you're practically even."

"I wouldn't call being down five bills practically even."

"Of course you wouldn't. You're a fuckin nit."

XV

Return to Platisville

"You picked a real beauty."
—J.D., gazing at Cole Dickson

DECEMBER 10—IT WAS 8 A.M. I GLANCED ACROSS AT COLE DICKSON, stretched out in the passenger seat of his truck, and swore under my breath. He was sleeping peacefully, which is what I wanted to be doing instead of picking my way through traffic and freezing rain toward the Casino Club. The Seattle reprise had looked like a soft spot, but Cole had already found a way to make it interesting. The enigmatic Cole Dickson was coming into sharper focus for me now. He started playing pool when he was fifteen, and before the year was out he was on the road, playing fabulously, gradually figuring out how to win. "After I learned a few things on the pool table, I had to learn my way around the people," he had told me a couple of days ago, as we left Reno. "For a while, everybody was double-steerin me, you know, play this guy, play that guy. I would have got beat a lot more than I did, at first, but they told me I had a lot of heart, and I guess that's right. I busted a lot of players that should have beat me." By the time he was nineteen he was beating champions, and he had launched his career as a professional gambler.

For a decade Cole made much of his living in the casinos of Nevada, playing blackjack. In 1987 the Washoe County District Attorney's Office accused him of cheating at cards, not a crime that the state of Nevada views lightly. Prosecutors contended he switched cards with a partner at the Flamingo Hilton in Reno, while a confederate distracted the dealer and another loitered behind the table to block any view of the exchange. The casino videotapes were grainy, out of focus, and inconclusive, but they were enough to convict him. Cole was sentenced to thirteen years in Nevada State Prison, but won a suspension of the sentence and probation, which he successfully completed.

His arrest and conviction had a profound effect on Cole Dickson. Since then he'd been trying to stay straight and work construction, but it was pretty dull stuff compared to his former life. I was reminded of Tony, trying to give up the game and get a normal job during his marriage. It is not an uncommon tug of war, but it can be psychologically trying. For a lot of years, Cole had equated hustling, making a score, making a lot of money, with his own identity, his masculinity. Another hustler-gone-straight told me once, "Everything was connected to my making quick money—even my sex life. I haven't been able to get it up since I quit gambling." It wasn't that bad for Cole, but it wasn't easy, either, and sometimes the call of the road was irresistible. Like last night.

We'd driven in Cole's Ford pickup through the frozen, desolate high desert of eastern Oregon to the outskirts of Davenport. But Cole hadn't wanted to go home yet. "Hang a right," he'd said. "We're going to Spokane."

"Cole," I'd said. "Spokane is in the wrong direction. We have to be in Seattle at nine A.M. to play Harry." This awful fact was true. Harry had insisted: He wanted to play Cole, but he had a busy day planned. It was nine A.M. or nothing. It could be a shrewd move, I thought; Harry probably figured mornings might be Cole's soft spot.

"I know, I know. But I know a card room where I can make some money tonight." This was not my normal road partner. Tony would have been ready for a little bean curd and a good night's sleep. Cole and I opted for a cheeseburger and a beer, and then hit The Shed, a ratty-looking card room next door to an equally shoddy poolroom in downtown Spokane.

"Slide me a hundred," Cole said. "This is the easiest spot in life, right here. I'll bury these guys."

By 1 A.M. the interment was complete, although hardly the way Cole had envisioned it: We were five hundred dollars stuck, and Cole hocked his cue to the house for the last hundred. He was getting horrible cards, and the ten-dollar limit didn't provide much opportunity to move anybody off a good hand. The low limit also made Cole less than cautious about staying in some hands. It was a bad combination. Of course, I unhocked his cue; he needed it to win my money back. And our visit to Harry had new urgency.

I was now dealing with the grittier aspects of being a stake-horse. I drove and let Cole rest; my player had to be as fresh as possible. It didn't matter that I'd slept only two hours, or that my head felt like it was full of wet cardboard, or that I could still smell the smoke from the card room and feel it in the rawness of my eyes, or that I could still taste the acidic tang of weak, burned 7-Eleven coffee in the back of my throat, guzzled while I gassed up the truck near Snoqualmie Pass. My job was to deliver Cole to the Gold Crowns in the back of the Casino Club in as good a shape as life would let me—and put up the jack for him to gamble against an intense, competitive, well-rested multimillionaire. But so what? As we turned off the freeway, it still looked like a soft spot.

The Jiffy Lubes and Kentucky Frieds and Kmarts and Nevada Bobs of Aurora were even more depressing today than they had been the first time I'd seen them, because after touring the country, I realized that more and more of it looked like this now. This endless schlock could be Baltimore or L.A. or Chicago or Miami or Philly or even suburban Toronto or Vancouver.

As we walked into the Casino Club I had a little déjà vu flash of Monk and Billy, but they weren't there. Neither was Harry. Most of the hard-core railbirds were, though; they'd obviously heard there was action. Zimmerman was there, and Vince. The house man was Timmy, the redheaded kid who'd played well in losing to Monk. J.D. was the first one to confront me: "So you're back for another piece of Harry, eh?"

"Not really," I said. "I'm just hanging with Cole a little bit."

"You picked a real beauty."

Cole did look a little rough, despite sleeping all across Washington. "Find me a Jack Daniel's," he whispered to me as he began to hit some balls.

"Sure?" I whispered back. He glared at me. "Fuckin A I'm sure. I gotta settle myself."

I watched him practice for a few minutes. He favored a spread-out stance, looking squat and powerful over the ball, Paul Newman eyes gleaming with concentration.

The place got a buzz and I looked up and there was Harry Platis, walking in the back door. When he saw me he stopped and smiled a narrow-eyed smile, looking at me like I was a surprise witness for the opposition. "Bucktooth's not here, is he? Or Tony?"

"No."

"You stakin Cole?" he asked gruffly.

"Yep, Harry, I am," I said.

"Well, let's get the fuckin money up, then," he roared, clouting me on the back with a big paw and giving me another smile, a real one this time. We each put a thousand on the light.

Harry won the toss and put a great break on Cole, but he managed to reverse it beautifully, sweeping a ball on to his side and leaving Harry shooting off the rail by his hole—at nothing good. "Oh, yeah, I remember now how much fun it is to play you, Cole," Harry said sourly. "Look at that fuckin shot, will you."

"Cole's already got him hot," J.D. whispered to me. "If Harry takes the heat he's fucked." He raised his voice. "Come on, Harry, put it back on him."

Harry didn't get it back on him, but he kept himself under control. He left Cole a one-rail bank, and Cole made it, ran four more, and then ducked. Harry wasn't about to go quietly. He hit a beautiful long two-rail lag, and when it fell in he was straight in on a ball out of the rack. "Fuck, Harry, great shot," Cole said. "Jesus."

Harry ran four balls but then he hit a cross-bank too hard, trying to hold position, and it jarred and rolled back over on to Cole's side. "Shit!" Harry said. "That's that fuckin rack." And it was. Cole cut the gift ball into his pocket and ran the rest.

Harry reached into his leg wallet and took out a banded thou and sidearmed it at me across the table. The stack of bills helicoptered through the air and I stabbed at it with an outstretched right hand, catching the packet just before it hit a guy in the row behind me. "Nice catch," Harry said. "You've had some practice with my money."

"Harry, you play shortstop, I'll play first base all day," I replied.

Harry won two of the next three to get even, but then Cole won three racks in a row. He came over to me and said, "This is george. I got the nuts now. He was shootin good but now he's in a losin funk. Get me another drink."

Funk or no funk, Harry hung tough. For an hour they traded racks, each winning on their own break. Cole had a beautiful, parsimonious control of the cue ball, but Harry knew how to move, too, and he rode inside his own fences, staying with the shots he could make and avoiding the ones he couldn't. I thought of Harry, proudly showing me where he grew up, the restaurant his father owned, the football field where he first found glory. He was a hard, prideful, disciplined, competitive, immensely successful man, and I admired him for his nerve and his ultimate faith in himself, enduring even when it was misplaced.

Finally Cole broke through, late in the rack on one of Harry's breaks, making a spectacular three-rail lag into the heart of the pocket. It was no flyer, but a beautifully constructed shot, executed perfectly. If the ball had hung, Harry would have had no shot. But it fell in, and Cole ran out easily.

When Cole won the next game, too, Harry said, "Aw, *shit*, Cole, that's enough, you're five grand up. I can't beat you today." He took the two thousand still posted on the light and handed it to me. And that was that.

Cole and I went to lunch at a cafe near Sea-Tac Airport and whacked up the money in the men's room, petrifying an elderly gent who doubtless thought he had walked in on a drug deal. So tired I could barely see, but very pleased, I said goodbye to Cole and called Tony from the airport. "Nice work, butthead," he said when I told him about the card game.

"I know, but I don't think Cole would have played that good today if he hadn't been worn out and desperate."

"Did Harry get hot?"

"Not really. He played good and he got beat and he knew it."

"You did good up there. Get your ass back, though. We're in action."

"Yeah? When?"

"This week. Morro wants to play at South Bay Billiards, that new joint in Hawthorne."

"How you hittin 'em?"

"Better than you, Bubba. Come on down. I need some Christmas money."

"I'm too tired to fuck with you. The flight gets in at six. Be there."

XVI

Liability

This'll be the Saturday you're reachin' your peak
Tonight'll be like nothing you've ever seen
Is it the crack of the pool balls, the neon buzzin' . . .
You're stumblin' onto the heart of Saturday night
                                                    —Tom Waits

DECEMBER 11—WE WERE BACK IN BELLFLOWER, BACK AT HARD Times, and back at our motel by the 91 freeway. We were upstairs, of course, because it was ten dollars a night cheaper, never mind the fact that we were proposing to bet a few thousand on a pool game.

My god, these sleazy motels were sapping my spirit. I'd come to expect a certain level of squalor on this trip, but that didn't help any when I found it: ragged towels the size of paperback books, matted shag carpeting, always beige or green, with dubious stains and brown flecks you hoped weren't moving. Awful lighting, no visible power outlet, so you had to horse the mattress off the bed in order to find one and plug in the laptop. No water pressure. Rust stains on the sink. Mildew in the shower. Bars of soap the size and thickness of business cards, always with some pretentious drivel about being "French Milled" on the wrapper. Telephones that only seem to work when it's the desk calling at 8 A.M. to find out just how long you propose to *stay* in room 216 (as if they had any demand for it) and why didn't you let the maid in this morning? An ice bucket, usually fake-wood-grain plastic, that won't hold enough ice to freeze a cockroach. A cigarette-burned particle-board nightstand big enough for the phone and the NO SMOKING sign and some piece of propaganda from the corporate folks about why their chain of dumps is so superior to any other, but not big enough to hold anything else, with a cheap cardboard-bound Gideons Bible and a two-year-old phone book, no yellow pages, in the drawer. A TV with vertical hold problems and four channels, all of which feature only inane local weathermen, test patterns, televangelists, and *Friday the 13th, Part 8.*

The view out the window was depressing in its familiarity: This was the ugly underside of sunny Southern California, where out-West dreams run out of real estate.

Of course the coffee search was as futile as ever. It was like looking for single-malt Scotch in Jiddah. I finally stopped at a doughnut shop near where Bellflower turns into Long Beach to get some regular shitty coffee, and I was left speechless by the woman ahead of me. She was somewhere in her sixties, with tightly curled grandmother's hair that should have been white. Now it was pink. And her pet toy poodle's hair was identically curled and identically pinked. She was wearing pink sweats and little pink running shoes. She bought—of course—two doughnuts frosted with strawberry icing. She broke one of them and gave half to Fifi.

It was a strange start to what promised to be a strange day. We were planning an assault against three of the toughest pool players in Los Angeles—Los Tres Amigos: Ernesto Dominguez, Francisco Galindo, and Ismael "Morro" Paez, or, as one player called them: *"Hasta Luego, Hasta La Vista,* and *Hasta Manana:* Three ways to say goodbye to your money." We had heard that Little Al Romero, a legendary road player who had a cue business upstairs at Hard Times, didn't play in the liability game anymore. He had accused Francisco and Morro of partnering against him. Others around the place told us it was just an alibi—that Little Al just didn't pocket balls the way he used to—but I saw him win an easy grand playing in the golf game last time I was there, and I knew he could still pocket balls and pocket money.

If Little Al, who'd been playing on this particular table for probably twenty years, didn't like the game anymore, what were we doing making plans to beat it? I considered that for a moment, but I still had to like Tony's snooker game against anybody on this side of the Atlantic.

As expected, Morro Paez had proposed that the game be played at South Bay Billiards, where he had just been named the house pro. He would have loved to get the place a reputation for high-dollar action, and if the golf game at Hard Times ever moved, it would bring a mountain of money in table time. So we went to South Bay to inspect the table, and Francisco also showed up to take a look. He was maybe five years older than Morro, but looked a lot more. He had a lined face and an unruly shock of hair that had turned half-and-half, black and gray. His hands were rough, callused. He made his living with a cue now, but he had obviously known serious physical labor in his life. In contrast to Morro, who was typically dapper in a crisp white shirt and Polo sweater over Perry Ellis slacks and expensive leather loafers, Francisco was wearing ancient chinos and a sweatshirt.

The table was very pretty, but useless: The pockets were buckets. "I told him to cut them tight," Morro said, managing to look disappointed for about twenty seconds. "He needs to fix it." Francisco just rubbed his chin, looked at the table, and shook his head.

"Oh, well, I guess we play at Hard Times, no?" Morro's high-beam smile was back.

Francisco nodded pleasantly, Tony a little grimly. If we wanted to play, it was our only choice. "Noon tomorrow," Morro said. Francisco nodded. Tony nodded. High noon. Before he turned to go, Morro handed Tony and me business cards. They announced:

Ismael Paez
"MORRO"
World-Class Pool Player

It was an absolutely accurate description.

DECEMBER 12—WE ARRIVED AT HARD TIMES AT 9 A.M. TO PREEMPT the morning golf game, so Tony could hit some balls on the mother of all trap tables.

The corner pockets were so tight a regulation US. snooker ball, $2\frac{1}{8}$ inches in diameter, would barely squeeze by the rails and into the pockets, by the thickness of a playing card on each side. The cloth was ancient, a parody of green. The surface was as slick and frictionless as blown glass—the polar opposite of the napped cloth on the snooker tables in Canada. The huge table looked like a key-lime pie baked in the shape of North Dakota.

The corner pockets were so small that they really didn't look like pockets at all, but rather like tiny nibbles out of the edge of the pie crust. The table had its own laws of physics: Balls once in motion tended to stay in motion. And they also tended not to go into corner pockets. The bottom left corner as you faced the rack was the evillest-looking pocket I have ever seen. In the daily golf game, it was the "one-hole"—the first one players shoot at as they try to make the holes in order. Over the years, the bottom rail and the side rail had been covered at varying tensions. People probably had parked their asses on the side rail too, and it swooped down lower than the end rail, giving the pocket a psychotic look, like Charlie Manson's left eye. It was a treacherous ball-spitting bankrupting heartbreaking bastard of a pocket. Snooker players familiar with the table would leave their opponents shooting toward the one-hole whenever possible. If Tony Annigoni or Buddy Hall or Efren Reyes or English snooker champion Jimmy White—or any other shit-fire snooker player you'd care to name—were to attempt the same long, straight-in shot at the one-hole twenty times, they might make, at most, four or five. They might make none.

Tony warmed up on the table, slowly figuring out where the cue ball might stop on various shots. I watched him slow-roll a couple of balls toward the right side pocket, and they rolled out and away toward the rail on the far side.

The golf-game regulars began to arrive, and they muttered and swore when they discovered a big liability game was planned. Playing snooker for a hundred dollars a point with three or four of the best players in the world following you is not for most people. It demanded the muscle-memory of Bo Jackson and the soul of Ivan Boesky. The game was played with three red balls instead of the full rack of fifteen. Playing for these stakes meant that somewhere between $3,000 (there is a minimum of thirty points on the table) and $5,100 (for a maximum of fifty-one) will change hands every twenty minutes or so, depending on which—if any—colored balls are made after each red goes down.

Tony and Morro and Francisco lagged for the break and to determine the order for the first game. Francisco broke, Tony was second, Morro third. It didn't take long to get a taste of what this game could do. Tony made the first two red balls, adding a blue ball with each, and Francisco came over to him with his bankroll. Tony referred him to me, and Francisco gravely counted $1,200. A few minutes later Morro left Francisco a shot at a side pocket, and he made the last red ball, followed by the pink, and then the yellow and green, neatly recouping at Morro's expense the $1,200 he had just paid me. I realized that this was by far the highest stake we had played for. Each game was worth ten times what we'd won in Savannah, each game worth more than we'd won in three days at Akron. In effect, one black ball today was worth more than Tony had won at the tournament in this room last month: It represented a swing of $1,400—$700 if you made it, minus $700 if the guy who followed you made it. It was the kind of action we'd been looking for the whole trip, but it cut both ways: We had a chance to double our bankroll, but we could also be out of business by the evening.

When Francisco finally missed, he left Tony a shot the length of the table on the brown. Tony almost got away with it. The brown doubled the corner and skidded down the rail while the cue ball slid around the table like a Formula 1 racer. The end result was a very difficult one-rail bank shot for Morro, who made it look easy, drawing perfect position on the blue in the side. He made the pink and black, too. End of rack. Score: Francisco even, Morro up a thousand, Tony down the same thou.

This game had a dynamic much different from a relatively simple head-to-head nine-ball match. The order was shifted between the three players after each game, so defensive strategies had to be reexamined. Also, in nine-ball, only one ball counted. Here, the pressure was incredible on every shot. Every ball made meant money—out of one pocket, into another. And each ball made carried the potential of starting a long run. Even a modest break of, say, twenty points—common in most snooker games—meant $2,000. I realized it was the only game I had seen where *any* shot could mean a four-figure swing.

I watched Tony closely. I'd never seen him play for this kind of cash, but he seemed exactly the same. If anything, I thought he was staying down a little better, perhaps because he knew how unforgiving the table was. Undaunted by Morro's run, he came back strong in the second game, running all three reds. After three racks, we were $1,500 ahead, and the growing crowd of spectators, used to seeing Morro and Francisco quickly empty visiting players, was clearly surprised. In the third rack, Francisco left Tony an almost straight shot, the length of the diagonal, on the blue, and Tony drilled it—remarkable on this table. Francisco came over and handed me ten fifties, shaking his head.

But the next few racks turned sour. The pockets began to take their toll; Tony jawed several balls. At the same time, Francisco caught fire and made several long runs, including a twenty-two-pointer, naturally following Tony. And both Morro and Francisco seemed to get better chances. One of the old golf players came up to me and said, "They're putting the team effort on you now." I just shrugged. I chose not to believe that, but by 3 P.M. we were $8,000 losers.

In the next rack, Morro left Francisco a relatively easy cut-shot on the first red ball, and Francisco ran all three of them, along with a brown, a blue, and a black, for a $1,900 payday. But he missed the yellow, leaving Tony a pretty good shot at it, albeit in the one-hole. Francisco and Morro then got in a vociferous argument in Spanish about whether Francisco's shot had been an illegal push shot. Tony thought it had been a push, but he wasn't involved in the money on the shot so he said nothing. It occurred to me briefly that the ruckus might have been staged to allay suspicions about their partnership, but I dismissed the thought. Tony bit his lower lip as he lined up the shot on the yellow. Two points, $200. At this stage it was not a major deal. But I saw that if he could get it to drop, he could get position on the green in the side. He stroked the shot boldly. The ball wobbled, but before I could swear at it, it fell in. Tony made the green easily and got the line he wanted on the brown. He made that, too, and the blue, and then the pink. He left himself a tricky cut-shot on the black, but he was in dead stroke, and somehow I expected him to make it, and he did. It was the first time all day anybody had run all the colored balls to end a rack, and it was worth $2,700.

As Tony prepared to break, somebody behind me said, "Hey, wait, let me in that thing." Grady Mathews shouldered through the crowd. "We'll have to draw for order," Morro said, and Mathews ended up last in the rotation, following Morro. It was an expensive draw. Tony made a red ball on the break and made the pink and another red ball. Grady was almost $1,000 stuck before he ever picked up a cue. He dropped a little over $3,000 in the first three racks and bailed out. The game settled into a grim pattern. The three players seemed uncannily even, in balls pocketed, defense, everything. But nothing important seemed to go Tony's way. He'd leave Morro tough and Paez would miss a shot and shit it in, off two or three rails. It happened twice on the *black*, which cost $1,400. On almost every rack, we were losing a little—$300, $200, $600.

I looked at Tony. By now I knew every little sign of his being down on himself, upset with getting bad rolls, whatever. He would miss a shot, then look up to the ceiling, trying not to let his anger show. He would chew nervously on his mustache. He would begin to rush his shots, as he did against Junior Harris. I was heartened to see no such signs. I knew how frustrated he was. I knew how much the money meant to him, with a cartel of business sharks out to steal his club. But he was not showing a millimeter of that. He wasn't loose or casual; that would have been equally worrisome, under the circumstances. He was quiet, focused, intense. It was a few minutes after seven when he came over to me and said, "Where do we stand?"

"Stuck fourteen thou and change."

He just nodded. "That's what I had it at. Fourteen six?"

"Yep."

He looked at me for a long moment. "Do you think they're sandwiching me?" he asked quietly.

"One, it doesn't really matter," I said. "Two, for the record, no, I don't. I just think they're damned good players who know this table."

"Me, too," he said, then he added, "We're okay, you know. It's not about yardage. It's about winning." A lesser player would have used his suspicions as an excuse to lose, and I had a feeling that had happened more than a few times before. That may be their real move, I thought: get other players so paranoid about the sandwich that they beat themselves. "You want something to eat?" I asked Tony.

"No. Just water. Keep the water coming, kid."

"You got it. Make some more fuckin balls."

He smiled. "Don't worry. I'm going to win this rack. You want to bet those five bills you owe me I don't?"

"Forget about it."

We were dead even on the rack when it got down to the black. Tony was following Francisco, who wasn't giving up much, but then, nobody was. Each player shot at the black four times, and nobody got a good shot. It was clear that somebody was going to have to make a terrific shot, or get lucky, to make it. Francisco left Tony with the cue ball on one end rail and the black on the other, and Tony hit maybe the prettiest safety I'd ever seen. It unfolded like the wings of a butterfly, the cue hitting the seven firmly a little less than half-ball, and the two balls traced mirror-image paths around the table, the black counterclockwise, the cue ball clockwise, and they ended in almost exactly the same positions in which they had started.

Morro and Francisco both played safe, and then Tony reached back into the Cochran's pay-ball games of his boyhood and hit a long three-rail shot: top rail, left side rail, bottom rail, rolling toward the right side pocket. I thought for a moment it would roll off and out of the hole, but as the black came off the bottom rail several things were revealed to me: First, that this was the epitome of the game, the finest contest I had seen in three months and thousands of miles, the perfect combination of firepower and defense and strat-egy and heart; second, that I had taken the right player on the road, a player smart enough and tough enough to transcend the fatigue and stress and fear and doubt; third, that he had *played* for the roll, and like a slow curveball the black would travel away from the near side rail and into the heart of the pocket, and as it did I realized, finally, that we would not leave any money on this table.

Tony won $1,000 on the next rack, and $1,600 the rack after that—catching a break when Morro, who followed him, cut the pink ball in and scratched. That meant he had to pay Tony $600. Then Francisco missed the black and left it for Tony. As he lined it up, a small figure came through the crowd and said, "I'm in, I'm in, next game, put me down, I'm in. José Parica."

Tony pulled up, glared at Parica, and got back down and nailed the black. Parica, sheepish, apologized. "I wasn't shark-ing you, man, sorry." It was impossible to be angry with Parica;

I just hoped his entering the game wouldn't kill Tony's momentum.

"I thought you were in the Philippines," I said.

"I'm back," he said, grinning.

A few months ago, Parica had come to L.A. and robbed this game, winning several thousand from Morro, Francisco, Ernesto, and a few others. Tonight, he held his own, but couldn't seem to put any big runs together. Tony, meanwhile, kept grinding it out, winning the money back the same way he had lost it, a few hundred at a time. He lost some ground when Francisco got loose for twenty-five points behind him, but by 11 P.M. he had pulled back to within $2,400.

In the next rack, the one-hole performed its voodoo on José Parica. Morro left him the last red ball, but aimed him at the cross-eyed pocket. Parica hit it well, but the ball bounced out of the corner like Sugar Ray Leonard. Tony, up next, sliced it neatly into the side and stopped the cue ball on time for the pink. But he didn't stop there. For the second time in the session he ran the colored balls in sequence. Add the pink and the red and he had run thirty-four points—the high run of the day and enough to put us on the plus side of the ledger for the first time in more than twelve hours.

After Morro kissed in the black following Tony in the next rack, Tony shook his head, turned to me, and unscrewed his cue. "That's enough," he said. Thirteen hours, thirty-plus racks, more than $120,000 worth of balls pocketed, and we ended up exactly $160 winners after I paid the $140 tab for table time. It was the sweetest cash I had collected the whole trip.

"Let's get something to eat," Tony said, slumping in his seat and rubbing his face with his hands. "I've never been so hungry, I swear. And I want a beer, too." We found an all-night Thai joint. As we sipped icy beers and waited for the kitchen to deal with our massive order, I looked at Tony and said, "We were damn near cashed there."

"I know."

"What turned it around for you?"

"I was too tentative, early in the game. I let the table and their knowledge intimidate me, and I was worried about them fucking me." He took a big sip. "Then I just decided I was going to loosen up and freewheel it. I know I shoot as straight as anybody on any table. All I had to do was play."

"After you made that long three-railer on the black ball I knew you were going to win it back."

"So did I. And so did Morro. He knows the value of running one of those in, and he could see I was playing with more confidence. Did you see him? He was shaking his head. He even got hot at Francisco for leaving me a couple of shots."

"You beat some champions tonight. At their own game."

"Yeah, but why are we so happy? We came down here to play this game, spent a few days to set it up, played all day, and won a hundred and sixty bucks."

"Yes, but—"

"I know. We came out of there with our nuts reattached."

"Amen."

WE HAD ONE MORE LITTLE THING TO ATTEND TO, AND THEN WE were going to break for Christmas with my family in Santa Barbara. On the way up the coast, we wanted to pay a call on a room owner in Oxnard who was reputed to play high. His name, for some obscure reason, was "Whataburger Al." Two Santa Barbara players had told me they'd made four-figure scores playing him.

Gold Coast Billiards was a drab little flyspecked room. Most of the tables were in execrable condition, but true to form there was a pretty good Gold Crown in the back, by the cash register, where Whataburger was glaring at us. He was a truculent little potbellied transplanted New Yorker with a square, bald head and an attitude. I introduced Tony and myself, and he just snorted. I liked him for his feistiness, but he didn't think too much of us.

"Would you like to play some?" Tony asked.

"Why should I?" he asked belligerently. "Did you hear that I was a score?"

"I heard you liked a game sometimes."

"What if I do? I'm a sitting duck for guys like you. I'm stationary, and you can move, you don't have to open a poolroom every day. You're not looking for a game, you're looking to win."

Tony shrugged. "Okay, I just thought I'd ask." I nodded at him, and we turned around to leave.

"If you're good enough to come in here and harass me, you're good enough to give me the seven."

"Absolutely not."

Whataburger Al shrugged and said, "Thought you wanted to gamble."

"I'll give you the wild eight for a hundred bucks a game."

"Fifty."

Tony sighed. "Rack 'em."

Whataburger Al proceeded to break in a nine and shit in an eight before Tony even got to shoot. Then Tony missed a five, and Al ran out to the eight to go $150 ahead. He almost made the nine on the break again, but it hung, leaving Tony an easy combination. "Shit, I never get no rolls," Whataburger said disgustedly. Tony shook his head, rolled his eyes at me, and ran four racks. Instead of racking the balls again, Whataburger said, "Fuck you, I quit."

On the way north, Tony said, "That was a hell of a hard hundred you steered me onto."

"Hey, I thought he was a sweetheart. I'd be a little touchy too, if a guy like you was trying to rob me. As a matter of fact, I am a little touchy, for that exact reason."

XVI

The Midnight Rodeo

"Somebody threw a cue ball at me once. It hit my wristwatch and took eight days off the calendar."
—Surfer Rod, Reno, Nevada

JANUARY 6—THE BANSHEE SCREAMED FOR JAMES DEAN AT A PLACE called Cholame. It's a dusty town in the flats east of Paso Robles, between the back side of the oak-studded hills of California's Coast Range and the vast Central Valley. Dean was out there on State Road 41 at dusk on a fine fall day for reasons of his own. When he collided with a farm lad's pickup truck in his racing Porsche, the script wrote itself, despite evidence that the accident wasn't his fault and that he probably wasn't even going all that fast. They say the local boys lifted his wallet on the ambulance ride, but by then he was past caring about his bankroll or his driving record.

Tonight I cared about both, but like Dean I needed to be someplace else in a hurry. The difference was, he had a lot better weather than we had. Gusting winds, black ice, sleet, and fog. Still, we had no choice. Without going horribly out of our way, we had to traverse this stretch in order to get from Highway 101 to Interstate 5. If we could make that link

successfully, we might sneak into Reno in front of yet another
nasty storm. "Fat chance," Tony said morosely, fiddling with
the radio to get a weather report. "We'll be lucky to get to
Reno by tomorrow this time."

We got to the junction with I-5 at Kettleman Hills, site of
one of the state's biggest toxic-materials dumps—as far as I
could tell, wonderfully located—a few minutes before 7 P.M.
"We're rolling now," I said. "We'll be in Reno in no time."

"I'll bet we don't make it by two A.M.," Tony said.

"How much?"

"When do you think we'll make it?"

"By eleven P.M., easy."

"You're nuts."

"Bet."

"I'll bet you you don't make it by eleven."

"You said two A.M."

"You said eleven."

"I'll bet you five hundred we make it by one A.M."

"No way. I'll bet you, let's see . . . You owe me six hundred
fifty . . . Let's see, I'll bet you two fifty we don't get there by
midnight."

"Done. Plus, say, a dollar a minute, either side of midnight."

"Okay."

"I can't believe I've just given you incentive to kill us both.
But you're going to look pretty stupid when Donner Pass is
closed and you're sitting there, leaning on the horn and
having a stroke, at eleven forty-five. You'll lose what little hair
you have left."

We were 250 miles away, which didn't bother me nearly so
much as the weather. It wasn't snowing at the moment, but
the fog was thick and visibility was terrible. And who knew
what was in store up on Donner Pass? I speeded up to 75 and

strained my eyes for taillights. The truck traffic seemed to be bunched up in convoys, and they were a bitch to get around. Tony began to snore.

I stopped for gas in Sacramento just before eight. As I was wheeling out of the station, back onto the freeway, Tony woke up and stretched. "What's the weather report there, ace?" he asked as we turned onto I-80.

"Fine, don't worry," I said. The attendant had told me Donner had been closed earlier in the day because of blowing snow, but I saw no need to tell him that.

Traffic was light out of Sacramento, and the road was dry. I kicked it up to 80 and Tony began to look a little nervous. As we started up the grade toward Donner, I was shocked at the amount of snow by the side of the road—it dwarfed the cars—but the road itself was scraped clean. I blessed CalTrans for its efficiency, and we rolled into the Hilton valet-parking lot at 9:45. Tony was morose. "I was counting on that damn pass being closed," he said. "They got three *feet* of snow yesterday. I can't tell you how lucky you were."

"I can tell you exactly," I said. "Two fifty plus a buck a minute, times, let's see, one thirty-five, comes to three eighty-five."

"Ah, you robbed me."

"Right. I robbed you. Let's see, there was the twenty-dollar-bill trick, the—"

"Save it. I just let you out, big time. All that work and you only owe me three bills."

"Not even. Two sixty-five, actually."

"Your tab hasn't been that low since we got off the train."

"I have a suggestion: Why don't you try mugging somebody else for a change?"

Tony was not planning to play in the tournament; he wasn't

ready to take his one-pocket game public. He was there strictly for the side action, which promised to be big with all the gamblers around. It would be a far different crowd from the other tournaments. The PBTA had barred its top thirty players from competing because of conflicting dates with a sanctioned tournament, and they had threatened to have a "spy" there to check on who played and who didn't.

Since the tournament was one-pocket instead of nine-ball, and since there was a hefty prize fund, a lot of gamblers who wouldn't get caught dead playing in a sanctioned event had shown up. Such as, for instance, Bucktooth. A lot of the really famous older players were there, genuine hustling legends: Cornbread Red Burge, Champagne Eddie Kelly, Boston Shorty, Johnny Ervalino, Bugs Rucker, even seventy-six-year-old Billy Amadeo. Amarillo Slim, the famous poker player, was there for a shot at the cheese. He was an accomplished one-pocket player, not as good as the top professionals but certainly capable of lighting the board—and his money would be in action, I knew, even if he wasn't.

The strength of the field and the nature of the players were no accident. Grady and the Hilton had put together a novel format: Entry fee was a thousand dollars in advance, with the guarantee that when the players actually showed up for the tournament, they'd get nine hundred of it returned to them immediately. That made the actual entry fee only a hundred dollars, astoundingly low for an event with a purse like this. The Hilton happily posted a large share of the prize money in anticipation of the overall business—and the guarantee that one-hundred-odd hard-core gamblers would each have a bankroll of at least nine hundred dollars over the weekend—not to mention the fact that the event would be a magnet for so-called professional gamblers of all types, pool players or not.

It was a pity the PBTA wouldn't sanction the event. It would have been fun to see Sigel and Hopkins and Hall and Davenport and Mizerak there, to name a few. But having these legendary road players and marquee names from decades past, all holed up in a snowstorm like the cast of *The Mousetrap,* was exciting enough for any serious aficionado.

The tables were set up on the third floor, and when we walked in we ran into Cornbread Red and Bucktooth, chatting like a couple of former cheerleaders at a high school reunion. The Seattle contingent was at least partly in evidence—J.D. was warming up on a table in the corner with Billy Cress. There were rumors that Harry was coming, but with his wife, which might both delay his arrival and cool his gambling.

The tables looked weird. They were sort of clumpy and boxy looking, with black rails and blinds and chrome corners. "Those are Globals," Tony said. "Actually, they're not a bad-playing table. But man, look at that light. It's grim." The lights were leaving two-inch shadows near the rails. The tables were good and tight, though, appropriate for one-pocket, and also appropriate for Mr. Annigoni. Compared to the six-by-twelve in L.A., they looked most welcoming.

"We'll get some nine-ball action here," said Tony. "This thing's open twenty-four hours. A lot of these guys like to play nine-ball and they'll want to stay in stroke after bunting at balls all day in the tournament. And I love these pockets."

It sounded reasonable to me—until I found out that Grady had imposed a no-nine-ball rule. "He doesn't want anybody breaking on them. The cloths are new and the break will put a track on them," Billy Cress told me.

Tony was horrified. "Maybe after they get some play he'll let up on that," he said.

"I sure as fuck hope so. Otherwise that hair-raising drive up here was for nothing."

JANUARY 7—THICK SNOW, PUSHED HORIZONTAL BY THE WIND, AND reports of subzero temperatures led me to abandon my plan of getting out for a walk to my favorite Reno breakfast joint, the Nevada Club, where friendly, maternal waitresses dished out pancakes, eggs, bacon, and bad coffee for a couple of bucks a throw. I settled for a crummy cappucino from a Hilton casino bar. On the way down the escalator to the casino I absently scanned the rows of corny five-by-seven publicity shots, showing big winners at slot, keno, and various other gambling tournaments—classic "grip and grin" shots I spent a newspaper career trying to avoid using. There on the wall, a third of the way down, beaming at the camera, was Harry Platis.

Twenty seconds later I did a double take. There was Harry in the flesh, having a flutter at the craps table, his wife at his side to make sure things didn't get too far out of hand. The casino was dotted with pool players: Keith McCready and Larry Lisciotti in the sports book, studying the California tracks' morning lines; Johnny Ervalino, fingers flying over the keys of a video keno machine; Cornbread Red, close by Harry, watching the shooter; Billy Cress slouching morosely at third base on a five-dollar blackjack table; Seattle player Mike Danner planted at a PaiGow table.

A couple of hours later the tournament was under way and I was in one-pocket-sweater's heaven: The world's best players, engaged in grim jockeying battles, each ball another skirmish. The dynamic was startlingly different from that of a nine-ball tournament, where most matches take maybe half an hour.

This was a race to five, and many of the matches went down to the ninth rack. Many of the spectators drifted in and out, picking up a match at several stages but not sitting and sweating every ball—but to me that continuum is the beauty of the game, seeing momentum and confidence ebb and flow, seeing the players who could handle the pressure best, watching shots I never knew could be made, position shots and defensive shots mostly, requiring mastery of the cue ball. I also began to understand the excruciating art of tempting an opponent with a dangerous shot, and the devastation that occurred when the challenge was accepted and the shot was made. I saw no sign of Tony all morning. I thought perhaps I'd better go check on him. On the way out I checked the pairings. Bucktooth's first match was scheduled for the afternoon, against a Seattle player named Jimmy Gottier, a relative novice. I'd met him on our first trip to Seattle and had liked him immediately. He was a young hipster who had talent and verve and grit, an antiques dealer who played pool with a beautiful old Robinson and a pair of thousand-dollar cowboy boots. He was a B-level player—he played Harry Platis a lot and mostly got the worst of it—but he really loved the game. "When I was nine or ten I saw *The Hustler,* and like most people in our generation that's why I play pool today," he'd told me. "That, and one day right after that I turned on the *Wide World of Sports* and there was Cisero Murphy playing Luther Lassiter for the U.S. straight pool championship. I was knocked out—these two handsome, distinguished-looking men in tuxedos, *almost never missing a shot.*

"And then when I moved to Seattle—well, it's a great one-pocket town anyway, but Harry being there, he has everybody around there playing one-pocket. I was a ball-runner, a rhythm player, and I'd always stayed away from one-pocket because I didn't understand it. But I became fascinated—it's so complex and interesting, and the momentum can shift so fast, and then shift back with the next ball. It's the best game."

I found Tony still in bed—and sick. Shortly after we'd arrived a player he wanted to make a game with had come up to him, sneezing and coughing, explaining he couldn't play because he felt so terrible, and Tony was convinced he had been infected with the player's bug. Whatever the cause, Tony's sickness was real enough; he was congested, running a fever, and suffering chills and body aches. I dosed him the best I could with cold pills and cough syrup and aspirin from the Hilton gift shop and got out of there and let him sleep.

I was back downstairs just in time to see Bucktooth put a beautiful break on Jimmy in the first game, and he won the first rack in ten minutes. Then he reversed Jimmy's break with a spectacular one-rail bank and coasted to a 2–0 lead, and it looked like it was going to be quick and ugly.

But it turned out slow and ugly instead. The Tooth scratched on the break in Game 3, and was so irritated at himself that he let Jimmy right back in it. Bucktooth, with his big lead and his petulance at the scratch, got too aggressive and tried to force the action. One-pocket does not allow such lapses in patience. If you gamble, and win, the game rewards you, but if you gamble and lose it will break your heart. Bucktooth took and missed some very hard shots, and Jimmy charged him for it each time, making one and duck, one and duck. In an hour the Tooth was on the hill, leading 4–2, but his shotmaking woes continued, and his irritation mounted as Jimmy played some of the best one-pocket of his life to tie the match at four. Now the crowd was focused on the case rack. They smelled blood, and Bucktooth knew it. He jumped to a two-ball advantage, but missed a long one-rail lag and left Jimmy an opening. It was one of those inexorable, excruciating situations that develop on a pool table. A player, clearly skilled, can't seem to get untracked, and as the number of mistakes and misfortunes mount, the talent differential matters less and less, and finally the player runs out of opportunities to put that talent to work. It reminded me of Tony versus Mario, and sure enough, Jimmy closed the Tooth out with a brilliant eight-and-out run.

When I told Tony about it, he shook his head, and snuffled, and chuckled a little. "You know, Tooie has always been real hard on tournament players. He gets on me for playing tournaments, and maybe he's right, from a gambling standpoint, but it takes another kind of skill. Tooie's a grinder; he'll lose for twelve hours but he'll beat your brains out in the three hours after that. He has the guts and the stamina to come back. But in a tournament, you got to come with the best you got right now or it's over. If you get down you better get your head straight and get back in it right then because you might not get another chance. It's a good lesson for the Tooth, in a way, but I'll tell you something else. He'll use this to his advantage. He'll get more action now that everybody watched him lose."

He didn't say what I was already thinking, but neither of us wanted to admit: Unless Tony recovered quickly, Bucktooth was the only chance we had to make any money this week. We were up maybe five thousand and change—but if we wanted to do much more on this trip than break even, we needed to cash a big ticket soon.

JANUARY 8—I TRIED TO STAY OUT OF THE SICKROOM AS MUCH AS possible. Besides, I was utterly entranced with one-pocket as performed by these virtuosi.

Like Chicago blues or Chinese cooking, it is quite simple on the surface; the complexity lies in the execution. What could be less complicated? One player gets one pocket, one the other, and whoever gets eight balls in his pocket first wins. But it is incredibly hard to play well. It requires pinpoint touch; a shot left four inches up the rail from your pocket is probably going to provide an easy one-rail bank to your opponent's pocket. Pinpoint cue ball control is a must for the same reason; the difference between leaving your opponent with nothing and selling out the entire rack is often no more than a quarter of an inch. Strategic thinking, banking ability, and, certainly, ball-pocketing skills are equally vital. For these reasons, one-pocket is not a universally popular game, unlike nine-ball—it is just too hard for 90 percent of pool players. Even ball-pocketers such as Tony who grew up on nine-ball admit that it is a true test of skill like no other. "It's also a great money game," Tony told me once, "because all these old farts who can't make a ball think they can outmove you. They think players like me have no appreciation for the poetry of it, but I do. The fact is I'd rather be making balls. That's why I love straight pool so much. But I think that when my biggest score comes, it will be playing one-pocket, because people think I don't know shit about it."

In this surreal little honky-tonk mountain town, one-pocket became my compass, my sacrament. I would watch matches for three, four, six hours at a time, studying the moves of players like Boston Shorty and Mark Tadd and Ed Kelly and J.D. and Billy Incardona and Johnny Ervalino and Grady and the Monk, then get the Cruiser out of valet parking and pilot it over to the Keystone Cue & Cushion, the air so dry and cold it seemed to crack and fall to the white streets in lethal bright diamonds. I'd get Table One if it was available and replay shot after shot, trying to get the sense of pace and spin, the contact point, trying to unlock the mystery of this magnificent game. Once Dan Louie, the great Seattle player, came in to practice for a match and watched me with polite amusement. "You like the game?" he asked rhetorically, and then I took the balls back up to Becky and watched Dan as he practiced, taking note of the way he seemed to stroke everything so *calmly*, killing the cue ball or running it, making a ball or making a safety. Like Jimmy Gottier, I'd watched Luther Lassiter as a kid, read his how-to articles in the magazines, and he'd talked about just what Dan Louie was doing now. *Calm speed*, Wimpy Lassiter had called it.

The tournament continued apace. Jimmy Gottier drew his nemesis, Harry Platis, in the next round after beating Bucktooth. I swore. I mean, I was happy for Jimmy, and maybe what had happened was good for Bucktooth in the long term, but it amounted to a huge opportunity squandered. If the Tooth had beaten Jimmy and played Harry, there would have been serious side action, and after the last time I knew the Tooth had Harry's number.

Predictably, Jimmy jumped out in front but did exactly the same thing that the Tooth had done: He got impatient, and Harry took full advantage, pulling out a 5–4 win that was the mirror image of the Bucktooth match. Jimmy Gottier was disappointed, but he didn't care that much. He already had his trophy. He would carry his win over Bucktooth with him the rest of his life.

BUGS RUCKER, ONE OF THE BEST BANK-POOL PLAYERS EVER, MAYBE the best black player since Cisero Murphy, was delayed by the storm coming in from Chicago, and wasn't present when his match was called with Wayne Niess, a player from Aloha Billiards in Orange County.

Bugs showed up an hour after the forfeit, and Wayne said, shoot, let's play the match. Grady Mathews agreed to this, which was pretty darned charitable of him, too; Grady was playing in the tournament, and Bugs was in his bracket.

Rucker was an imposing, distinguished-looking man. He was tall, perhaps six-three, and his hair was going to gray. His style was very distinctive. Despite his size he got down on the ball with straight snooker player's legs, his long body folded at a right angle, his chin down on the cue just like Tony's. He was an overpowering player, and if he was bothered by his rough trip or the rush to arrive on time, it certainly didn't show. He defeated Niess easily.

Wayne Niess showed his class when somebody asked afterward, "Why did you let him back in? You had a free pass." He replied simply and with some asperity, "This is a gentleman's game, and people need to know that."

I'D BEEN WAITING ALL DAY FOR THE 8 P.M. MATCH BETWEEN J.D. AND Cornbread Red Burge. Cornbread was a big favorite, a champion playing a relative unknown, but I'd seen enough of J.D. to think it might be a good match. I thought again about what Jimmy had said about the one-pocket world in Seattle, and I remembered how eager the crowd at the Casino Club had been to try to hook Bucktooth with J.D.

Cornbread was certainly formidable. He was a legend in pool halls across the country before J.D. was born, and it was easy to see he still had it. Just a few weeks previously he had had open-heart surgery, but he looked in perfect health, and there sure wasn't anything the matter with his stroke. A small man, with red hair turning white as only red hair does, he looked like a little bird with fancy plumage in snazzy warm-ups, a gold chain glittering around his neck. Red grinned and drawled wisecracks to his buddies as he warmed up, but there was nothing amusing about the way he attacked the balls.

J.D. started wonderfully. Playing inspired defense, he took the first game and should have won the second, but Corn-bread came back from three balls down and outdueled him on the final ball to tie it at one apiece. The opportunity lost seemed to enervate J.D., and his game slipped a couple of notches—enough to put Cornbread up 4–1, only one game away from victory. He is not a player to squander opportuni-ties. He moved the cue ball so surely and elegantly that for a while it seemed J.D. would never get a shot at anything make-able.

But J.D. was known in Seattle for his heart, and he showed it to the world in this match. Playing with incredible disci-pline, he took care of the cue ball every time, and whenever Cornbread opened the door a crack, he took advantage, making banks, combinations, reversing tough leaves. On the edge of elimination, he won three straight games to tie the match at four apiece.

J.D., a very deliberate player under any circumstance, had left the table to collect himself several times during the match. After reaching the tie, he walked out before the case rack and got a Pepsi and let Cornbread stew for a while, to think about how he had lost the last three straight and let a sure win turn into a fifty-fifty proposition. Cornbread, by contrast, played pretty fast as a rule; he seemed to like to get into a rhythm, catch a gear, and go. He shook his head in exas-peration as he watched J.D. leave the room.

But if the stratagem was designed to unnerve Cornbread, it was doomed to failure. He'd experienced every shark in the book, and he wasn't about to lose his head. If anything, it gave him time to gather himself and concentrate on the case game.

J.D. put up a great fight, but finally Red, leading 5–3, got an opening and made two balls to get to seven, leaving himself an eminently makeable cross-table cut-shot on the match ball. He looked up then, and smiled a little ghost of an executioner's smile, and quietly laid down his cue on the table and walked out of the room and let J.D. think for a few moments about the consequences of trying to shark a champion. Then he came back in and slammed the ball into the pocket for the win.

Quite a few players stepped up to congratulate J.D. on playing Cornbread as well as he had, but he seemed to take little comfort in that. He just shrugged, "What can I say? He kicked my ass."

Bucktooth shook his head. "That's what I fuckin hate about tournaments. That kid just put a major knock on himself. Everybody will be talkin about how great he played Cornbread Red. Shit. He won't get a game for a fuckin year."

Bucktooth woofed at Harry a little bit afterward, but Mrs. Platis just looked at the Tooth like he was a cur fixing to piss on her prize hydrangea, and said, "Harry, I don't want you to play that man." Say goodnight, Tooth.

I went upstairs to find Tony pallid, coughing, feverish, congested, breathing shallowly, complaining of chest pain. "Can you get dressed?" I asked him.

"Yes," he said, "but I sure don't want to go anywhere."

"Tough."

I called the concierge, found an urgent-care center a couple of blocks away, and got my car pulled up to the door outside. An hour later, I was standing at the prescription window at a Pay-Less Drugstore, awaiting heavy-duty antibiotics and decongestants. My player, it seemed, had pneumonia.

JANUARY 9—NOW IT WAS TIME FOR REALISM. "KEEP YOUR EYES OPEN down there for some action for Tooie," Tony croaked when I got up. "That's our only hope to make the nut this week." I thought about Surfer Rod, getting eight days knocked off his watch calendar, and I thought we were in danger of having the same thing happen. Privately, I doubted Tony would be ready to play competitively in two weeks; maybe a month.

It was 9 A.M. and the tournament room was nearly deserted. Grady Mathews, for once, was not too busy to chat. I liked him a lot. He had a great sense of humor, and his professorial mien was occasionally eclipsed by a devilish grin. He was universally acknowledged to be one of the most knowledgeable, and therefore one of the best, one-pocket players in the world.

This morning he was engaged in some lighthearted banter with Billy Incardona. The two could not be more contrasting in appearance—one Omar Sharif, the other Don Knotts with glasses—but they shared a wealth of experience and wisdom, and a mutual respect of the kind I had found among the top few players in the game.

Billy, knocking some balls around with his new Cognoscenti, said, "I wish there was somebody around here to give me a ball."

Grady: "You can have two, and the thing that goes with them."

Grady began to goad Billy about how careful he was, matching up, which is a polite way of saying he was a lock artist. "You haven't played a good player even in twenty-five years," he said.

Faced with the truth, Incardona grinned and said, "I don't have to play good players to make a living. But if somebody around here would just give me one ball . . ." If anybody understood the veracity of George C. Scott's admonition about yardage versus winning, it was Billy Incardona. He hit a few more balls, and when nothing in the way of a game materialized, he took off in search of breakfast.

Grady sighed. "I'm just about off gambling. If you play any of the new guys there's always something wrong with it and the good players all want something. Look at this kid J.D., nobody much knew him, trying to get a game, and then he plays Cornbread like that. There just isn't any percentage in playing any of these guys any more." He smiled at me, knowing that I didn't precisely accept the fact that Grady Mathews, stone gambler, was proposing to quit betting on pool.

"And Cardone," he said. "Talk about careful. Man he's the most careful book I've ever seen. You know I've booked at a lot of tournaments, maybe fifty, maybe more. I lost a little in two of them, and made an average of five or six thousand each in the other forty-eight. And every time I went to the promoter and gave him a little, maybe five hundred, maybe a grand, and said thanks. Then when I promote a tournament and somebody books they don't give me a pretzel. And then when I go up to one of these motherfuckers and ask them for five hundred up front and wish them luck, they act like I just tried to assassinate them.

"I'll say one thing for Cardone, though," he added after a few moments. "At least he plays with his own money. Most of these kids never play with their own money. They may never know the feeling of walking out of the room busted and not having a meal, but they also don't know the absolutely or*gasmic* feeling of walking out with all your pockets filled with hundreds and not having to whack it up with anybody.

"Stakehorses. Shit. Horse-faced motherfuckers. I got so I can't even stand to look at them. You got to watch them blow-dry their hair, they tell you where to eat, what clothes to wear, where to stay. Who needs that?" Grady Mathews looked up sharply, remembering to whom he was addressing these remarks. "Oh. Sorry. Nothing personal."

THE TOURNAMENT SHOOK ITSELF OUT BY LATE AFTERNOON. ONE BY one, the players dropped away, even some of the great ones: Cotton LeBlanc, Bugs Rucker, Mark Tadd, Grady himself. Finally, there were two, to play for the championship (and the twenty thousand dollars) the following day: Cornbread Red and Champagne Ed, a match for the ages.

At 4 P.M. I took the news to Tony. He said, "Kelly used to be a champion, and he's been playing pretty good lately, but I bet Cornbread gets him."

Then I said, "The Tooth's got a game."

"What?" Drugs or no drugs, Tony was alert now. "What kind of a game? Harry?"

"No. You know Toby Flaherty?"

"Yeah, I do. Tough little fucker. From Oklahoma, lives in Vegas now. Plays good."

"How good?"

"Real good. As good as I do, maybe half a ball better. Tooth's not playing him straight up is he?"

"One-handed, even."

"One-handed?" It would have been a shout, but it came out as a croak. "Fuck, man, that's great. The Tooth can play one-handed one-pocket with anybody. I mean, *anybody*. Good for him for going straight up with someone. How much?"

"Thousand a game."

"When?"

"About six."

"Flaherty have the money?"

"Apparently he's got a syndicate. Oklahoma guys, the Tooth said."

"How much did the Tooth offer you?"

"A third. I told him I needed to talk to you."

"Fuck, grab it, it's our only shot."

"That's what I thought."

"Keep him as calm as possible," Tony said. "Don't let him get real upset. Stay out of his way but make sure nobody gets at him."

"How the hell do I do that?"

"Fuck, I don't know, you're the stakehorse."

"Thanks. Take your medicine, you wheezy little bastard."

TOBY FLAHERTY LOOKED LIKE EXACTLY WHAT HE WAS: A SCRAPPY little pool hustler, Irish by heritage, Okie by birth, now head-quartered in Las Vegas. He was short, dark, intense, flat-bellied, and well muscled, with an underslung jaw and eyes as old as the game, eyes that squinted and flashed with competitive fire and irritation when he missed a shot. I watched him warm up dispassionately, wondering about his heart and his stamina.

I knew his backers—or at least, I knew the type. They took me back to my time on bush racetracks in Texas and New Mexico. They wore jeans, fancy cowboy boots fashioned from the hides of exotic reptiles, metal-tooled belts, Western shirts, and leather jackets, and had hooded eyes. I knew they'd have bankrolls and a penchant for Jack Daniel's, Texas hold 'em, and lowball, and I wouldn't trust one of them.

So this is what it comes down to, I thought. This is post-graduate stakehorse training, and this is what I get: Reno, Nevada, in the killing zone of winter. My player in bed with pneumonia and a third of somebody else's action. Betting my bankroll on a loudmouthed, white-haired pool hustler named Bucktooth, playing a one-handed game against a Las Vegas sharpie with his roots deep in horseshit and red Oklahoma mud, a bona fide investment opportunity if I ever saw one.

"Hey, Tooth," I said, motioning with my head. "Friend of yours."

"I saw him," Bucktooth said.

Chatting easily with Flaherty's backers, lounging back in his seat with one snake-booted foot propped in the air, white Stetson cocked back on his head like the hammer of a Buntline Colt, was Amarillo Slim, poker champion, pool player, and gambler—not known for booking losers.

"He told me he doesn't have any of it, but of course he knows 'em," the Tooth said. "No big deal, either way."

I pulled out some cash to post, and the Tooth waved it away. "We'll settle up when it's over," he said, and flipped ten Cecils onto the cloth. One of Flaherty's crowd did the same, and Bucktooth picked it all up and stacked it on top of the light.

Both players were a little nervous at first. The Tooth showed it by being overly aggressive, Flaherty by being tentative, which is safer. They split the first four racks, but Flaherty won the next two.

Tony appeared at that moment, the first time he'd been in the tournament room for two days. He looked like hell. He nodded his head in greeting, and the gesture looked spasmodic, forced. "The Tooth's trying to make everything," I whispered to him. "He needs to ratchet back a few notches, take care of whitey." Tony nodded grimly, and went over and whispered in Bucktooth's ear. The Tooth nodded his head emphatically. Tony wobbled back over and sat down next to me. "He says he's figured that out," Tony said. "He's way too hyper, but he'll settle down in a minute."

"Good," I said, "because this kid plays pretty strong, one-handed."

As I spoke Flaherty, left deep in his own pocket, banked a ball three rails around the table and made it, then lagged a ball close and left the Tooth buried. Tony winced, whether from the turn of events or from pleural pain I couldn't tell.

But the Tooth was hardly intimidated. He eyed his options carefully, then picked a ball out of the rack, lagged it one rail to the lip of his hole, and managed to kill the cue ball on the far rail, hooking Flaherty on the ball hanging in his own pocket.

"I feel like shit," Tony whispered. "I've got to get out of here. He'll be all right. Just remind him that it's okay to leave the ball out in the middle of the table where the kid has to jack up." With that, he raised himself painfully to his feet, managed a wave in the Tooth's direction, and shuffled toward the elevator.

He had made a good point. Playing one-handed, it's much easier to make a shot when you're able to rest the cue on the rail. When the cue ball is out in the middle, you have to poke at the ball with no way at all to support the cue. If you've never done it before you'll be lucky to hit the cue ball at all, much less hit it in a precise direction, and hit a specific point on the cue ball, and hit it with anything approximating a powerful stroke. Bucktooth had developed terrific skill at doing all of that. He would point to the ball, lining up the shot, the cue well above table level to avoid fouling, then slowly lower the cue until it stopped for an instant, about an inch above the cue ball. Then he would snap the cue down and through the shot. He looked quite fearsome, like a Minoan statue, arm straight, cue extended like a jousting lance, bulging eyes gleaming, a scowl on his face as he eyeballed the shot, then skewered the cue ball with a sudden, violent stab. Flaherty's midtable form was neither as dramatic nor as effective, but when he was able to rest the cue on the table, his ratio of successful shots increased dramatically.

The two players traded racks, each probing for weakness in the other's game like a dentist checking for cavities. The thousand dollars each rack represented seemed almost incidental. How did Toby react when the Tooth won a tough rack? How did the Tooth handle it when Toby threw a little tantrum? The players and their seconds watched, and analyzed, and whispered. "Don't let him push the tempo on you, Bucktooth," I told him. "He's happiest with an all-out slugging contest. Duck a few times, leave him stymied, and he might get reckless. But don't get reckless for him."

"Yeah, I know it," the Tooth said. "He don't play bad but I can kick his ass, see, and I think he knows it."

"Lie in the weeds and wait for him," I said. "He's not going to run out on you from where you can put the white ball." Slowly, Bucktooth began to win more skirmishes, and at 9 P.M. he went ahead by three racks for the first time. Toby's response was quick. "Play for two thousand," he said.

"Yep," said the Tooth.

Both players had been blooded now, the Tooth by his early loose play and Toby by his opponent's return to form. They settled into a tight pattern, volley and return, driving balls up the table and away from the other's pocket, picking off strays, making banks, jockeying for advantage. A cautious game of one-pocket is played in two parts. In the first, from the break onward, the balls are all fairly close to the scoring pockets, most or all being below the side pockets. Gradually, as players drive balls away from their opponents' pockets, the balls all move up the table to the opposite end, and every shot is a bank. This was particularly true in this one-handed game, where scoring opportunities were harder-earned, and fifteen minutes or so into each rack the shift would be complete. I began to think of this moment as "halftime," because the pace of the game switched so dramatically, with the players trying to lag balls back into or near their pockets with one- or two-rail banks, trying to make sure they didn't play short and give up an easy cross-bank, or kick out another ball with the cue ball and give away a more or less straight shot. Each ball became a well-defined battle. Toby would lag a ball down the table, and the Tooth would shoot it away. Back and forth. If Toby made a mistake and Bucktooth didn't have to take the ball back out of the pocket, and could lag a ball of his own, the momentum would shift. Each would make the occasional brilliancy, a two- or three-rail shot that would make, or a ball hung in the pocket with no way to shoot it out, and the racks would turn on shots like that.

Neither player ate. A little after nine I offered to get Tooth something, but he waved me away impatiently. "He broke the balls bad," the Tooth said. "I should be able to get up on him. It's time to send this kid to Nebraska." Every time the Tooth used this phrase to describe closing somebody out, busting them, I felt a little twinge of chauvinistic irritation. "Do worse than that, Tooth," I said. "Send him back to fuckin Oklahoma."

Bucktooth smiled, and walked to the table, looked at the rack, and picked a combination one-rail bank out clean, then spun the cue ball back straight in on the next ball, and down on to the end rail for the next, and then back out into the rack. He was playing as deliberately as ever, and it took him perhaps ten minutes to run eight and out—the first time anyone had done it in the match. That was the breakthrough moment, I thought—eight and out off Flaherty's break. Seven thousand winner.

But Flaherty, grinding on it now, played a flawless game off the Tooth's break. Bucktooth scratched early in the rack, before he had made a ball, and put a coin on the rail to indicate he owed a ball. Later in the rack, with the score tied at four balls each, Flaherty walked by the rail, saw the coin still sitting there and said, "Hey. You owe a ball."

"No, I don't," Bucktooth said. "You slept it. If you didn't call me on it when I first made a ball, you can't call me on it now."

"Bullshit. You owe a ball. Spot it up."

"No. That's the tournament rule. You can ask Grady." It was true.

"*Fuck* tournament rules. This ain't no tournament. This is you and me, playing for two thousand bucks a rack, and you owe a ball."

"No way." The Tooth was getting hot, and I was afraid that more than a ball would be lost if the argument continued. I walked over to him. "Bucktooth, fuck this. Pull up. You don't need this. Make him pay you off and let's get out of here."

"No, I want to drive this little fucker into the ground."

"Look," Flaherty said. "Either you spot a ball, or you forfeit the rack and we quit right now."

"I ain't forfeiting nothing. This rack is dead even right now."

"Nope. You owe a ball."

"Shit!" Bucktooth walked over and spotted a ball.

I shook my head. "I can't believe you let him get away with that."

"I'll kick his ass anyway and then he's really going to be buggy. He'll be talking to himself all night."

But it didn't work that way. Buoyed by his triumph, Flaherty played flawlessly the rest of the rack and won. Weirdly, it played out that way for the next four racks, each player winning on his opponent's break. I marveled at the quality of the play, and I knew the few spectators who had sweated the match felt the same way, from the low whistles, the exchanged glances and nods when great shots were made. I couldn't believe the touch both players showed, coasting balls to the hole, killing the rock on the end rail, hiding it behind the stack, weaving it between balls to get position—all with no bridge hand.

Toby asked to raise the stake to three thousand, and the Tooth wordlessly complied. Now there was six thousand on the light, and the Tooth was still seven thousand ahead.

At midnight, the Tooth was ten thousand dollars to the good, and then he made the greatest break of the night. The balls seemed to flow to his side of the table, and the cue ball killed up the side rail from Toby's pocket, leaving him nothing. It was a picture-perfect break, the break every player tries to achieve in one-pocket. The Tooth turned back to me, gritted his teeth, and clenched a fist in triumph. "That'll hold him," he whispered to me. "He can't fade that."

Toby Flaherty circled the table once, then rubbed a hand across his jaw and shook his head. "Fifteen minutes," he said. "I need some coffee."

"Okay," the Tooth said. Tall Paul, a player Tooth knew from San Francisco, was sitting nearby, and he said, "Paul, watch the money on the light." Paul agreed, and we departed for the head. Bucktooth took a paper towel, dampened it, and scrubbed his face. "I've got him now," he said to me. "He can't get out of that break, and if I play him smart this rack, see, I'll be thirteen grand up. I don't know how many bullets those guys have but we've got to be pretty close to busting them. They can't be wanting to put much more into this."

Just then the door to the men's room swung open, and

Amarillo Slim ducked his Stetsoned head and walked in. "Hi, Slim," Bucktooth said breezily, drying his hands and preparing to walk out.

"Now, Bucktooth"—Slim made a two-syllable word out of "now" and at least three out of "Bucktooth" as he stood in front of the pisser and unbuttoned his jeans—"Bucktooth, don't y'all blame me for this. I didn't have a damn thing to do with it, and I think it's really an accident anyway—"

"What?" Bucktooth said sharply, alarmed.

—"but one of them old boys from Oklahoma out there is movin the cue ball."

"WHAT!! I'LL WHACK EVERY ONE OF THEM MOTHER-FUCKERS!" Bucktooth and I bolted for the door, leaving Amarillo grinning at us over his shoulder as he took a leisurely piss all over our complacency.

Sure enough, we got out there in time to see one of Toby's backers, his blue denim haunch up on the rail, idly flipping the cue ball back and forth, into the cushion and back, talking to somebody else in the stands.

"WHAT THE FUCK DO YOU THINK YOU'RE DOING??" the Tooth bellowed. "GET YOUR GODDAMNED HANDS OFF THAT CUE BALL!"

The guy stood up, a little guiltily, and said, "What difference does it make? You guys aren't playing right now, anyway."

"*Not playing?* I just broke those balls and put your boy in jail, and I want that cue ball back where it was NOW."

"Sure, okay, man, don't get upset, put it where you want it," the guy said. "I didn't realize you broke. Place it where you want it."

Bucktooth put the ball back where he thought it was, and it looked right to me. He was breathing hard, shaking his head and muttering. "My God, I seen some moves before but that takes the fuckin Kewpie doll, right there. Jesus." He turned on

Tall Paul, who was still sitting where he was when we left. "Paul, why didn't you stop him?"

"Man, I watched the money, just like you said. I didn't know what he was going to do until he did it, Bucktooth, come on. I couldn't help it."

Bucktooth shook his head again in disgust. "Where's Flaherty?" he demanded. "Let's get this thing going." A couple of minutes later Toby came back into the tournament room, walked over, took one look at the table and snapped, "Who moved the cue ball?"

"Moved it, nothing," I said. "Your man there"—I pointed—"decided to pick it up and play with it while we were in the head."

"I told him he could put it back wherever he wanted," his backer said.

"That's where it was, right there," Bucktooth said. "It was your guy's move, not ours. Come on, it's your shot."

"Bullshit. I ain't playing with it there. Break the balls again."

"Oh, now I see this move," Bucktooth said bitterly. "I break the balls DEAD FUCKIN PERFECT," he shouted, "and then you decide to take a break because you're *tired,* and your guy here comes along and fucks up the table, and that gives you an excuse to get out of this box I got you in. Well, horseshit, you ain't pullin that on me."

"All I know is I ain't playin from there," Flaherty said.

"Where do you think the ball was?" the Tooth demanded.

"Don't matter where I think the fuckin ball was. Rack 'em."

"Tooth, pull up!" I said. "For God's sake this is the second raw move they've put on you. Are you going to let them fuck you out of your money, and mine too? Pull up, we've won ten grand, that's a good night's work. Forget about it. Let's go."

Bucktooth hesitated for a moment. "I hate to let them pull

this on me," he said quietly, "but I know I can beat this kid. I'm going to play."

He rebroke the balls, and of course he didn't get nearly the break he did before, and he swore, and Toby Flaherty reversed the break on him perfectly, and the next three hours passed like kidney stones. Bucktooth's legs were tired, and it showed in the way he moved around the table. Flaherty, for the first time since the first few racks of the session, was outplaying Bucktooth, moving better, making balls better.

Finally Bucktooth tried a tight cross-bank and missed it, the ball jarring out and rolling to the middle of the table, and Flaherty made it and two more to win his fifth straight rack, seven out of the past eight. Tooth wearily reached for his pocket to pay off, but Toby swept the money off the top of the light. "I'll just take this," he said. "We're done."

"Yer quittin me?" Bucktooth asked incredulously.

"Yep. It's three A.M., man. I got to get some sleep. Play again sometime." And with that, Flaherty, his backers, and eight thousand dollars of our money walked out the door. Bucktooth just stared. He'd had Flaherty trapped, and let him out. He had, against his better judgment, allowed his opponent to outmaneuver him, outpsych him, and finally beat him.

"I got greedy," the Tooth said, the fatigue seeping into his voice like radiator water from a bad hose. "Don't worry, I'll play him again, and I'll know what to expect, and I'll empty him." He was still bent over the table, practicing the cross-bank that didn't go, as I got into the elevator.

I staggered out to the garage and asked for my car. It was shockingly cold, probably ten below, and the wind was blowing; the pain of it on my face and in my lungs was exquisite. The car's engine was growling unnaturally, like a horribly wounded animal; the oil was so cold it would barely run. The abandoned snow-humped streets were tinged with the blood-red reflection of casino lights, and the signal at Virginia was blinking an impotent yellow. I reached for the heater-fan switch; there was ice on it. I recoiled and switched on the stereo instead. The tape player squeaked in protest against the cold, but finally engaged. Lyle Lovett was wailing as I got onto the freeway going east:

> He almost made it to the buzzer
> but somehow he gave up in the end
> . . . it's the classic contradiction
> the unavoidable affliction
> it don't take much to predict, son
> that's the way it always goes
> push will always come to shove
> on that midnight rodeo

I drove for half an hour, until the adrenaline began to ebb and I realized that the pain behind my eyes had nothing to do with the cold. I turned around and cruised slowly back, thinking as I thumped over the tracks by the strip about that interminable Coast Starlight to Seattle where this had all begun. We were still on that train, I thought, helpless to go anywhere but where it would take us.

"We're fucked," was Tony's succinct reaction when I returned to the room, and I had to admit he had a point. He was as sick as he had ever been in his life, and before long he would be heading back off the road to face his life, full of hostility and betrayal and litigation and uncertainty. After our $2,640 loss, it turned out we had spent three and a half months winning $3,500. We could have done almost as well bagging groceries. But we would not have had the magic of the road, the emotional progression of winning, then losing, then sucking it up and winning again. We would not have been in the arena, and for both of us, not trying was infinitely worse than losing, and we would never allow the losing to prevail. As I slipped into sleep I thought, as long as Tony could play, and we had a bankroll, we still had a chance.

XVIII

The Man with the Golden Gun

"A man would have to be a lunatic to quit an all-day-long sucker-fool like you."

—Paul Lyons, *Table Legs*

JANUARY 20—WE WOULDN'T GET ANY KIND OF A CHANCE AGAIN FOR some time. Tony was still out of it the next day. Cornbread Red won the tournament in the afternoon, and Toby Flaherty refused to play Bucktooth again. I spent the day in a bit of a daze, trying to rest, discussing our options with Tony, all the while replaying Bucktooth's match in my head.

The next morning I took Tony to the airport and got him on a flight to San Francisco. Until he was healthy, we were out of business, and he also had to deal with the Q Club mess. "Call me when you find work," I said.

"Don't worry. I'll find a game. And if I don't, you and I can play."

"Wonderful."

I flew to L.A., tired of the snow, and went to Hollywood Billiards every night to see who was playing high. The answer seemed to be nobody. Morro was out of town. The place seemed to be gripped with some odd lassitude; it rained, most nights, and Hollywood Boulevard was damp and bleak. I knew I was running out of time; I needed to get on with life, but I was like a weanling colt: I didn't want to give this up quite yet. I played golf on a fine six-by-twelve in the evenings with Tom Salter, the manager of the Hollywood Athletic Club, and a couple of straight-pool and nine-ball games with Jan Hacker, the sweet, talented club pro, and her boyfriend, cue maker Jerry McWhorter. One night I watched McWhorter catch fire playing nine-ball, a race to nine for a C-note against a regular Hollywood Billiards scuffler named James. McWhorter ran six racks, never looked like missing, and I started getting wistful for serious action. I played long, intricate sessions of one-pocket against myself during the cool smoggy afternoons at the Athletic Club. I waited.

Ten days later, the call came. "Hey, bubba, we're in action."

"You sound alive."

"I actually feel like it."

"What's up?"

"Boy George," Tony said. "He's been coming around, beating a few people, trying to make a game with me. I've put him off a couple of times, because I've been getting my strength back, practicing a lot, and I'm playin real good."

"I'll take the train up tomorrow. Why don't you meet me at the Oakland station?"

"If I can find it."

JANUARY 21—"THIS IS PERFECT," TONY SAID AS WE HEADED TOWARD the Bay Bridge, rain pelting the soft top of his ancient Datsun roadster. He looked thinner, if that was possible, but his eyes had the old fire. "Georgie is in the club tonight. I told him I had a friend who stakes me coming into town, we were going to go have a few drinks, and I might come back down afterward. He said he'd be there all night."

"Let me guess. We're going to your place, and you're going to take a nap in your clothes."

I didn't need to sleep in my clothes; I had already done that on the train. I reread Ross MacDonald and listened to Stan Getz in the parlor of Tony's elegant restored Victorian—I did drink a little red wine, strictly for professional reasons—then woke Tony up about 1 A.M.

As we turned past the swirling inchoate clump of crackheads at the corner of Golden Gate and Jones and parked in the familiar lot behind the Q Club, Tony said, "This is probably my last game here." He looked through his tiny windshield at the dark brick walls of the club he'd created, shaking his head, the corners of his mouth pulled downward. "We're headed for court. We can't agree on anything and they're tryin to rob me. I'm going to stay out of this place until it's resolved."

I didn't say anything about it being the end of our tour, as well; I knew he knew that. I got out of his little car and closed the door gently. "Let's make it a winner, then," I said, and we went up the stairs.

The club was dark; there were only a couple of tables going. At a table near the bar, Boy George was bent over a shot, the table light glinting off three heavy gold chains around his neck, his little gold gun dangling from one of them.

Tony called out, "Hey, George, you ready?"

"Sure I'm ready," Boy George replied, "If you're ready to give me a fair game."

"Come on, rack 'em, I'll give you that game you've been wanting," Tony said, a little loudly. "Orange Crush. Five and the break. But you got to freeze up some cash."

"Tony, that's a lot of weight," I said sharply.

George looked at me, then at Tony. "What do you want to do?"

"If I give you that game, it's gonna be worth my while," Tony said. "I'll play you five ahead for two thousand." He looked at me, almost pleadingly, and I snapped, "Jesus, I can't believe this. You bring me down here, drinking all night, you're giving away the store, and you want me to put up *two large?*"

"I'll do that," Boy George said to Tony, "if you can get your boy there to go."

I shook my head exasperatedly and walked a little way away from the table. Tony came after me. "Perfect," he whispered. I shook my head again, violently, for Boy George's benefit. "Are you going to slow-play it?" I asked.

"No," he replied. "I don't have to. We made a game, he likes it, it's a fair game, and I'm going to beat him. I think he'll stay with it. It's not like it's easy. It *is* a hell of a lot of weight."

In a few minutes we came back to the table, and Tony had the two thousand in his hand.

Boy George broke and made nothing. As Tony surveyed the table, my mind wandered from this match and our dwindling bankroll to the unremitting pressure of the game. Much has been made of the pool hustler's need to understand psychology, and thus understand his opponents. Easily as important is a clear self-understanding. Tony was of necessity the ultimate realist: In making each new game, he had to ask himself: Exactly what do I need here to win? How many balls can I give up? How many do I need? He had to be able to answer those questions accurately, and he had to know his heart would carry him where his stroke wouldn't. He made his living by knowing more about his own skill, and that of others, than they did; this game was a case in point. On this night he knew he could win giving Boy George the five and the break. He was able to win money not just because he could get out that way, but because he *knew* he could, and Boy George didn't.

As I watched him assume the now familiar stance, line up shot after shot, I found that I could almost perfectly predict when he'd miss, or get out of line, and when he wouldn't.

Anthony Chenier Annigoni ran all nine balls in that first rack. Nothing fancy, no extreme English, just calm, honest center-ball position and relentless accuracy.

He won the first set at about 3 A.M. It wasn't a shutout; Boy George won some racks, and made some nice shots. But he couldn't consistently get to the five ball from the break, and when he missed, Tony almost invariably got the five off the table, so they were even the rest of the way, and as often as not Tony ran the balls right out.

Boy George doubled up on the second set, and when he lost it he was six thousand dollars down, and out of cash. "Hey, Rickie," he said to the guy with him. "Lend me four bills, will you?"

"No way, George. You can't beat this game. Let's get out of here."

Boy George took the gold from around his neck—all of it, even the little gold gun—and wordlessly handed it to his partner. "That's worth twice that much," he said, and his partner shook his head, and posted the four thousand.

By 6 A.M. that was gone, too, but George didn't want to quit. "I'm gonna go get some money wired here from Stockton," he said, and he went in search of a Western Union.

The gray light fluttered in like wisps of lint from the huge old windows over Market Street. I sat back by the snooker table with a big cup of coffee, leaning on my cue case, and watched the sleepless old men as they arrived for the live sex show downstairs at the Regal Theatre. I watched Boy George as he strode down the street toward the wire office. I watched the *Chronicle* truck come and fill the box, and wondered what Herb Caen had to say this morning. I watched Tony, sitting across the table from me.

"That's it, he's done," Tony said, chewing on a corner of his mustache.

"No, I bet he scores some cash," I said.

"If Boy George called you at 6 A.M. and wanted you to wire him ten grand, would you do it?" he said. "Fuck, no, you wouldn't. He's tapped. He'll be back next week or next month and he'll try me again but I'll have to give up more weight. It was a bad roll he wasn't carrying heavier."

A couple of minutes later I said, "You have a lot of heart, and we won some money."

"We did." He said nothing more for a moment, and I watched a wino lurch down the street, tipping his cap elaborately to everyone he met. "You're done, hey?" he said then.

"Yeah, I have to be." I took my bankroll out, and counted out Boy George's $10,000, and another $3,200. I split it into two stacks, and then picked up mine and counted out an additional $265. I shoved the rest back in my left-hand pocket, where I will carry my cash for the rest of my life.

"Square?"

"Hey, you don't have to do that. We can play some gin. Or maybe you'd like to play some straight pool, forty no-count?"

"Maybe you'd like to find somebody else to rob," I said.

He smiled. "Maybe I would." He looked at me, eyes hopeful. "We could go on the road again. Germany. They're playing a lot of nine-ball there. We should go to Germany, Italy, and then England, try some snooker against those boys. Hey, maybe I could even get on that English tour. We could make some serious money over there, man, serious. Maybe we could even take Bucktooth."

I called a cab, and as we walked out of the club, Boy George came wheeling around the corner, out of breath. "Where are you going?" he demanded.

"I'm going home," Tony said. "If you get any money, let me know."

"Hey, you can't quit me."

"I'm not quitting you. I'd be crazy to quit you. I just beat your brains out. But I'm not playing on the wire. Post the cash and I'll play you all you want."

"I'll get some today."

"Then I'll play you some tonight." He got into the Datsun and gave me a salute as Boy George and his partner walked away.

"Fuck you, we're not taking Bucktooth," I said, and I could hear him laughing as he drove down Golden Gate Avenue in the soft morning rain.

ACKNOWLEDGMENTS

I am deeply grateful to Suzanne Gluck, my fabulous agent, who, I'm certain, can be ferocious and maternal at the same time; and to Ann Godoff, the kind of editor most writers are never lucky enough to get. Also, many thanks to Susan Jensen and Enrica Gadler.

I sincerely appreciate all the players mentioned herein, particularly my road partner, Tony Annigoni, without whose talent and heart and humor I would have had nothing to write about; also Rich Cook, Cole Dickson, Keith McCready, and Harry Platis.

Thank you, Sarah Jackson, for your encouragement. Thanks to Marcia and Maurice Neville, those charming facilitators; to HST, as always, for inspiring; to Uncle Alan and Aunt Jan, for putting up with a couple of pool bums; to Mike and Julie Shamos, for the same thing, and Mike, for all of your valuable assistance. Also, thanks to Lori Dickson, Mort Luby and Mike Panozzo, and Barbara Woodward at the Sands Regency, for their help; and to Ron Becker, Ed Beitiks, David Dayton, Jon A. Jackson, Greg Keeler, and Chuck and Susie Rathbun; and to two most disparate Walkers, Carter and Jerry Jeff, each for reminding me that many things go many ways, many times but once, until your life is past and love is but a thought.

DAVID MCCUMBER is an award-winning journalist who worked for more than twenty years as a writer and editor at newspapers and magazines across the West. He was founding editor and publisher of the regional literary magazine *Big Sky Journal*. McCumber lives in Livingston, Montana, where he is at work on his third book of nonfiction as well as a novel and a collection of poetry.

ABOUT THE TYPE

This book was set in Baskerville, a typeface that was designed by John Baskerville, an amateur printer and typefounder, and cut for him by John Handy in 1750. The type became popular again when the Lanston Monotype Corporation of London revived the classic Roman face in 1923. The Mergenthaler Linotype Company in England and the United States cut a version of Baskerville in 1931, making it one of the most widely used typefaces today.